Bismi Llahi r-Rahmani r-Rahim
In the name of Allah the Most Compassionate, the Most Merciful.

Goodness does not consist in turning your face towards the east or the west. The truly good are those who believe in God and the Last Day, in the Angels, the Scripture, and the Prophets; who give away some of their wealth, however much they cherish it, to their relatives, to orphans, the needy, travelers and beggars, and to liberate those in bondage; those who keep up the prayer and pay the prescribed alms; who keep pledges whenever they make them; who are steadfast in misfortune, adversity, and times of danger. These are the ones who are true, and it is they who are in awe of God.
(2:177)

Other Titles By This Author:

My Little Lore of Light
The Light of Muhammad
Links of Light: The Golden Chain
The Story of Moses
Who Are You? A Book of Very Serious Questions
The Animals of Paradise
The Animals of Paradise: Coloring Book
My Little Lore of Light: Coloring Book
Every Day A Thousand Times
As-Salamu 'Alaykum Ya Rasul Allah (sas)
Ibrahim Khalil Allah (as)
Animal Salams
A Book of Angels

Copyright © 2020 by Karima Sperling
All rights reserved. This book or any portion thereof may not be reproduced or used in any manner whatsoever without the express written permission of the publisher except for the use of brief quotations in a book review.
Printed in the United States of America ISBN 978-0-578-79622-2
Little Bird Books littlebirdbooksink@gmail.com

The Family of 'Imran:
Mary, Jesus, Zachariah, and John

By Karima Sperling

Dedication

This book is dedicated to Mawlana Shaykh Nazim al-Haqqani and Hajjah Aminah, who by their example and service showed us what it means to be a loving slave of God. And to Hajjah Emine Teyza, a true friend to them and to us. May Allah shower them with His blessings and raise their stations forever higher and higher.

Thanks

Thank you to Shaykh Mehmet Efendi for extending his blessing, support, and strength.

Thank you to Hajja Rukiye Sultan for being an example of the form of Fatima (rah).

Thank you to Shaykh Bahauddin Efendi for his kindness and humor.

Thank you to Hajj Mehmet Nazim for being always an available source of knowledge and good sense.

Thank you to Aminah Alptekin for her endless patience and expertise and once more turning a file into a book.

Thank you to my patient and attentive readers, Alia Nazeer, Fatima Sperling, and Dr. Munir Sperling.

Thank you to Mahmoud Shelton for guidance on the esoteric. To Yasmine Motawy for her kindness and expertise. To Fatima Maringele for good suggestions.

Thank you to the children for whom this was written, Haniya, Humayra, Layka, Ishaq, Jacob, Hamza, Ghalib, Khalil, Noura, Karima, Tarik, Hala, Musa and the one on the way.

But most of all thank You to the One who made them all.

Abbreviations

(sas) – sall Allahu 'alayhi wa s-sallam. The peace and blessings of Allah be upon him. Prayer said after the mention of the name of the Prophet Muhammad (sas).

(as) –'alayhi s-salam meaning on him be peace. Prayer said after the mention of the name of a prophet or archangel.

(ahs) – 'alayha s-salam, on her be peace. Prayer said after the name of Maryam bint 'Imran (ahs).

(ra) – radhia Allahu 'an. May Allah be pleased with him. Prayer said when the name of a male companion or family member of the Prophet Muhammad (sas) or other prophet is mentioned.

(rah) – radhia Allahu 'anha – May Allah be pleased with her. Prayer said for a woman from the family or companions of the Prophet Muhammad or of earlier prophets when her name is mentioned.

(q) –qaddas Allahu sirrahu – May Allah sanctify his secret. Prayer said when the name of a saint is mentioned.

A Note About the Pictures

Pictures have become problematic for most Muslims. Depicting the human form and face has been discouraged if not condemned outright. However, the stricture on images has not always been consistent or universal. This is best illustrated by the paintings themselves that come to us from many different times and regions. There is even sufficient evidence from the hadith literature that the Prophet (sas) himself respected the paintings he found inside the Ka'ba, of Ibrahim (as), Maryam (ahs), and 'Isa (as), and that he protected them with his own hand from being demolished with the rest of the images and idols.

I have used many pictures in this book. They have a purpose other than just decoration. They took almost as much time, thought, and care to assemble as the text itself. When I used human figures, I tried to use those done by Muslims for Muslims. These works of art were painted to be enclosed in books, as in a box or chest. They were not hung on a wall or displayed. I use them as they were intended to be used. If there are faces, they are generic. They are not portraiture. Most of the people have the same face without individuation. Often they wear the clothes and have the physical features of the audience for whom they were made, rather than of those they are supposed to portray. They are representative rather than realistic because the artist was interested in portraying a spiritual truth rather than a physical form. I have used very few European Christian images because they tend to be too 'real', and also because the artists have a penchant for portraying their prophets naked. I have used some however, because they illustrate, in the most effective way, points I feel are important.

In the world we live, images of all kinds surround us, and no one forbids their use. Books, films, television, photographs, newspapers, social media - we are inured to these images. Pictures have, in many ways, superseded words. Hopefully we do not worship them.

In my personal opinion, it is not right to portray a prophet, not right and not possible. They are inimitable. Their features are full of light, perfect and beautiful. Neither the human hand nor imagination can do them justice, and it is not proper to try. However, I feel that pictures enhance the text, and make it easier for people in today's visual world to connect, respond, and remember. I seek refuge in Allah from error and *kufr*, and Allah knows best.

Table of Contents

1. Introduction..1
2. Setting the Scene – The First Temple...5
3. Setting the Scene – The Second Temple......................................13
4. The Family of 'Imran (ra)..21
5. A Promise 29
6. Becoming Maryam (ahs) 35
7. A *Mihrab* for Maryam (ahs) 41
8. Above the Women of the Worlds..49
9. The Female Form..61
10. Zakariyya the Prophet (as)...63
11. The Fruit of Prayer...69
12. Eastward Bound...77
13. A Sign for Mankind 81

14. The Good News of Yahya (as)..87
15. Saint Josef (ra) 93
16. A Thing Forgotten..99
17. A Stream Beneath Her 105
18. Silence Is Golden 111
19. The Unwise Wise Men..117
20. The *Rabwa* 123
21. A Wise Child..133
22. From the Source of Life...139
23. The Teaching of Yahya (as)...145
24. The Hidden Years 149
25. Dyers, Bleachers, and Helpers 157
26. Life and Spirit...163
27. On a Silver Platter...169
28. *Masih* 'Isa ibn Maryam (as)...175

29. A Prophet and A Slave 181
30. A Word and A Spirit 189
31. His Name Will Be Ahmad (sas) 197
32. The Man with Two Tombs 203
33. The Table Spread 209
34. 'Isa's (as) Invitation 215
35. The Last Supper 223
36. The Substitution 229
37. After Seven Days 237
38. Hierarchies 245
39. The Three Righteous Men of the Last Days 253
40. The End 261
Glossary 268
Bibliography 278
Picture Credits 285

Muhammad (sas) on a camel and 'Isa (as) on a donkey, riding together. Illustration of the vision of Sha'ya (as) (Isaiah 21:7) for the History of Al-Biruni, 16th century.

1.
Introduction

Allah commands us to **relate the stories that perhaps they** (people) **may reflect.** (7:176).
    As a wise man once said, "The Qur'an doesn't order us to teach law or doctrine but it does order us to tell the stories. Tell the stories from The Qur'an, the Hadith, about the prophets, their companions, and the saints. It is not our responsibility to verify the details, only to relate the stories. People may think on them and take something. Don't worry if the stories actually happened, where or how. Just remind the people so that they may reflect and so that their hearts may incline towards the hereafter. Tell the stories - they will have an effect. They lead to an understanding of how the prophets used to live; what they did, their manners, their conditions, their thinking. They show how the world was through their eyes. This is what is important." (Shaykh Nazim al-Haqqani: 9/10/11)
    Allah sent us His Books to be our maps and His prophets and saints to be our guides. The accounts of the lives of the prophets are not intended to be bedtime stories to put us to sleep. Their purpose, on the contrary, is to wake us up and make us think about what Allah might

have had in mind when He first molded our father Adam (as) out of mud. These stories are an important part of the "User's Manual" with which our Most Generous Maker has sent us out into the world to see how we will act. They have as many levels of meaning as there are storytellers and as many levels of understanding as there are listeners. Told and retold they release new and renewing insights every time they are encountered. They never get old. They were designed for all of us to use in our daily lives for comfort and support, for understanding and inspiration. Their deceivingly simple images open to reveal whole worlds of meaning. They should be our trusted companions as we journey homeward through one door of life and out the other.

According to a hadith of the Prophet Muhammad (sas), "Whoever testifies that there is no god other than God, One, having no partner, and that Muhammad is His slave and His Messenger, and that 'Isa is His slave and His Messenger and His word which he bestowed upon Maryam and a spirit from Him, and that Paradise is real and that Hellfire is real - God will grant him Paradise no matter what deeds he may have done." (Al-Bukhari).

This book is neither polemical nor ecumenical. Its purpose is neither to emphasize nor to minimize the differences of belief that exist among the People of the Book. It simply aims to tell the story of the Muslim prophet 'Isa ibn Maryam (as) and his family, referred to collectively in The Qur'an as the Family of 'Imran: 'Imran, his wife Hana, their daughter Maryam and her son 'Isa, Hana's sister 'Ashya and her husband Zakariyya, and their son Yahya, peace be upon all of them. It is a story of three special births, three unjust murders or attempted murders, and seven remarkable lives of patience, compassion, nobility, and love for God. These are the last prophets of the Banu Isra'il. After them Allah established His religion, Islam, for the whole world.

The details of the story are based primarily on what is found in The Qur'an itself and in the Hadith. Secondarily, it is based on what sincere, knowledgeable, and wise Muslims for generations have culled from Christian sources that they carefully reinterpreted from a Muslim perspective. Without apology or excuse, it relates the wide variety of their explanations and understandings.

This book is meant for Muslims and for those who want to know what Muslims believe. Its aim is quite simple: to tell a story in an engaging way that encourages the reader to spend some quality time in the company of a few of the greatest men and women who have ever walked our planet; to create the space to consider their words and their actions, to think about their lives and characters, to get to know them more intimately and, hopefully in the process, to establish some kind of a personal relationship with them.

Everything that a Muslim believes must be checked against the life and advice of the last prophet, Muhammad (sas). No story can be told without also telling his story. The Prophet Muhammad (sas) said, "The prophets are brothers of one father; their mothers are different but their religion is one. Of all men, I have the most rightful claim to 'Isa ibn Maryam because there was no prophet between him and me. He will be my successor – *khalifati* – over my community. He will surely descend. When you see him, you will recognize him." (Al-Bukhari).

Perhaps this work can help us to be able to recognize 'Isa (as) when we see him, to believe in him and learn from him whether we see him or not, and to feel our hearts stir with love for him and his brother prophets. The Prophet (sas) has promised, "You will be with the ones you love." (Muslim, Al-Bukhari). So when our journey finally finishes, Allah willing, we will be together in their blessed company.

La ilaha ila Allah. There is no god except God. Alhambra, Spain.

PALESTINE IN THE TIME OF JESUS, 4 B.C.–30 A.D.
(INCLUDING THE PERIOD OF HEROD, 40–4 B.C.)

2.
Setting the Scene – The First Temple

After having been forced to leave his homeland, the prophet Ibrahim (as) and his companions traveled under God's guidance to the land that stretches along the eastern edge of the Mediterranean Sea. This land, which so many have called by so many names, Canaan, Palestine, Judaea, Israel, is known to all as the Holy Land, the land promised by Almighty God to the descendants of His prophet Ibrahim (as).

Ibrahim (as), his companions, and their descendants lived as pastoralists, in tents that they moved from place to place as their livestock required. Nothing distinguished them from their neighbors except a fierce and relentless devotion to their Creator, the One Lord, Allah. For more than two hundred years, their children prayed to Allah in their homes and in the holy places that He designated for them, places where angels had descended, where miracles had happened; places made sacred by divine communication or manifestation. Some of these places had even been sacred long before the arrival of Ibrahim (as). Some of them had been chosen at the time the world was created. These still exist today, special places where the world of spirit connects with the world of matter, and the

The well into which Yusuf (as) was thrown by his brothers and from which he was taken into slavery, Galilee, Israel.

unseen can sometimes be miraculously seen.

The grandson of Ibrahim (as), Ya'qub (as), who is also known by the name Isra'il, had twelve sons all of whom were prophets of differing ranks. A famine caused the family to leave the Holy Land and seek provision in Egypt. Yusuf (as), the great grandson of Ibrahim (as), having been previously sold by his brothers into slavery and having been awarded by Allah with good fortune and power, forgave his ten half brothers and invited them to move to Egypt. There they settled and were slowly robbed of their freedom and reduced to slavery over a period of approximately four hundred years until the coming of the next great prophet.

During the time they were living in exile in Egypt, each of the sons of Isra'il (as) generated a tribe of people. This resulted in what are known as the twelve tribes of Isra'il, the Banu Isra'il. Each tribe took the name of the son of Ya'qub (as) who fathered them. When their safe refuge in Egypt turned into bondage, Allah empowered the prophets Musa (as) and Harun (as) (Aaron), descendants of Ya'qub's (as) third son Lawi (Levi), to set the Banu Isra'il free and return them to the land He had promised their great grandfather Ibrahim (as). The prophets led the Banu Isra'il out of Egypt, out from under the tyranny of Pharaoh, through an opening in the sea to freedom in the land Allah had chosen for them.

Although these tribes descended from brothers, they neither got along nor were they able to act in unison for any appreciable length of time. When they left Egypt, each tribe marched through the sea as an isolated group. It is even said that Allah opened twelve paths through the sea so that each tribe marched alone. And when they reached safety on the other side, they set up their tents separately. For the forty years that they struggled in the desert of the Sinai, Allah assigned separate areas for each tribe when they encamped. Allah gave them a boulder that served as a miraculous source of water which they carried with them on their daily migrations. From it Allah caused twelve springs to flow so there was no need to even share their water (2:60).

The most precious thing that Allah gave the Banu Isra'il, however, was the Tawrah, His holy Law in the form of a book inscribed on tablets of stone which He sent down to Musa (as) on Mount Sinai around 1500 BCE. They were told to build a chest, the Ark of the Covenant, in Arabic *Tabut*, to hold the remnants of these tablets and to be the place from which their Lord would address them. They were also instructed to build the first temple to enclose and protect this holy chest. The Temple, or Tabernacle, was an arrangement of tents and leather fences that could be disassembled and carried on wagons to be reassembled each time they encamped. They carried their *qibla* with them wherever they went, a portable mosque. **In it there will be tranquility from your Lord and relics of the family of Musa and the family of Harun, carried by the angels.** (2:248).

The rock said to be the one from which 12 sources of water flowed for the Banu Isra'il in the desert, Wadi al-Lija, Sinai Egypt.

Every day this moveable sanctuary was rolled up and loaded on wagons that led the caravan of the children of Isra'il in the direction their Lord had chosen for them for that day. Every night the tent was unloaded from the wagons and erected. The *Tabut* was placed inside the

Holy of Holies, and the protective fences and screens were set up around it demarcating the sacred space.

After forty years and the deaths of both Musa (as) and Harun (as), Yusha (as) (Joshua) took over as the prophet, guide, and military commander of Isra'il. He led them, as a conquering army, into the land that Allah had promised to the descendants of Ibrahim (as). They settled there and each of the twelve tribes was assigned its own territory. However, the descendants of Harun (as) of the tribe of Levi were designated by Allah Almighty to be the priests and so they worked in the Temple rather than on the land. They ate from the alms of the worshippers and they owned no farms. This is the direct reverse of the later Muslim law that makes the taking of alms (*zakah* or *sadaqa*) forbidden to the descendants of the prophet Muhammad (sas).

Sometimes the Tabernacle rested in Bethel, sometimes in Shechem. It was owned by no one but it was believed that as long as it remained with them, the Banu Isra'il would be safe and victorious. The Tribes fought with each other constantly and worse, they rebelled against their Lord, adding gods to the worship of God until finally the *Tabut* was taken away by Allah. The heart of the Tabernacle remained empty for the next four hundred years.

One day, the tribes asked their prophet Shamwil (as) (Samuel) to implore Allah on their behalf to appoint a king behind whom they could unite and fight as one for the Lord. **"Appoint for us a king, that we may fight in the cause of Allah." He said: "Is it not possible, if you were commanded to fight, that you will not fight?"... Yet when they were commanded to fight, all but a few of them turned away: God has full knowledge of those who do wrong. (2:246).**

Allah appointed a man by the name of Talut (Saul) to be their king and after four hundred years of absence, the *Tabut* was miraculously returned to the Tabernacle. The Tribes finally accepted Talut, united and were led by the Ark to victory over their enemies. Then Dawud (as) (David), a descendant of Harun (as), was given to them to be both their prophet and their king. He held the disparate tribes together in the worship of the One God. Dawud (as) built himself a city and a palace near the village of Salem or Jebus (Jerusalem) and he decreed that since he now lived in a house built of stones rather than a tent, that Allah also should have a house of stone.

So it was that on a mountain in Jerusalem, over the sacred rock which they believed had served as a sacrificial altar for Ibrahim (as) and was the first earth Allah had created, the navel of the world permanently connecting the Creator to His creation, the temple of stone was built. The *Tabut* however, remained in a sort of tent made of woven curtains in the innermost court, the Holy of Holies. It was to serve the people as a universal *qibla*. From wherever they were, they would turn towards it – one God, one people. Dawud (as) did not live to fulfill his dream. His son Sulayman (as) (Solomon) followed in his footsteps as both prophet and king and completed the temple around 1,000 BCE. This building was the most magnificent structure in its form and ornamentation that the world has ever seen. It is even said that the Jinn were put under the command of Sulayman (as) in order to design and execute the most marvelous decorations in precious metals and gems.

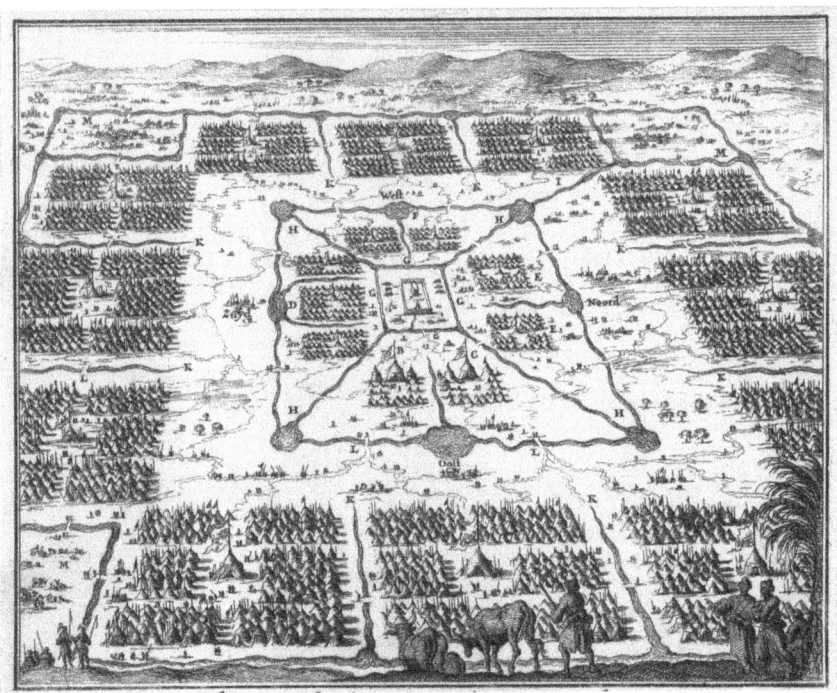

Illustration of the encampment of the Banu Isra'il around the *Tabut*. Jan Luyken, 1673.

Now the Banu Isra'il had a stone building, resting on the rock of Ibrahim (as), embracing in its very core the stone tablets of the Law. For forty years the Banu Isra'il functioned as a single state, united under a just and wise ruler, worshipping the One Merciful God. But when Sulayman (as) died, his sons could not hold the kingdom together and they could not even hold fast to the worship of Allah. Immediately after the death of Sulayman (as) the kingdom split into two warring kingdoms, Isra'il in the north under the son of Sulayman (as), Rehoboam, and Judah in the south under one of his disillusioned commanders by the name of Jeroboam. Within a hundred years the kingdom and Temple of Sulayman (as) were gone.

Somewhere between 945 and 925 BCE Canaan was invaded by an Egyptian army under pharaoh Shoshenq I. The temple was stripped of its precious metals which were then used to decorate temples to the gods of Egypt. It was partially rebuilt and robbed again in 700 BCE by Sennacherib, the king of Assyria. And then in 586 BCE Nebuchadnezzar, king of the Babylonians, finished the job and leveled the temple to the ground so not one stone was left standing upon another. The Jewish Tribes were taken into exile. Some of them returned but most did not. And so began the dispersion of the Banu Isra'il. Some stayed in Babylon. Some migrated to Alexandria and Southern Egypt, some to fertile oases in the Arabian desert, some eventually to Rome and Byzantium.

The ones who returned, rebuilt the Temple on the holy mount in Jerusalem. It was a simple building, not the grand edifice of Sulayman (as) but a small building on the same spot. They began to perform the ritual sacrifices once more and the rites that belonged to the Temple. But it was essentially an empty building. The *Tabut*, the sacred relics, the link with the divine, was gone. And this time it would not return, until perhaps the end of times.

An artist's rendering of the Temple and Jerusalem at the time of Sulayman (as).

The Western Wall. The massive stones at the bottom were built by Herod in order to enlarge and retain the Temple Mount.

3.
Setting the Scene – The Second Temple

After the Babylonians destroyed the Temple in 585 BCE, the Persians ruled for two hundred years. Then Alexander the Great conquered the whole area. The Greek culture that he introduced had a heavy influence on the language, customs, and life of the region. There was rebellion resulting in a brief hundred-year period of Jewish self rule which collapsed due to internal rivalries.

By 65 BCE the Romans had essentially become the most powerful force in the area. In 37 BCE they appointed a Jew as their deputy to rule for them in the Holy Land whose name was Herod. Although he was intelligent and capable, power turned him into a tyrant. He wanted to please his overlords without abandoning his heritage. He was a friend of Antony and a business partner of Cleopatra. He used the massive amounts of wealth at his disposal to transform the second Temple from a simple unadorned building into a great monument that would impress the hard to impress Romans. He doubled the size of the Temple platform to what it is today by building a retaining wall of huge stones, what is now the Wailing Wall, and he built the fortress that encloses the graves of Ibrahim (as) and family at Hebron. He covered the Temple itself in sheets of gold and precious stones in an effort to outdo his predecessor, the prophet Sulayman (as), and in order to be remembered in the annals of history. He is still remembered, not for what he built but rather for what he destroyed.

All the while the business of the Temple went on. Its altar was busy from dawn to dusk with its main function, the sacrifice of animals to God. Twice daily the sluices had to be opened to allow running, living, cleansing water into the inner courtyard of the Temple where the altar stood directly in front of the Holy of Holies. This running river of water was needed to wash away the bloody remains of sacrifice. The temple was so crowded with professional priests, living off the donations of the poor and pious, that it is said in the Gospels that there were more priests than worshippers. Although still the house of God, in some way this grand new temple was an ornamented box that had been robbed of its treasure.

The average man aspired to the Greco-Roman culture that he saw in the ruling privileged classes around him. He admired their great literature and philosophy as well as their dress and appearance. He wanted to be accepted into the Roman men's club that was known as the Gymnasium. This is where the men of consequence met to exercise, play sports, and discuss the events of the world. It was both gym and university. Whether playing ball or discussing philosophy, the one requirement was that it was done free of clothing, naked.

Adam (as) and Hawwa (rah). Ethiopia, Abreha and Atsbeha Church. 17th century.

Imagine the impact of just this single cultural norm on a people who believed that the first man and woman lived without want or sin in a garden until their disobedience of the one and only rule Allah gave them, caused them to be stripped of their heavenly clothing and plunged into the world naked. Shamed and humiliated by the sight of their own nakedness, Adam (as) and Hawwa (rah) ducked behind trees, using leaves and bushes to cover themselves. Think of Nuh (as) whose nakedness was witnessed by one of his sons who was then cursed with having to be a servant to his brothers. Think of Musa (as) whose, as yet ignorant, people whispered that he must be deformed because no one had ever seen him naked. Then Allah gave legs to a rock which ran away with his clothes while he was washing in the river. Following after the rock to retrieve his robe he was seen by his people to be perfect in every way. Consider the Prophet Muhammad (as) who was also never seen naked even by his wives; who did not uncover himself completely even to bathe, and who informed us that angels will not remain in the presence of a naked human. The Banu Isra'il were strict about their modesty, covering their bodies, both men and women.

The unintended consequence of the Roman and Greek penchant for nakedness was to expose the believer. As a result, there were at least two remedies for reversing the appearance of circumcision. One was stretching the remains of the foreskin by means of a weight called a *pondus judaeus* and the other was a surgical procedure (epispasm) that somehow restored the semblance of a foreskin. It would turn out that this small removal of skin, a practice abhorred by the Romans, would serve to be a huge obstacle to the spread of monotheism. And it did not help that the favorite food of the Greeks and Romans was pork. Rather than being regarded as unclean, the pig was considered the choicest offering to the gods, a symbol of fertility and divine generosity. It was not just a culinary preference but a moral and religious one as well. Hippocrates, the father of western medicine (370 BCE), recommended pork as the healthiest meat.

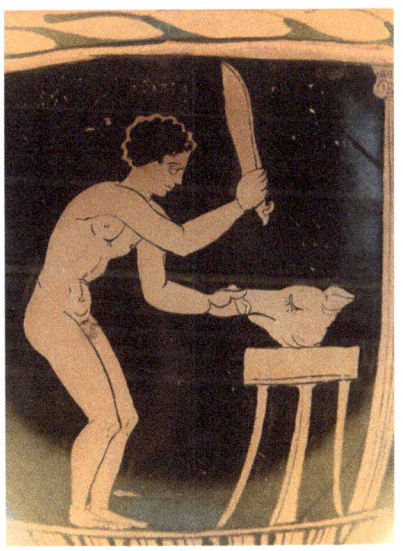

Greek amphora depiction of naked youth preparing a pig head before a temple, ca. 360 BCE.

Incidentally, the Romans can be credited with being the first to express anti-Semitic rhetoric. First Cicero (7 – 43 CE) then Tacitus (56 -120 CE) wrote of the shocking people of Judaea who refused to worship Roman gods and who also turned other people against the gods of their ancestors. And these 'disgusting barbarians' rebelled against the newly instituted Roman law that declared the emperor, in all his hairy human frailty, a god. Caesar walked in the footsteps of Pharaoh who said to Musa (as), **I am your Lord Most High.** (79:24).

Similar to what the polytheists of Mecca would say six hundred years later about the Prophet Muhammad (sas) and the early Muslims, Tacitus complains: "The Jews regard as profane all that we hold sacred; on the other hand, they permit all that we abhor." "They sit apart at meals, and they sleep apart... they abstain from intercourse with foreign women. They adopt circumcision to distinguish themselves from other people by this difference. Those who are converted to their ways follow the same practice, and the earliest lesson they receive is to despise the gods, to disown their country (Rome), and to regard their parents, children, and brothers as of little account."

These views seem almost like a parody. But it should serve to caution us that tradition and normality can masquerade as truth and deceive even those deemed to be the most clever and discerning. The Qur'an says that the people of Lut (as) vilified their prophet by saying: **Drive them out of your city; these are indeed men who want to be clean and pure**. (7:82). How dare they even think of being either clean or pure?

There was some truth in the words of the Romans. The Banu Isra'il had amassed a ponderous body of prohibitions and prescriptions. These served to isolate and so also to protect the believers from the influence of the unbelieving world but made it very difficult for that world to learn about Allah and join in His worship. There was, however, a category of people called proselytes who, although they believed in the God of the Banu Isra'il, did not have to follow all the laws. They were allowed to worship with the congregation but because they did not circumcise, they could not marry into it.

There were several reactions on the part of the Banu Isra'il to the prejudice of their overlords. There was one elite group of priests and their privileged families (called Sadducees) who hoped to survive and thrive by accommodating the rulers. They supported making a compromise that would allow them to hold onto their inherited power and yet rise in the political system of Rome. They hoped to enjoy the best of both worlds. They clung to the Tawrah of Musa (as) but they interpreted it with minds trained in a philosophy borrowed from the Greeks and Romans. They rejected the idea that there is life after death. They saw no evidence for there being a resurrection or a final judgment. For them there was no reward or punishment, no destiny, and no unseen or angelic realm. They were materialists. After death the best that could be hoped for was a shadowy existence in Hades, a sort of limbo that continued indefinitely. They were the majority of priests serving in the Temple and on the board of governors, the Sanhedrin. They were the priests in power.

Opposing them were other priests (called Pharisees) and those educated in the law (Scribes), most of whom officiated in the small regional synagogues or places of prayer outside of the great Temple. They were in closer contact with the people but they had less prestige and power. They held on to the Tawrah of Musa (as) and they also held tightly to the oral traditions of their rabbis as a way to practice what they found in the Tawrah. They rejected the religion and philosophy of their alien overlords. They also objected to the compromised way of the Sadducees. They believed in life after death, the coming of the Day of Judgment, Angels, Heaven and Hell. Eventually, after the final destruction of the Temple in 70 CE, their understanding of Judaism predominated.

However, the Pharisees believed that in order to achieve Heaven it was necessary to follow the minute details of the letter of the law which had been elaborated by their teachers and Rabbis. They tightened the rules, added laws to the laws and made judgments without mercy. Their legalistic approach is exemplified by their definition of the Sabbath. The Tawrah says not to do work, carry burdens, or light a fire on the seventh day but to rest and fast and keep the day holy for remembering the Lord. The Pharisee priests devoted themselves to defining what is work and what is a burden. They fought and argued with each other over their differing opinions. They said you could milk an animal on the Sabbath but only the amount of one swallow. You could lift a spoon but only if it weighed less than a fig. They argued about whether a mother could pick up her child or pin her shawl, about whether a lame man could carry his crutch.

In addition, the Pharisees were obsessed with avoiding contamination, with being defiled. They added to the already long lists of the things that caused such pollution. They had to avoid contact with the dead, including certain species of rodent and reptile, and contact with anyone or anything that had had such contact. They had to shun all contact with people who had any kind of skin disease from leprosy to psoriasis. They could not touch a woman who had her period or any object or person that had been touched by such a woman. If they did it would cause such impurity that it took up to seven days and numerous submersions in ritual baths to cleanse.

There was a third group (the Essenes) who tried to revive the spirituality of the religion of Ibrahim (as). They rejected the whole establishment, including the Temple and everyone in it. They separated themselves into their own communities on the edges of settled areas and practiced their religion in isolation. Although no one knows for sure exactly what they believed or how they lived, it is thought that they took ritual baths every day and dressed all in white and did not marry. It is also thought that there were no women accepted to live among them. There are some who think that 'Isa (as) was an Essene but that seems unlikely if just because of his love and respect for his mother and because he had so many close disciples and companions who were women.

So, by far the majority of the Banu Isra'il, the common villager, man or woman, had no one to follow, no rope to hold on to. The state was taxing them to death, and they were angry. They were open to whatever political group promised change. There were those who found in the holy Books the promise of a messenger from God who would clean His religion of corruption and falsehood and let His light shine brightly for all people to see. There were passages in their holy books that referred to a coming savior, a messiah. He would be a Jew of the family of King Dawud (as). It was written that he would be born near Jerusalem in a town called Bethlehem. He would revitalize the religion of Ibrahim (as), defeat their enemies, establish them in the holy land as rulers over all people and call the dispersed tribes to return to their homeland. His signs would be military triumph and the obliteration of belief in gods other than God. United under one God, the Banu Isra'il would live in prosperity and peace, heaven on earth, until the Judgment Day and the final destruction of life on earth as we know it.

In conclusion, it is said that at the time of the second Temple in the last centuries BCE, there was not one Judaism but many Judaisms. Even those who believed in Allah differed seriously about how to worship Him and how to interpret His words. They argued about it incessantly, and sometimes they even fought and killed each other over it. The believers in divine unity could find no unity among themselves. They had fallen prey to the tyranny and taxation of foreign powers who felt no shame in taking themselves for gods and who had absolutely no appreciation or respect for the chosen people of the one true God. The pious waited for a messiah who they hoped would save them.

Aerial photograph of the ruins of a first century Essene settlement, Israel.

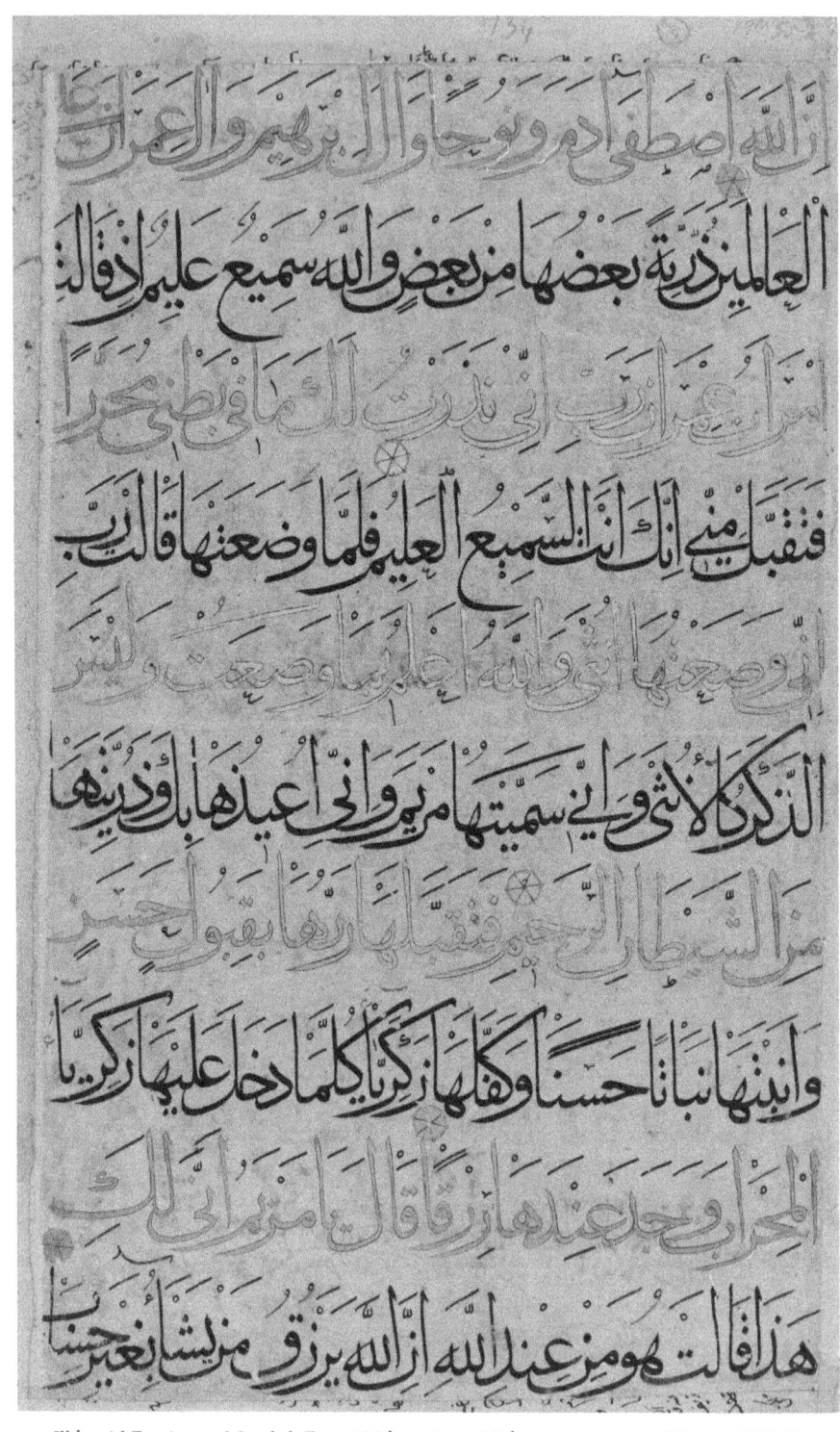

Ilkhanid Persian or Mamluk Egypt 14th century. Muhaqqaq script. Aal 'Imran 3:33-36

4.
The Family of 'Imran (ra)

I ndeed, Allah chose Adam and Nuh and the family (*Aal*) of Ibrahim and the family (*Aal*) of 'Imran above the worlds, descendants one of another. And Allah is Hearing, Knowing. (3:33-34).

There was one family, living at this time near the Temple in Jerusalem, who managed to rise above the discord and divisiveness of the world around them; who managed to keep their hearts connected to the One who never changes. They are said to have had a special relationship with their Lord. Allah says about them in The Qur'an: **Indeed, they used to rush to do good deeds and they called upon Us out of longing and awe, and humbled themselves before Us.** (21:90). This family is identified in The Qur'an as the family of 'Imran, *Aal 'Imran*, for whom the third surah of The Qur'an is named.

The early commentators say that 'Imran (ra), whom the Christians call Joachim, was probably a wealthy man who functioned in the Temple and in the community as both a religious and a political leader. He was generous and respected. His word was trusted, and his favor was sought. It seems he was, that most rare of creatures, a good and honest man. It is permitted for Muslims to hold a wide variety of opinions about the things not considered *'aqida*, the established fundamentals of belief. So although there is no indication that he was either a priest or a prophet there exists a mosque for him called *Nabi* 'Imran (prophet 'Imran) in Yemen. And Allah knows best.

Genealogy of 'Imran with picture of his daughter Maryam (ahs) and his grandson 'Isa (as).

What we do know is that he was married. Although the name of his wife is not mentioned in The Qur'an, the Christians tell us it was Hana or Anne (rah). A Hadith of the Prophet (sas) informs us that Hana (rah) had a relative by the name of 'Ashya (rah), who is known in Hebrew as Elisheba and in Christian tradition as Elizabeth. She was married to a Temple priest and prophet, Zakariyya (as). 'Imran (ra) and Hana (rah) were gifted with a baby girl whom they named Maryam (ahs) and who then had, in a miraculous way, a son, *Masih* 'Isa ibn Maryam (as) whom the Christians call Jesus Christ. 'Ashya (rah) and Zakariyya (as), at around the same time, also had a son named Yahya (as) whom the Christians call John the Baptist.

Three prophets and the holiest woman ever born are what constitute the *Aal* of 'Imran (ra). They are the last links in the unbroken chain of prophets that Allah Almighty sent to the Banu Isra'il through the line of Ishaq (Isaac) (as) and Ya'qub (Jacob) (as). There was an earlier man who is named Amran in the Tawrah and 'Imran in the Muslim accounts although not mentioned in The Qur'an. He was also the father of two prophets and of a saintly woman. His children were Musa (Moses) (as), Harun (Aaron) (as) and their sister Miriam (rah) whom the Tawrah even calls a prophetess (*nabbiyya* in Hebrew). It is clear that The Qur'an is referencing this earlier family when talking about the later one. Maryam (ahs) is even called (19:28) the sister of Harun (as) because they are **descendants one from another** (3:34) both genetically and spiritually. Two pious men named 'Imran, whose personal stories have not been considered of enough relevance to be revealed to us but whose families were honored and chosen above the worlds. Two good men, who were humble before their Lord, who were so obedient and pure hearted that they were honored to be the vehicles by which prophets came into this world.

The word *'imran* itself comes from the root *'-m-r* meaning to inhabit, to prosper, bloom, to live long, to fill a place with life. The phrase *'amara rabbahu* means he worshipped his Lord. It is the same root from which the name for the smaller hajj, the *'umra*, stems, which means to visit but particularly to visit an inhabited, settled place. *Aal 'Imran* then conveys the meaning of a blessed house, a thriving family full of worshippers.

There has been some controversy over the fact that The Qur'an calls Maryam (ahs) the sister of Harun (as) (19:28) and the daughter of 'Imran (ra). Skeptics have said that The Qur'an has confused the family of 'Isa (as) with the family of Musa (as). Believers have posited that perhaps Maryam (ahs) actually had a brother named Harun which was a common name at the time. Nothing in Allah's Book, however, is frivolous or insignificant. The fact that both families are called 'Imran is, of course, not a mistake. Rather it serves to call our attention to the ways in which the stories of the two 'Imrans reflect and reveal each other.

Both families of 'Imran (ra) were steadfast in their worship of Allah through long periods of difficulty. The 'Imran father of Musa (as) held on to belief in the one God despite four hundred years of subjugation to and immersion in an overwhelmingly polytheistic society. Many of the other Banu Isra'il had succumbed to social pressure and tried to adapt to Egyptian ways and forgotten or deserted the religion of their ancestor Ibrahim (as) in order to improve their lot. In much the same way, the 'Imran (ra) of our story held fast to the religion of Ibrahim (as) in the age of Greco-Roman polytheism when it was neither advantageous nor safe to do so. The descendants of both 'Imrans (may Allah bless them) delivered a new form of the one and only religion and changed the world in very significant ways, forever.

These two families of 'Imran (ra) demarcate the boundaries of the dispensation of the Banu Isra'il. Judaism began with Allah speaking to Musa (as) *Kalim Allah*, the intimate of Allah, on Mount Sinai and ended with the birth of 'Isa (as) *Kalimat Allah*, word of Allah, on Mount Moriah. It is suggested that the spelling of the name 'Isa was deliberately chosen to mimic the spelling of Musa, reflecting their symbolic functions as

Mount Sinai where Musa (as) received the Torah, with the name Musa in Arabic.

bookends of the Jewish scripture of which the two 'Imrans (ra) and their families represent the beginning and end.

In addition, there has been some scholarly discussion about why Allah uses the word *Aal* as opposed to *Ahl*. They both can mean family, tribe, or people. Some linguists think that *Aal* is just a variation of *Ahl*. In general, *Aal* is considered the more inclusive, broader term although there are others who contend the opposite. According to Lane, *Ahl* can be used for the family of any person and even as a polite way to refer to the women of the house. But *Aal* is only used for people of distinction, only a prophet or a king technically has an *Aal*. So in the *Salawat Ibrahimiya* we ask for blessing on the *Aal* of Muhammad (sas) just as Allah blessed the *Aal* of Ibrahim (as). The Qur'an also speaks of the *Aal* of Pharaoh that He punished by drowning in the sea (2:50).

Ahl refers to the close family or household of a man. *Ahlu l-Bayt* is the phrase used to designate the family of the Prophet Muhammad (sas). Depending on the source, it includes all his wives as well as his children and their descendants or it is limited to his daughters, in particular Fatima (rah) and her husband 'Ali ibn Abi Talib (ra) because they are the only ones with descendants who survived. However, the Prophet (sas) also

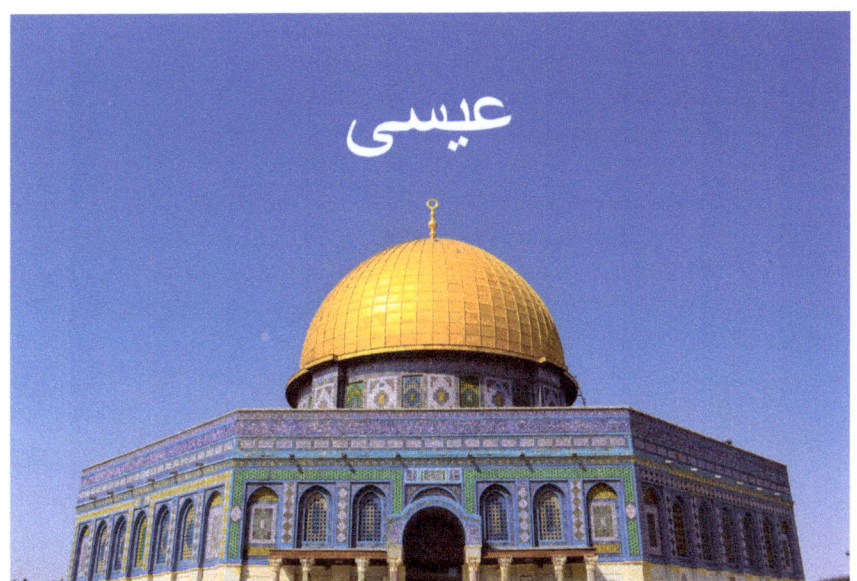

The Dome of the Rock on the Temple mount with the name of 'Isa (as) in Arabic.

included his companion and retainer Salman al-Farsi in his *Ahlu l-Bayt*. The Prophet's (sas) *Aal*, on the other hand, are all of those for whom the taking of charitable donations is forbidden, his extended family including his cousins and uncles and his descendants up to today. When he was asked directly who comprises his *Aal*, he responded, "All pious people".

'Imran (ra), however, did not have a large family or following. His *Aal* only seems to designate a small group consisting of his wife, their daughter and her son, his wife's sister, her husband and their son, a group more consistent with an *Ahl*, a household. So it is thought that by using the word *Aal* for 'Imran (ra), Allah is elevating his status in the eyes of people to emphasize his spiritual rather than his social distinction.

Descended from Ibrahim (as), according to the Muslim genealogies, through Ya'qub (as), Harun (as) and somehow also Dawud (as) and Sulayman (as), the Family of 'Imran adhered firmly to the laws of their ancestors not only in their words but also in their actions and, most importantly, in the depths of their hearts. They exemplified the true meaning of purity, which doesn't lie in the number of baths they took or the whiteness of their clothes or their lack of contact with the sick and the poor. Instead they guarded an inner purity that kept envy and greed, selfishness and heedlessness from soiling their hearts. They kept the remembrance of Allah before their eyes at all times, and they actively sought His pleasure with their hearts and hands at all times. They have been raised by Allah Almighty into the blessed company of the family of Ibrahim (as).

The mission of these last prophets of Judaism seems to have been to burst open the thick walls of rules and regulations that had fortified the religion of Ibrahim (as), protecting as well as isolating the ones inside and serving to deter outsiders from entering. The result was to put an end to the worship of other than God in the West and in most of the world. The fact that the last two prophets of the line of Ishaq (as) did not marry or have children could be seen as a sign that the line had been completed and a new dispensation was coming. The way was opened for the advent of Allah's last messenger, the Seal of Prophets, Muhammad Mustafa (sas).

The *surah* in which this family is introduced, *Aal 'Imran*, in comparison to all the other chapters of The Qur'an, contains the most number of words derived from the root s-l-m meaning peace and submission. In it, the phrase *la ilaha illa Allah*, there is no god but God, occurs all of four times. In Surah Maryam, which tells their story, Allah calls Himself the Merciful, *Ar-Rahman*, sixteen times and mentions His *rahma* (compassion) another three. It tells the miraculous and moving stories of the opening of the wombs (*rahm*) and consequent miraculous births of Yahya, Maryam, and 'Isa, may Allah bless them all. These words seem to best characterize these remarkable men and women. It could be said that the *Aal* of 'Imran (ra) is the *Aal* of *Rahma* and *Salam*, the family of compassion for others and submission to God.

Family of Prophets
(Allah's peace on them all)

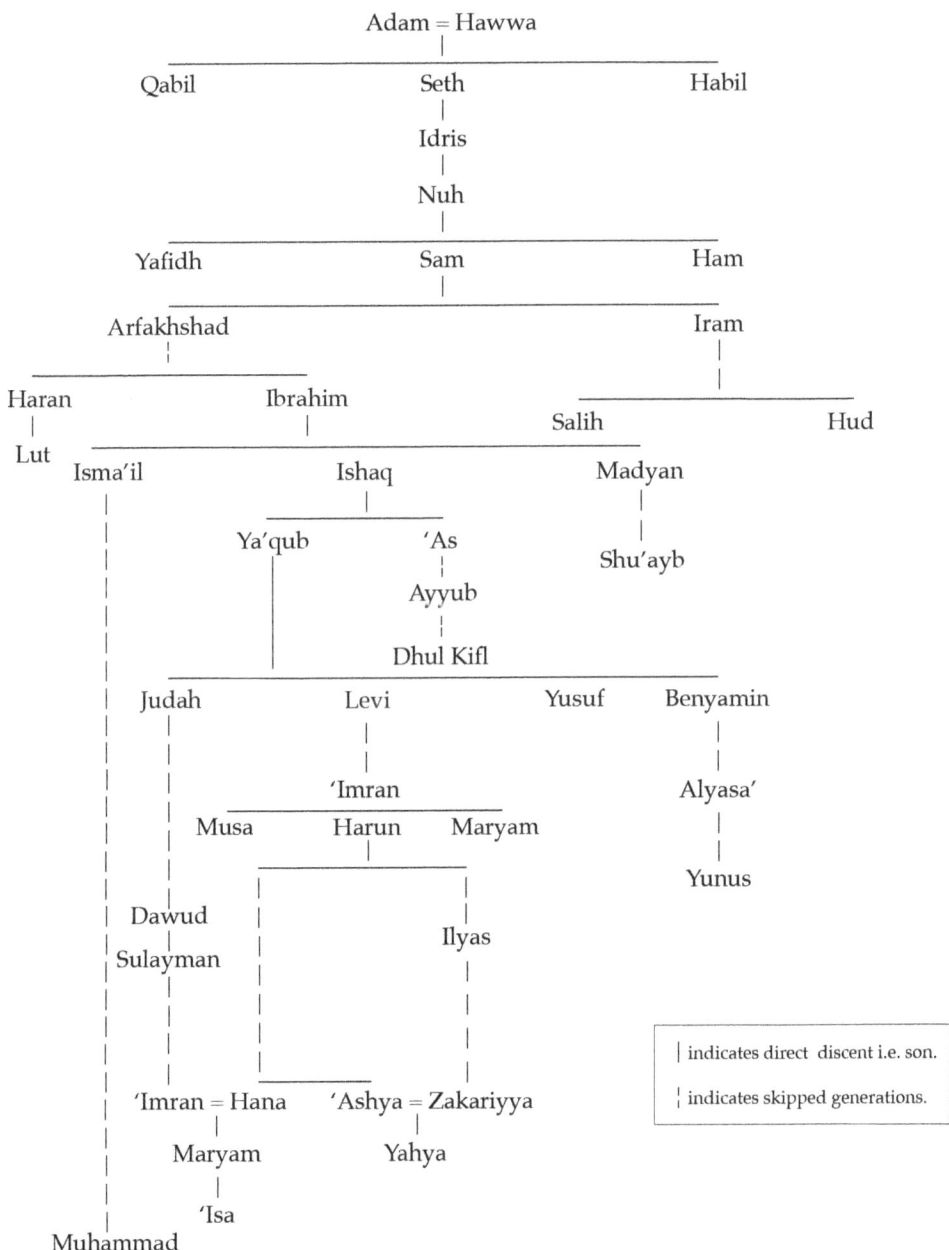

A painting by Ching Hsun.

5.
A Promise

Some say that Hana (rah) and 'Imran (ra) had been blessed with many children, all boys or both boys and girls. Late in life, Hana (rah) found herself unexpectedly pregnant once more. Others assert that, like her sister 'Ashya (rah), she had never been able to have any children. Being childless was a particularly unfortunate and even shameful condition in a world that honored a woman primarily for her fertility. One day Hana (rah), sitting in her garden in the shade of an overhanging tree, heard a soft chorus of chirping. Looking up, she saw a tiny nest crowded with open beaks. Five baby birds, their mouths open and their eyes shut, were crying insistently to be fed. She watched as the mother bird darted back and forth bringing food for her children. Hana's (rah) heart melted in sorrow. From the depths of her longing, she asked Allah to give her what He had seen fit to give even the wild birds, a child of her own. Allah Almighty heard her heartfelt prayer and, it being the decreed time, granted it.

The men and women of Allah's choosing do not have children just because they love each other and share a bed. Their children are not born in order to perpetuate the race of Adam (as) or to carry on the family business or to be the delight of their parents. Their children, and perhaps all children, are prayers come to life, miracles who manifest the divine compassion. They are Allah's answers and gifts to His loving servants and they do not come lightly. Many of the prophets of the Banu Isra'il had to wait long and pray hard for a child. Ibrahim (as) was an old man before he was given Isma'il (as) and Ishaq (as). Ishaq (as) had no children for many years until Rifqa (rah) gave birth to the twins, Ya'qub (as) and 'As. Now it was the turn of 'Imran (ra) and Zakariyya (as) to receive their gifts.

When Hana (rah) realized she was with child, it came to her heart to dedicate this precious gift to serve Allah. It surprises us that she had wanted a child so badly, and then when she got what she wanted she gave it up. But she had not wanted a child just to sleep warmly in her arms, or to play at her feet as she worked, or to skip beside her when she went to market. She had not wanted a child just to feel their small arms around her neck or their sweet breath on her cheek. She had wanted a child so that they would inherit her faith and that of her ancestors, so that there would always be a child of Adam (as) on earth remembering their Lord and praising in the way that is pleasing to Him.

Baby Musa (as) in the *tabut* being rescued from the river by the wife of Pharaoh. Illustration from the History of Rashid al-Din Hamadani (14th century Mongol).

The traditional scholars say that Hana's (rah) promise was not made on a whim, nor was it calculated to impress. On the contrary, it was the result of an inspiration from Allah Almighty although of a lower order than revelation. Hasan al-Basri compares Hana (rah) to Yuchabad (rah), the wife of the first 'Imran (ra) and the mother of the prophet Musa (as). She was inspired to place her infant son in a box and commit him to the waters of the Nile, an inspiration that sent him into the arms of the one from whom he was fleeing. He compared Hana (rah) to Ibrahim (as) who was inspired in a dream to sacrifice his only son, to slaughter with his own hand the child for whom he had prayed a lifetime. Hana's (rah) heart transmitted the wish of her Lord clearly and she obeyed without question, even if she had no understanding why.

To give a child to the Temple as a charitable act was neither novel nor shocking at that time. It was common for members of the priestly families, the tribe of Levi, to commit at least one of their sons to enter Temple life and continue the family tradition of service there. In fact, Herod is said to have passed a law forbidding the practice because there were so many toddlers being left on the Temple steps by their pious parents. Hana (rah) talked to her husband 'Imran (ra) and, although he did not object, he thought it might be wiser to wait until the child was born to see first if it was a boy or a girl. But Hana (rah) did not wait. She went forward with her intention on the assumption that her prayer had been answered so the child must be a boy. She would not or could not change the impulse of her heart and her sacred vow was made. **Imran's wife said, "Lord, I have dedicated what is in my womb entirely to You; so accept this from me. You are the One who hears and knows all," (3:35).**

'Imran (ra) was cautious about dedicating their unborn child because, although it was common to dedicate boys, it was rare to dedicate girls. The menial duties, such as cleaning and carrying water, were considered too strenuous for young girls and the priestly duties were restricted to males. The Muslim accounts state emphatically that there were no girls ever admitted to Temple service. However, scholars today are quite sure that in fact there were some special, very young girls who were selected to live in the proximity of the Temple and serve. In fact, it is stated they lived in a three story house within the precincts of the Temple. They wove the curtains that veiled the holiest part of the sanctuary. They baked the 'showbread' that lay all week on the main altar in the inner sanctuary and could only be consumed by priests within the confines of the Temple. They prepared the incense that was kept smoldering and smoking on the incense altar and served to cover the smell of the animal sacrifices that were taking place on the other side of the curtain.

"And the virgins also that were shut up, came forth, some to [High Priest] Onias, and some to the walls, and others looked out of the windows. And all holding up their hands towards heaven, made supplication." (2 Macc 3:19-20). The Mishna (the written oral tradition, first part of the Talmud) states that there were eighty-two girls who were taught to weave the very intricate curtains or veils that were specified to enclose the Holy of Holies. These were made of linen, silk, and gold thread. "The veil of the Temple was a palm-length in width. It was woven with seventy-two smooth stitches each made of twenty-four threads. The length was of forty cubits and the width of twenty cubits. Eighty-two virgins wove it. Two veils were made each year and three hundred priests were needed to carry it to the pool." (*Mishna Shekalim* 8, 5-6).

The small, flexible fingers of the young girls were the best for this task, just as until today in some countries of the Middle East, young girls work at knotting the intricate oriental rugs that carpet the houses of the world. These girls had not yet reached maturity. They were considered pure and could move about the temple freely and perhaps act as intermediaries between the grown women worshippers and the priests. The main ritual of the temple was the offering of sacrifice. This sacrifice could be anything from a basket of grain or fruit to a pigeon or a cow. It could only be offered to the Lord by the priests of the Temple at the altar which was situated just outside the Holy of Holies. As the quotation from Maccabees shows, the girls had some access to the High Priest and were even perhaps expected to offer certain prayers at certain times.

The practice was to turn the baby over to the Temple authorities some say at birth before they had ever even nursed from a worldly mother, others say at three years after the obligatory period of nursing was over and they were weaned. Then they entered into the Temple to be trained and educated. The parents could only visit them on special occasions. They served until they reached maturity. For the boys this meant fourteen or fifteen. For the girls it was younger, at least by twelve or whenever they began to menstruate. At that time, the boys were given a choice to remain in the Temple or to go home and lead a secular life with their families. If they chose the Temple, they were married to whomever the priests chose as suitable and they continued their duties. Marriage was considered the duty of every Jewish male, as it is in Islam also. However, the stated purpose in Judaism is to procreate and maintain the population of believers. For Muslims, marriage is considered to be half of one's religion, a spiritual journey, and the way to avoid sin. The girls, on the other hand, due to the ritual purity requirements of traditional Judaism, usually were not permitted to remain in the Temple once they matured. They were married to righteous suitors and left the Temple grounds.

Despite her husband's wise counsel, Hana (rah) knew the inspiration came from her Lord and that the child she carried inside her was meant for the service of Allah. She felt so sure that what she did was what was being asked of her that she made her sacred vow anyway and resolved to present the baby at the temple gates once he was weaned, a sacred vow that would either have to be fulfilled or ransomed. It is believed, however, that before the child was born 'Imran (ra) died, may Allah give him peace, and Hana (rah) was left a widow and the unborn child an orphan.

Coptic icon of 'Imran (ra) and Hana (rah) and the birds.

Opening of Surat Maryam by Muhammad al-Qandusi, (d. 1861, Morocco).

6.
Becoming Maryam (ahs)

As 'Imran (ra) had perhaps known, the baby he did not live to see was a girl. Hana (rah) on the other hand, appears to have been completely surprised. She had felt so strongly that this baby was meant for service in the Temple that she never doubted it would be a boy. However, Allah knew best what He had given her.

'Imran's wife said, "Lord, I have dedicated what is in my womb entirely to You; so accept this from me. You are the One who hears and knows all." But when she gave birth, she said, "My Lord! I have given birth to a girl." God knew best what she had given birth to: the male is not like the female. (3:35-36). Hana (rah) was stunned. She had felt so strongly that this child, born so late in her life and in answer to her sincere prayer, was a gift from Allah with a special purpose. This child belonged to Allah, to be His servant. But in what way, she wondered, was a girl child going to be able to serve her Lord? And so Hana's (rah) statement of surprise is really a question: "How, O my Lord, is a girl to be dedicated to You?" And He answered her by saying that it was neither by chance nor mistake that she had given birth to a girl. Allah had chosen this child above the worlds because a female is not the same as a male. She has different qualities and different strengths. As they say, if men and women were the same, why would Allah Almighty have made two of them? This time, for His special purpose, Allah had chosen a woman.

"I name her Maryam and I seek refuge in You for her and for her offspring from satan the accursed." (3:36). And so Hana (rah), newly widowed, chose a name for the child in memory of her beloved 'Imran (ra). She named her baby Maryam after the daughter of the first 'Imran (ra) and the sister of the two prophets Musa (as) and Harun (as). It was that first Maryam (rah) who, as a rightly guided child, counseled her father not to avoid his wife for fear of conceiving a boy in the year when Pharaoh was killing the baby boys. It was that first Maryam (rah) who, in obedience to her mother, followed the little wooden casket (*tabut*) with Musa (as) sealed inside as he was set afloat on the Nile, by Allah's order, to meet his destiny. It was that first Maryam (rah) who ran along the shore, her heart pounding, to see where the casket would come to land; afraid it would be tipped over or caught in the tangled stems of the water lilies or drowned in the currents and eddies of the great river. It was that first Maryam (rah) who in terror saw it drift into the canal that watered the palace gardens of the Pharaoh himself. It was that first Maryam (rah) who, hiding in the reeds, saw Musa (as) plucked out of the river by the royal attendants and cradled in the arms of the Queen. She watched as the baby rejected all the wet nurses the Queen could find and she risked her own life to suggest his own mother to nurse him and still his sobs. That first Maryam (rah) was strong and sure. She was unafraid to act on the inspiration Allah sent to her heart. The Banu Isra'il even consider her to have been a prophetess, one guided to right action and inspired by Allah to give tidings of the future. According to the Tawrah, throughout their lives, she was consulted by her prophet brothers, and could connect with her Lord to give them wise and prophetic counsel. This was a good role model for Hana's (rah) newborn fatherless daughter.

The Muslim traditional scholars all say that the name Maryam means 'Handmaid of Allah' which accurately portrays her mother's intentions for her. However, there is no derivation that we know of today to support this claim, in either Hebrew or Aramaic, the spoken language of that time. The Jews say rather that the name Maryam stems from two Hebrew words, *mar* (*murr* in Arabic) meaning bitter, and *yam* (the same in

Arabic) meaning river or sea. They say she was so named because she was born while the Banu Isra'il were enslaved in Egypt, and it expresses the bitter tears shed by her captive people.

Others suggest that it is from myrrh, the bitter incense that was associated especially with the marriage ceremony. Today the linguists say that since the Muslim form of the name is Maryam, rather than the Hebrew Miriam, it comes through Syriac from the original Hebrew. In Syriac her name is Maryamo, and it is derived from the root *r-w-m* meaning to elevate, to be from a high place. There are also those today who in deciphering the ancient Egyptian hieroglyphics have found many names similar in sound. In ancient Egyptian *mar* or *mari* meant love or beloved. It was common to name women as beloved of one god or another. For example, the name MeritAmun translates as "Beloved of the god Amun". Since Hebrew and ancient Egyptian belong to the same family of languages, shared vocabulary is not unlikely and the existence of loan words, after four hundred years of living together, is not improbable. Even the name Musa they believe stems from the Egyptian word for 'son

Grotto of the birthplace of Sayyida Maryam (ahs), Jerusalem.

of', like *ibn* in Arabic and *ben* in Hebrew. For example, the name of the pharaoh Thutmose means son of the god of wisdom Thoth, and Ramses means son of the sun god Ra.

So the nicest and most appropriate translation of the name Maryam might be from *mar*, meaning either beloved or exalted and *ya* from the Hebrew word for Allah, the first syllable in Yahweh. She sincerely loved her Lord and was loved in return, and she was raised by Him above the women of the world: Maryam (ahs), the beloved of Allah.

As Hana (rah) named her child she also made a prayer. She prayed: "**I seek refuge in You for her and for her offspring from satan the accursed.**" (3:36). The Prophet Muhammad (sas) said, "With the exception of Maryam and her son, there is no human born who is not touched by satan at the moment of their birth and who does not begin to cry out because of it." This exceptional exemption is credited to the prayer of Hana (rah).

Some claim that after three days Hana (rah) swaddled Maryam (ahs) in a shawl and took her to the main temple in Jerusalem with the intention of handing her over to the priests. However, most accounts say that Hana (rah) nursed Maryam (ahs) at home for the prescribed term of three years. During this time, she was lovingly guarded in an inner room of the house. She was not taken out and about to the markets or passed from arm to arm among her neighbors and relatives. Her playmates were carefully chosen from the purest and best behaved of the believing families. Nothing impure or even worldly was allowed near her. She grew lovely and healthy as Allah says that He made her to **grow in goodness and beauty** (3:37). She flourished.

Maryam's (ahs) first seven steps from the Chora Church 12th century mosaic. Istanbul.

Maryam climbs the stairs to the temple by Father Jerome Xavier for the Mughal Prince Salim 1602.

7.
A *Mihrab for Maryam (ahs)*

At the age of three Maryam (ahs) was weaned and taken by her mother to the Temple to be presented to the priests. Hana (rah) had no second thoughts nor any doubt that this is what her Lord required of her. It also seems that there was little hesitation on the part of the priests to accept the small girl. The Qur'an makes it clear that **Her Lord graciously accepted her** (3:37). This is understood to mean that He fully, completely accepted the vow of her mother and that He fully accepted Maryam (ahs) as His servant. If the priests were at all responsive to their Lord, they could only also agree to what was already accepted regardless of whether girls were normally dedicated or not. This is regarded as being the first miracle delivered on behalf of Maryam (ahs).

It is related that Maryam (ahs), although only a toddler, managed the massive stone steps by herself without asking to hold the hand of her mother and walked, head held up and eyes wide with wonder, through the high arched gate into the great Temple of Allah. She stood serenely in the middle of the circle of critical priests who were waiting for her. She did not turn to look back at her mother. She was neither shy nor assertive, neither proud nor afraid. She simply stood before them relaxed and at ease. She was a beautiful, sturdy child, big for her age and radiant with light. She trusted that she was in the place she belonged, and that calm assurance was visible to everyone. There was not one among those usually disapproving men who could help smiling as they saw her. She watched her mother go with neither a tear nor a question. She was home.

These are accounts from the Unseen, which We reveal to you. You were not with them when they cast their pens as to which of them would take charge of Maryam; nor were you with them as they quarreled (3:44). The Temple was not set up perhaps to house and care for a toddler girl, and, even if it were, Maryam's (ahs) father had died and she was required by law to have a male guardian. Zakariyya (as) immediately offered himself since his wife was her kinswoman. But for some reason the other priests would not accept this very simple solution, perhaps because of his age or venerability. It could be that because her family was wealthy and prominent, the other priests hoped either for favors or prestige by becoming her guardian. Or it could be that because she was such a special and unusual case, out of curiosity they wanted to be part of raising her. Or it could be that because of her character and the signs of her having been divinely chosen, they wanted to be of help to her in the hope of pleasing God. But it might also have been that none of them really wanted to shoulder the heavy responsibility of protecting and guarding a young orphan girl in a world of men just as none of the Bedouin women wanted to foster the small orphan baby Muhammad (sas). By drawing lots, therefore, the choice was left up to Allah.

It is said that they went down to the river, perhaps the Jordan, taking with them the reed pens with which they wrote copies of the sacred Tawrah. Others say that by *qalam* Allah meant their canes or sticks, and still others say iron rods. Each had the name of its owner inscribed upon it. They threw their pens into the water. Some say that they all sank except the pen of Zakariyya (as) which floated down stream. Some say they all floated down stream except the pen of Zakariyya (as) which either sank to the bottom or stood on end in place, defying the current. However it was, the pen of Zakariyya (as) was clearly set apart. Not willing to take the chance that the first throw was a mistake, the priests insisted on throwing them again two more times into the river. Three times the pen of Zakariyya (as) was chosen. Finally, they all consented that Allah had

The Mihrab of Maryam (ahs) in the Al-Aqsa Mosque, Jerusalem.

appointed Zakariyya (as) to be the guardian of Maryam (ahs).

So Zakariya (as), the prophet of God, Maryam's uncle, became her guardian and her spiritual guide. He prepared for her a sanctuary in the Temple, called in the Qur'an a *mihrab*, a small secluded chamber oriented towards the Holy of Holies, the direction of prayer at that time. The commentators say that he protected this space with seven walls each closed with a locked door. He was the sole possessor of the keys. The outer door could only be accessed by a moveable stair or ladder in the manner in which the Ka'ba door is accessed. After her lessons and duties were done, Zakariyya (as) would lock her inside this room for safekeeping. However awkward and unkind this might sound, and unlikely for practical reasons, it serves as a strong image to portray the reality of her divine protection and her inner inviolability.

The word *mihrab* in Arabic comes from the same root as *harb* meaning war. Its derivatives were used to designate the highest and most honorable area in a king's house. Some understand the connection as being the symbol of what is worth fighting for. Others say it was where wars were initiated and concluded. In a religious context, it is the place of honor where the *imam* stands, but also the place where one fights with *shaytan* and one's own rebellious self.

Some commentators say that her *mihrab* was, in fact, the Holy of Holies itself. Like the contents of the *Tabut*, Maryam (ahs) was another **remnant of what the family of Musa and the family of Harun left behind,** (2:248) and so was safeguarded carefully in the innermost sanctuary of the Temple. She was a precious gift from God like the Ark itself. She was protected by visible and invisible veils and walls. Even shaytan himself was not able to approach her.

The possibility of her actually inhabiting the Holy of Holies seems most unlikely since only the high priest was allowed to enter the inner sanctum of the Temple and then only once a year to pray for the welfare of the nation. If he was not properly prepared and purified, he would be burned to a crisp by a bolt of lightning sent from the Lord of Heaven. This had actually happened to the two sons of Harun (as) who had been the first high priests.

The Holy of Holies was a stone walled room originally lined in wood and gold at the far back, far west of the Temple enclosure. The Temple in Jerusalem at the time of Herod still had a Holy of Holies that could only be visited by the High Priest on the Day of Atonement, but it was mostly symbolic. The room was empty with a raised area indicating where the Ark of the Covenant should have stood. Interestingly enough, in the modern reconstructions of the Temple, there are three levels containing thirty-eight small storerooms that surrounded and formed the outer walls of the Holy of Holies on three sides and another room that had access to it directly above. These small spaces could only be reached by ladder. It might have actually been possible that Zakariyya (as) commandeered one of these storerooms to house Maryam (ahs).

For the Christians, the idea that Maryam (ahs) replaced the Ark in the Holy of Holies is most appropriate and symbolic. She physically represented the new Ark as she was to become the living container of Allah's word which He was to manifest in 'Isa *Masih* (as) just as the wooden ark held the heavenly tablets of God's word, the Tawrah. In much the same way the Shi'a Muslims contend that Sayyiduna 'Ali (ra) was born inside the Ka'ba and exited through the split stone in the southern corner.

However, the Sunni Muslims have honored another place as the *mihrab* of Maryam (ahs). Several floors below the mosque built over the place where Sayyiduna 'Umar (ra) prayed in Jerusalem, the Masjid al-Aqsa, there is a small room accessed by stairs leading down rather than up. In it is a prayer niche, *mihrab*, that is known as the *Mihrab* of Maryam (ahs). In this sacred place it is recommended for Muslims to pray, and to read the nineteenth chapter of The Holy Qur'an called Surah Maryam. It was in this place she is supposed to have lived and worshipped. Nearby is the *mihrab* of her guardian Zakariyya (as) and a large stone said to have served as the cradle for the baby 'Isa (as). It is reported that Abu Hamid al-Ghazali visited this *maqam* with a large group of men. He recited some lines of poetry that caused one of them to fall into a state of ecstasy and the other men to weep and tear their clothes. A man named Muhammad al-Kazaruni died in ecstasy in the middle of it all (Matar).

But there is no consensus as to where exactly the original Temple of Sulayman (as) stood or even the historical Temple of Herod although the second is assumed to have been built over the ruins of the first. Surprisingly, there exists neither recorded accounts nor hard evidence to

The cradle of 'Isa (as) in the Al-Aqsa Mosque, Jerusalem.

point conclusively to the spot where the Holy of Holies was located. Some say it was over the rock (*sakhra*) that is now enclosed beneath the Dome of the Rock. Some say it was somewhere beneath where the Masjid al-Aqsa now stands. Some say it was where there is now a grove of trees between the Dome and the Aqsa Mosque or at the spot where the ablution fountain stands. A fourth opinion is that it was to the north of the Dome. Although most say that, judging by the layout of the only remaining wall of the second Temple of Herod, the Wailing Wall, the area of the Masjid al-Aqsa would lie outside the Temple enclosure. All the possible locations, however, are within easy sight of each other and can be considered as one sacred space. All of them have been made holy by Allah and by the touch, breath, and light of hundreds of His prophets, His saints and believers. Of the rest, Allah knows best.

Ayah 37 from Surah *Aal 'Imran* is used from the most simple to the most elaborate of mosques. This is the simple yet elegant *mihrab* of the Shaykh Nazim Mosque, Lefke Cyprus.

The ornate *mihrab* of the Prophet Muhammad (sas) with the same *ayah* inscribed above in the blue medallion, **Whenever Zakariyya entered her** *mihrab* (3:37). Madina, Saudi Arabia.

Maryam (ahs) at the peak of the dome surrounded by women saints. 14th century mosaic from the Chora Mosque, formerly Church, Istanbul Turkey.

8.
Above the Women of the Worlds

Here in this space the little Maryam (ahs) grew up. When she was not helping to sweep the Temple, she might have helped prepare the incense or bake the bread for the altar. She may have been one of those girls taught to weave the elaborate and intricate designs of the thick curtains that the Tawrah required to veil the innermost sanctuaries. She would also have probably had lessons to teach her Hebrew because the Jews at this time no longer spoke the language of the Tawrah, rather they spoke Aramaic and Greek. She was undoubtedly taught to read the Tawrah and to memorize the prayers and rituals of common practice.

When not performing whatever duties were assigned to her, she remained in her seclusion, praying and worshipping. It is said that she felt no boredom or fatigue. She did not know the meaning of loneliness. The angels spoke to her as it is written: **The angels said, "O Maryam, God has chosen you, and has purified you. He has chosen you over all the women of the world. O Maryam, be devoted to your Lord, and prostrate, and bow with those who bow down"** (3:42-43). One can imagine the angels ministering to her needs, perhaps even playing gently with her, their quickly moving lights making games and shadow plays for her amusement, enveloping her in their love, and singing the praises of their Lord in harmony with her own.

Her entertainment and her joy lay in worship. Most children are naturally drawn to prayer and imitate with pleasure what they see their elders do out of obligation. It is only later that they are taught to hold things other than worship in higher regard and hurry through their prayers in order to be free to return to the business of the world.

In The Qur'an Allah orders Maryam (ahs) to be devoted and obedient, to prostrate and to bow. When things became difficult in the world for her she was commanded to turn her face steadfastly to God. The commentators describe this station by saying that it meant that she stood in prayer and contemplation until her ankles were swollen and her feet were sore. She did not take notice of her physical state or needs, and she did not let them distract her from worship.

She is ordered to bow among those who bow in prayer (*raki'in*) (3:43), and she is counted among the devout (*qanitin*) (66:12). In both instances Allah has employed a masculine plural noun to designate the group in which Maryam (ahs) belongs. The masculine plural covers both men and women when the company is mixed. She is not being told to be a worshipper among or like a group that consists solely of women worshippers. She is also probably not being ordered to worship like or among the men. Rather she is told to be among the group that includes both men and women, the group in which no distinction is made on the basis of physical properties, the exalted group where worshipers are simply that, and equal in the eyes of Allah. She was pure, she was chosen, she was devout. She was beautiful both inside and out.

Under the spiritual guidance of her uncle and Allah's prophet, Zakariyya (as), Maryam (ahs) flowered as Allah had ordained for her. It is said that she grew faster than most other children. In an age when the death of children was a commonplace occurrence, a child who grew vigorously and developed early must have been considered the recipient of Allah's special blessings. It is recorded that the prophet Ibrahim (as) also grew at double the rate of other children. When he was just a few months old he appeared to be like a year. We are told that Maryam (ahs) didn't just grow, however, she developed in a goodly way (3:37). Her skin was radiant, her body well developed, perfectly proportioned and sturdy. Her eyes were bright and intelligent. Her character was both peaceful and pleasant, not sullen nor sad. She dwelled in the constant remembrance of her Lord, not forgetting Him as she went about her daily tasks, her heart never leaving Him although she remained present and aware of all that went on about her. It was clear to anyone who saw her that she had been favored by her Lord, and that she was someone special.

Many of the prophets have been protected in some way from growing up immersed in the normal materialism of the world. They have been selected, often by tragedy or difficulty

Tree of life, 19th century Persian rug from the Claremont collection.

although sometimes by privilege. They have been selected out and set apart. Deprived of father and/or mother, orphaned or persecuted, hidden or exiled, they were left to grow undamaged by the heavy expectations of their family and society, often in the care of angels. There is a natural state of being in which all of mankind is born, a state of complete belief and trust in their Creator. This is called the *fitra*, the perfect nature in which all the children of Adam (as) are made. **And so, set thy face steadfastly towards the [one ever-true] faith, turning away from all that is false, in accordance with the natural disposition (*fitra*) which God has instilled into man: [for,] not to allow any change to corrupt what God has thus** created this is the [purpose of the one] ever-true faith; but most people know it not. (30:30).

Everyone is born in this state, but most people lose it early in their lives due to the influence of the unbelieving world around them. So the Prophet (sas) said that all children are born muslim (submitted) only their parents raise them to be otherwise. Maryam (ahs) like her grandfather Ibrahim (as) grew up in a cave but a cave that was created for her in the very heart of humanity rather than in the wilderness among the innocent beasts. Flourishing in a walled garden, safe from wind and weather, safe from thieves and poachers, **like a good tree, its root firm and its branches in the sky, yielding its fruit at all times by permission of its Lord.** (14:24). Protected and open, as in the cupped hands of the one asking (*du'a*) and receiving from Allah - this was the childhood of Maryam (ahs).

Allah Almighty mentions only one woman by name in The Qur'an, that is the name of Maryam bint 'Imran (ahs). And He made it explicitly clear, **The Angels said to Maryam: "O Maryam, Allah has chosen you and made you pure: He has truly chosen you above all women."** (3:42).

And so the question arises as to whether Maryam (ahs) should be considered a prophet, a *nabiyya*, as her namesake Maryam (ra) (Miriam) is called by the Banu Isra'il. At different times, in different places, Muslims have seriously considered whether the mother of 'Isa (as) can be considered a prophet in her own right. And in our time in particular the question is being raised anew. She received revelation directly from Jibra'il (as), the angelic messenger who delivered revelation to all the prophets. Her book was in the form of a miracle child whom Allah has told us was **His word which He conveyed unto Maryam,** (4:171). So she received revelation, and she received a Book. Allah calls her the best of women. Her qualifications are not in dispute. If she were a man, there would perhaps be no debate. But the problem is that she is not a man and **a male is not like a female** (3:36). Almost all the scholars agree that to be a prophet one must be male. They cite these verses of The Qur'an as the proof: **And We sent not (as Our messengers) before you other than men whom We inspired** (12:109, 16:43, 21:7).

She was pure, she was devout, and she was faithful. She was strong enough to withstand the insults and vitriol of her whole world. But in the end she was not asked to be a public figure. She was not asked to **Arise and warn** (74:2). That function was taken up by her son, 'Isa ibn

Maryam (as). Perhaps it could be said that while the two were joined, while she held 'Isa (as) within her, she was like a prophet but not once they became separate because Allah says that together they comprise one sign. **And We made the son of Maryam and his mother a sign** (23:50). There is a Hadith of the Prophet (sas) in which he said that "no one will enter Paradise before the first believers of my Nation except a few. Among these few will be Ibrahim, Isma'il, Ishaq, Ya'qub, the ancestors of the Banu Isra'il, Musa, 'Isa, and Maryam bint 'Imran." (al-Qurtubi).

Allah calls Maryam a *saddiqah* (5:75), a woman of sincerity, testifying to the Truth. This is one of the highest degrees of sainthood. **Whoever obeys God and the Messenger will be among those He has blessed: the messengers, the truthful (*siddiqin*), the martyrs, and the righteous - what excellent companions are they!** (4:69). And it is said that the Prophet Muhammad (sas) repeated these words of The Qur'an on his last breath, asking to be among this excellent company.

However exalted, the spiritual station of *siddiq*, it is not that of a prophet or messenger. This is the consensus of Muslim scholars. However, Ibn Kathir, although he is one of the formulators of this *fatwa*, still cannot but show honor to Maryam (ahs) by writing after her name, *'alayha salam*, on her be peace. This is the blessing that is traditionally bestowed exclusively on prophets and angels and on no others.

Gate to the Hall of Justice, Bab ash-Shari'a, Alhambra, Spain. The outer arch has the hand of Fatima carved on the keystone which is original to the Muslim building. The inner arch has a mosaic of Maryam (ahs) which was added after the Spanish conquest..

9.
The Female Form

Maryam (ahs) was chosen by Allah Almighty above all the women of all the worlds. She is presented to us as a model of the spiritually perfect woman. **Allah has given examples for those who believe: Pharaoh's wife, who said, "My Lord, build for me a house near You in the Garden. Save me from Pharaoh and his actions; save me from the evildoers," and Maryam, daughter of 'Imran, whose body was chaste, therefore We breathed therein of Our Spirit. And she put faith in the words of her Lord and His Books, and was of the devoutly obedient. (66:11-12).**

And so the Prophet Muhammad (sas) has said that there have been many men who attained to the state of perfection but only these two women. But he has also said that there are four women who serve as role models and leaders (*sayyidat*) of all of womankind. In addition to Maryam (ahs), daughter of 'Imran (ra) and Asiya (rah), Pharaoh's wife who saved Musa (as) as a baby, believed in him as an adult, and was ultimately martyred for her faith, he added his own first wife Khadija (rah) bint Khuwaylid, and Fatima (rah) bint Muhammad (sas), his youngest daughter.

Statue of Ramses II and his wife, possibly Asiya (rah) Luxor, Egypt.

Khadija (rah) as a mature and widowed woman chose the Prophet (sas) for her husband because of his fine character and moral qualities. She was intelligent and clever and held her own even in a man's world of business. Her vision was not restricted to the material world, however. She recognized the exalted nature of the Prophet (sas) perhaps even before he knew himself. Throughout her life she loved and supported, served and sacrificed for him. She was the mother of all his children who lived to adulthood. And she was the first believer in his mission. She witnessed the visit of the Archangel Jibra'il (as) and was given the good news that she had attained to Paradise while she was still alive. The Prophet (sas) never stopped extolling her virtues and honoring her memory throughout his life. She was an example of faithfulness and constancy, of love and kindness. She was a staunch witness to the truth.

But of Fatima (rah), her youngest daughter, we actually know very little other than that she was the beloved of her father. He would stand to receive her whenever she entered the place he was sitting, and he would spread his cloak for her to sit beside him. He would always kiss her because, he said, her kiss had the taste of Paradise. Sayyida 'Aysha (rah) said that Fatima (rah) resembled her father the most of any of his family, in the way she walked and gestured, and in the way she talked and the matters that concerned her. She was entirely devoted to him. After her mother died, as a small girl she watched over him. When the Meccans reviled him and threw filth on him while he was praying she, like a little mother, grieved for him and lovingly cleaned it away. That is why she was known by the cherished epithet, *Umm Abiha* – 'mother of her father'.

She remains a figure of purity and piety, so much so that the same extreme qualities that are ascribed to Maryam (ahs) by some, are also hers. She never suffered from either monthly or postpartum bleeding. As a result, she was never without ablution and never excused from the opportunity to pray or to read scripture. Even though she married and delivered five children it is said her virginity remained intact. The Qur'an praises Maryam (ahs) several times for her chastity, **Maryam the daughter of 'Imran, who guarded her chastity** (66:12) and she is known in the Christian world as the Virgin Mary. Fatima (rah) is known to the Muslim world as Fatima Batul, the virgin, the one who keeps apart, separates herself, and remains untouched. Batul is also the word used for the offshoot at the base of a date palm that, when removed and planted separately, is an exact replica of the parent tree. The Prophet (sas) said "Fatima is a part of me. Who hurts her, hurts me." (al-Bukhari). Like Maryam (ahs) and 'Isa (as), Fatima (rah) and her father (sas) were so closely connected that in some ways they could be considered one.

The Prophet (sas) getting ablution with his wife Khadija (rah) holding the towel. Siyer-i Nebi, Ottoman, 1388.

The phrase, **guarded her chastity,** is perhaps not best translated as virginity because a married woman who remains faithful is considered chaste. Rather it means to be modest, to restrain lust, to guard the cleft places, the openings, the private parts. It is used for both men and women in The Quran. It is a description of the proper behavior of believers in general as in the often quoted verse in which Allah proclaims the spiritual equality of men and women. **For Muslim men and women, for believing men and women, for devout**

Mosaic of Maryam (ahs) in the Aya Sofya, Istanbul, Turkey.

men and women, for true men and women, for men and women who are patient and constant, for men and women who humble themselves, for men and women who give in charity, for men and women who fast (and deny themselves), for men and women who guard their chastity, and for men and women who engage much in Allah's praise, for them has Allah prepared forgiveness and a great reward. (33:35). It is used once specifically as a command for all men: **tell believing men to lower their gaze and guard their private parts: that is purer for them. God is well aware of everything they do.** (24:30) and once as a command specifically for all women in a verse that mirrors the preceding one. (24:31).

However, the virginity or chastity spoken of here is not only a physical state. More importantly, it is a spiritual and moral reality. Maryam (ahs) was pure, untouched by worldly distractions, her perfect God-given nature (*fitra*) remained unbroken and intact from birth until death. The virginity of Maryam (ahs) and of Fatima (rah) has been compared to the illiteracy (*ummiy*) of the Prophet Muhammad (sas). Allah kept him pure of the influences of the other Books and their adherents in order to make it crystal clear that the words he uttered were solely of divine origin. His heart and mind were chaste, clean. So it is stated that Maryam's (ahs) womb was virgin, untouched by man, in order to emphasize that what was delivered out of it was the pure Word of God, uncontaminated and direct from the source. Nothing came from her that was not from Allah. It is not her virginity that is honored but it is her being filled with her Lord. And Fatima (rah) also partook of this same kind of ultimate purity, a purity that was not just empty of sin but replete with light.

Although it is true without doubt that both Maryam (ahs) and Fatima (rah) grew up immersed in holiness, never having taken a single breath that was not steeped in the consciousness of God, neither woman was spared the sufferings of life. On the contrary, their worldly lives were stripped of adornments, luxuries, and even common comforts. Their loss of loved ones began early. Fatima (rah) lost her mother as a child. Maryam (ahs) lost her father before she was even born. They were both poor, exiled, and persecuted by their own people. Fatima (rah) grew up under the tyranny and mistreatment of the enemies of her father. She suffered along with all those who first followed the new revelation. She watched the ones she loved die too young. She was the only one of the Prophet's (sas) children to survive him, and she lived only six months after his passing.

She, like Maryam (ahs), is also known mostly for the children she bore. Her two sons, Hasan (ra) and Husain (ra), were the only immediate descendants of the Prophet (sas) who had children of their own. In fact, the family of the Prophet (sas) is preserved exclusively through the sons of Fatima (rah). Like Maryam (ahs), Fatima (rah) seemed to be eclipsed by the men in her life. Once 'Isa (as) is born we are told very little more about the life of his mother. This is not because they were no longer important but because the world only takes notice of what it cannot overlook.

Fatima (rah), although the daughter of the Prophet (sas) and the wife of Sayyiduna 'Ali (ra), played no central role in the outward life of the community. But quietly she helped whoever needed and gave to them whatever she had, holding nothing back for herself or her family. She did not draw attention to herself or set herself above the other believing women either as a teacher or as someone of privilege. She led by her example, working hard, grinding grain between two mill stones to help feed those answering her father's call. She shared her great wisdom and knowledge only with those who came seeking it. But she was not weak or timid either. She stood up for what she believed to be right and she defended herself and her family even as a child. Like Maryam (as) who, although raised in the shelter of the Temple and never having lived in the world, came to face her people openly and bravely carrying her miraculous child when it was Allah's order to do so.

It is related (Musnad al-Bazzar) that one day the Prophet (sas) asked his companions what is the best characteristic of women. No one had a response, and so the topic passed without further comment. Sayyiduna 'Ali (ra) was present in that gathering, and afterwards he went home and mentioned it to his wife. Sayyida Fatima (rah) answered by saying, "The best trait of a woman is that men do not see her and she does not see men." Sayyiduna 'Ali (ra) later repeated this to the Prophet (sas)

The marriage of Fatima (rah) and Ali (ra). Siyer-i Nebi, Ottoman, 1388.

who verified it, stating "Surely Fatima is of me."

She was the Prophet's (sas) daughter, of course everyone knew her by sight and by reputation. Even after the order to cover, she was a recognized and familiar figure. But although she was sighted, she was not really seen, and although she was recognized, she was not really known. Nothing in the way she walked or moved, the way she spoke or dressed, attracted the eyes of people and especially not that of men looking as men look at women. She did not attract that kind of attention by her actions or her appearance. She was protected by her own innocence and purity, and she remained hidden in the bright shadow of her men. She was God's servant first and foremost, and she had no need to take this relationship into the public eye. The hiddenness of both Sayyida Fatima (rah) and Sayyida Maryam (ahs) is perhaps the brightest trace of their greatness. Like a luminous pearl in its lustrous shell, each was light upon light shining inward, veiled only by her own radiance. So it might be that there are many more perfect women than the ones we know but that Allah protects their secret with His silence.

Sayyida Fatima (rah) gave birth to five children in the nine or ten years of her married life. In spite of the weaknesses this naturally entailed, her sons related that they remembered their mother praying long into the night when most other people were asleep. 'Aysha (rah) said that Fatima (rah), just like her father, was most concerned about the poor. Even though she herself worked hard for most of her life and had no servants to help and no luxuries, she gave what little she had to those Muslims who were even poorer. Sometimes she let her own family go to sleep hungry if she thought that another family was more in need. The only dowry she requested on the occasion of her wedding was to be given the power of intercession for the Nation (*Ummah*) of the Prophet (sas).

It is told that once, at a time when there was very little food in Medina, the Prophet (sas) went to Fatima's (rah) house to see if she had anything he could eat. She also had nothing but, shortly after he left, a neighbor brought her a bowl of bread and a few pieces of meat. She immediately sent her sons to bring their grandfather back so that he could share in the food. He ate, and Fatima (rah) and her children ate, and they gave to the Prophet's (sas) other daughters and their families and to the Prophet's (sas) wives. And still there remained food in the bowl to be shared with neighbors. The Prophet (sas) asked Fatima (rah) from whom she had been given such miraculous food, and she answered in words similar to those of Maryam (ahs**) "From Allah who provides for whom He pleases without measure."** (3:37). And the Prophet (sas) extolled his Lord and said "Praise be to Allah who made you the equal of the Lady of Isra'il for when Allah gave her food and she was asked about it, she answered with the very same words."

The opening of Surah Maryam. 19th century Dagestani Qur'an.

10.
Zakariyya the Prophet (as)

Her Lord graciously accepted her and made her grow in goodness and beauty, and entrusted her to the charge of Zakariyya. (3:37). Maryam (ahs) was put under the care and guardianship of her uncle, a priest and prophet by the name of Zakariyya (as). His identity is not easily traced in either the Old or the New Testament. There are at least two prophets by that name in the Hebrew Bible whose stories have become confused with each other. The Gospel of Matthew mistakenly refers to him as Zacharias son of Barachias who was actually a sixth century BCE prophet, while Luke leaves out any reference to the name of his father.

    What we know from The Qur'an is that he was a priest who served in the Temple and so he must have been of the tribe of Levi descended patrilinealy from the prophet Harun (as). Some Muslim scholars repeat the mistake of Matthew and call his father Barachiah. Some, such as Ibn Kathir, say his father was named Ladun a descendant of Dawud (as) who they then claim was also a descendant of Harun (as). This conveniently gives Zakariyya (as), and by extension the family of 'Imran, both the Davidic lineage necessary for the Messiah and the Levite lineage required for a priest. But this is inaccurate because Dawud (as) was not of the patrilineal line of Harun (as), he was from the tribe of Judah (ra) not Levi (ra). However, Harun (as) and his son both married wives from the tribe of Judah. So probably 'Imran (ra) was a Judahite, but Hana (rah) and 'Ashya (rah) were Levite. In this way the children of Zakariyya (as) were descended from Harun (as), and the children of 'Imran were descended from Dawud (as) with a link to Harun (as) only through the mother. Yahya (as) could be a priest, but 'Isa (as) could not. 'Isa (as) could be the foretold Messiah, but Yahya (as) could not.

In consequence, we do not know the parentage of this holy prophet of Allah. He was married to a sister or cousin of the wife of 'Imran (as), and it is assumed that he was also some sort of relative since that was the preferred form of marriage especially among the priestly class. It is believed that he, like Maryam (ahs), was dedicated by his parents as a baby, to serve in the Temple. He grew up in that religious environment, and was trained and educated in the main Temple on the holy mount in Jerusalem. When he reached maturity he chose to remain as a priest in the Temple.

Zakariyya and 'Ashya (rah) at home.
James Tissot, 1886, French.

He was married to a lady by the name of 'Ashya (rah) which is the Arabization of the name found in the Gospel of Luke, Elizabeth, Elisheba in Hebrew. Ibn Kathir says that 'Ashya (rah) was the niece of Hana (rah) the wife of 'Imran (ra) mother of Maryam (ahs). Others even say she was Hana's (rah) oldest daughter and so the sister of Maryam (ahs). But most agree that she and Hana (rah) were sisters or cousins since the Prophet Muhammad (sas) said that their children were maternal cousins. These women are mentioned in The Qur'an in the course of the narration of their stories but they are referred to by the names of their children or husbands rather than called by their personal names.

The only woman named in The Qur'an is Maryam (ahs). This might be out of respect for the custom of the Arabs at the time of the revelation and still today, where it is considered impolite to mention the women of a man by their given names. Rather they are referred to in circuitous ways, such as the 'people of house' or by their relation to others, daughter of, mother of etc. Maryam (ahs) alone is named perhaps because in life she also stood alone. She was singled out for a unique destiny, chosen above other women and not really part of the household of any particular man except her son and he is referred to by her name rather than she by his.

The name Zakariyya (as) is usually considered to be related to the Arabic root meaning pure, *z-k-y*, but in Hebrew it comes from the root meaning to remember or remind and is commonly translated as 'the Lord has remembered'. In Arabic then this name would be translated as *Dhakariyya* from the root *dh-k-r*. *Dhikr* is also used to refer to the ritual remembrance of God. **Remind (warn, teach), for the reminder benefits the believers**. (51:55). He was a pure and pious man who remembered his Lord at all times and who was remembered by Him in return. In fact, Zakariyya (as) is best known for turning to Allah when he was in need and for getting an immediate response.

When we are introduced to Zakariyya (as) he is already an old man. He says of himself: **My Lord, indeed, my bones have weakened and my head has turned white,** (19:4). He has become old and his growing weakness has impressed upon him the nearness of his departure from this life, and he is worried about the state of the people he will leave behind. He continues by saying, **but never have I been unblessed in my supplication to You.** (19:4). He remarks that Allah has in the past granted him what he has asked for. This is in itself a remarkable distinction. Either he has been very fortunate indeed to have been granted most of what he has asked for or, more likely, he has been content with what he was given and asked for very little. Certainly we know that although he had no children, he never asked to be given a child before old age had set upon him, and then he was not thinking of his own benefit, but rather he asked out of concern for his people and the religion itself.

We don't know anything about his youth or even his early manhood. He had grown up, married, and chosen to remain as God's servant, a priest in the Temple. It was the only life he knew or cared about. He and his wife 'Ashya (rah) had reached old age together without having any children. It is said that 'Ashya (rah) had never even been able to conceive a child. This was not an uncommon condition of the wives of the Hebrew prophets. And yet, unlike some of the other prophets of the Banu Isra'il, she and Zakariyya (as) had remained devoted to each other, and no second wife had been added to the family for the purpose of providing children. 'Ashya (rah) was a good woman, faithful and included in The Qur'anic statement about the family of 'Imran in general, eager to do goodness, always aware that everything comes from Allah, a grateful and humble servant of the Lord. They were content with each other and with whatever their Lord chose to give them or withhold from them.

Zakariyya (as) was busy with his priestly duties, busy fulfilling the mission with which Allah had entrusted him, guiding the Banu Isra'il and watching kindly over the children and adults put under his care. It is thought that he received the divine call to prophethood when he was already in middle age or older and that he may have actually risen to the rank of High Priest. Although, from what we know of the history at that time, the office of High Priest had become more of a political appointment rather than a spiritual one. Perhaps Zakariyya (as) was the last of the authentic High Priests, prophet and priest. His duties would have involved overseeing the other priests and all of those dedicated to or serving in the Temple. He would have been a teacher, delivering sermons of advice and counsel, and have overseen the daily program of animal sacrifice and maintenance of the incense and showbread in the anteroom of the Temple.

As High Priest, on the Day of Atonement, he would have been the one entrusted with the heavy task of entering the Holy of Holies to make *sajdah* to his Lord and to ask forgiveness for the Banu Isra'il. Before entering the Holy of Holies, the High Priest bathed in a special pool and dressed in simple white garments. He was checked by his fellow priests to make sure everything was in order as carefully as an astronaut for a space mission. If something should go amiss, if something was not exactly as it was required to be, Allah's divine anger would descend. Then there was no one who could enter to save him. Just in case, the priests tied a strong rope to his ankle, also reminiscent of the tether of an astronaut. If they heard some unexpected sound they could drag him out quickly. Maybe they thought they could save him from his Lord or at least retrieve enough of him to bury. When he exited it was common for the High Priest to make a prayer of thankfulness for having survived intact. His purity and sanctity would have been visibly confirmed by the fact that year after year he emerged unscathed, unconsumed by divine wrath and that his prayers for the forgiveness of his people had been accepted.

Zakariyya (as) was chosen to be God's prophet, and so we know he was a man of truth and devotion to God, a man whose sole aim was to serve his Lord and to bring as many of His creatures to salvation as possible. We can imagine the kind of man chosen by Allah Almighty to be His prophet: strong but compassionate; acutely aware of his own short-comings but tolerant of others; loving and supportive to the believers but stern in respect for the law and its transgressors. Like all the prophets before him he was familiar with the state of the people to whom he was sent, and he knew how far they had strayed from righteousness because one of his functions was to be a witness over them.

Zakariyya (as) as a priest in the Temple. William Blake, 1799.

He is mentioned by name seven times in The Qur'an, four of these being about his involvement in the lives of others, Maryam (ahs), and Yayha (as), and three of them about himself. He is mentioned as being among the righteous children granted to Ibrahim (as) (6:85). He is called by the most honorary title in Islam, the title by which the Prophet Muhammad (sas) was proud to be known, the slave of Allah (19:2). And along with the other members of the family of 'Imran (ra) Allah says: **indeed, they used to hasten to good deeds and supplicate to Us in hope and fear, and they were humbly submissive to Us.** (21:90). He was kind, humble, submitted, and he relied on no one other than Allah.

Opening of Surah Maryam, 1778, Dagestan.

11.
The Fruit of Prayer

Every day Zakariyya (as) brought food and necessities to Maryam (ahs) in her small room. When she was around eleven or twelve, as she was nearing the time when she would be released from her mother's vow and be too old to stay on the Temple grounds, he was startled to find, when he visited her, that she already was well supplied with food. He was immediately concerned that someone had managed in some way to make contact with Maryam (ahs) without him knowing. He was worried that the security measures he had installed around her had been breached. She was a young girl and vulnerable, and he became frantic with worry.

He saw no evidence that anyone had broken the locks or made a forced entry, but he was shy to confront or accuse her. When Zakariyya (as) calmed down and looked more closely he saw that the fruits in her room were not those that were available anywhere in the markets of the land. It is said that she had summer fruit in the middle of winter and winter fruit in the middle of summer. Zakariyya (as) also knew in his heart the innocence and purity of Maryam (ahs) who had been his charge and his pupil for almost all of the twelve years of her life. It was a mystery that troubled him very much, and one day he decided that the best course was to simply ask Maryam (ahs) about it directly.

Whenever Zakariyya went in to see her in her sanctuary, he found her supplied with provisions. He said, "Maryam, how is it you have these provisions?" and she said, "They are from Allah, Allah provides for whom He wills without measure." (3:37). And he knew she spoke the truth. This unquestioning, pure child was the recipient of Allah's miraculous bounty.

Her words plunged like a knife deep into his heart releasing a need and a hope he had kept hidden perhaps even from himself. He yearned for the closeness with his Lord that he saw on the face of the child. He wanted this experience for himself. He wanted the taste of a miracle on his own lips and the voice of the divine in his own ear. He wanted to feel Allah's touch on his own heart. And so Zakariyya (as) hurried on his stiffening limbs, his soul bursting with the need to reach out to his Lord. **He cried to his Lord, "My Lord, do not leave me childless, although You are the best of inheritors."** (21:89).

Inspired by the child Maryam (ahs), it came to Zakariyya's (as) heart that he might be permitted to ask his Lord for a son. He felt old, and he saw no change or improvement in the state of his people. They were being inevitably drawn into the pagan ways of the foreign powers that ruled them, the Babylonians, the Persians, the Greeks, and now the Romans. Zakariyya (as) did not see, in any place he looked, someone with the wisdom and spiritual power to guide the people. He was old and his power was waning. He was concerned for the house of Ya'qub (as), for the prophetic line that had been continuous since his ancestor Ibrahim (as). However, he was submitted to his Lord's will, and he thought that he had long ago accepted that he would have no heir. He had comforted himself that Allah would protect His religion. But here was this beautiful saintly girl child, who would protect her when he was gone? It came to his heart that he had a responsibility to ask for what he saw was needed. **"Call on Me and I will answer you."** (40:60). Ask and you will be given. Ask, for Allah is the most Generous who says, **And whenever My servants ask you about Me, surely I am Near: I respond to the call of the one who is calling whenever he calls upon Me. So may they respond fully to Me and may they have faith in Me, that they might be guided rightly!** (2:186).

He left her room in haste and hurried to the corner where he prayed in the Temple, his heart intent on the need to speak privately with his Lord. His hands shaking, raised in sincere supplication, he pleaded that Allah Almighty, who could bring fruit out of season to delight a little girl, could also give him and his wife out of their season, an heir. **Then and there, Zakariyya prayed to his Lord. He said, "My Lord, bestow on me good offspring from Your presence. You are the Hearer of prayers."** (3:38).

Zakariyya (as) continued in the outpouring of his heart, in the immediacy and honesty of the moment: **"Lord, my bones have weakened and my hair is ashen grey, but never, Lord, have I ever prayed to You in vain. And I fear for those who depend on me, and my wife is barren. So grant me, from Yourself, a *wali* to be my heir and the heir of the family of Ya'qub. Lord, make him well-pleasing [to You]."** (19:4-6).

It is said that when approaching Allah for a favor it is important how you do it. There is a correct way to ask. Zakariyya (as) did not just ask for a child. He asked for a son, a male child. And he did not just ask for a male child, he asked for an inheritor, one who would inherit his spiritual station and continue guiding the people. The Turkish thirteenth century writer, Nasru d-Din Rabghuzi says: "O true believer! If you ask for a son, don't simply ask for a son. Don't you see that a son can be good or bad?" Zakariyya did not just ask for a son; he said, **"My God, grant me a son. May he be a *wali* (a friend of God), and may he be well-pleasing [to You]!"** (19:6). Just as Asiya (rah) the adoptive mother of Musa (as) did not just ask for any house in Paradise, she said: **"O my Lord! Build for me a mansion in the Garden near to You."** (66:11).

After Zakariyya (as) prayed for a son, he performed the ritual prayer in the Temple. At that very moment Jibra'il (as) descended with Allah's response. **And the angels called to him as he stood praying in the sanctuary, "Allah gives you the glad tidings of (a son whose name is) Yahya [who comes] to confirm a word from Allah, lordly, chaste, a prophet of the righteous."** (3:39). And so Rabghuzi goes on to say that "Zakariyya was performing a ritual prayer in the sanctuary. He didn't say he was wandering about in the streets. He didn't ask for a son while shopping in the bazaar. In this way it was made known that the proper way to ask God for something, is to ask for it after prayer in the *mihrab*, standing up facing the *qibla*."

It might appear then that Hana (rah) had asked for a child in all the wrong ways. She had asked for a child while sitting under a tree in her garden. She just asked for any child although what she really wanted was a good son to dedicate to the Temple. But since a woman is different than a man, perhaps her prayer in the garden of her house was more acceptable than if she had made her way through the busy streets to the Temple to pray. Her desire for a good child, a servant of the Lord and who would be pleasing to Him had no relation to gender, although this was a fact not known to her at the time. And so her sincere prayer was answered by the birth of the best of all the women of the world. Sometimes we do not need to be aware of just what exactly it is we are praying for because Allah always knows best.

Mihrab of Zakariyya (as) Al-Aqsa Mosque, Jerusalem.

Allah Almighty sent an angel immediately to His servant Zakariyya (as) with the best of news, his prayer had been accepted. **The Angel said: "Zakariyya, We bring you good news of a son whose name will be Yahya - We have chosen this name for no one before him."** (19:7). The Lord was going to grant him a righteous son who would be a prophet to inherit after him. And Zakariyya (as) was astounded and wanted to know how such a thing would come to be. **He said, "Lord, how can I have a son when my wife is barren, and I am old and frail?"** (19:8). Zakariyya (as) did not question Allah's ability to grant his request. He was not doubting that it was within the great power of the Lord of Creation to do such a thing. He was instead asking for an indication of the manner in which Allah Almighty would choose to manifest His creation. Should Zakariyya (as) look for a younger, healthy new wife who could bear a child as Ibrahim (as) had taken Hajar (rah) the handmaid of Sarah (rah) or as Ya'qub (as) had taken the servants of each of his two wives? Would Allah give Zakariyya (as) back his youth as He had to 'Uzayr (as) who slept for a hundred years and then found his son to have grown older than he himself? Would his wife be healed of her barrenness, like Sarah (rah) the wife of Ibrahim (as) or Rifqa (rah) the wife of Ishaq (as)? What would be the manner in which Allah would carry out His promise, and what should Zakariyya (as) be prepared to do on his part?

The angelic messenger said, **"This is what your Lord has said: 'It is easy for Me. I created you though you were nothing before."** (19:9). The Angel replied that Allah had created Zakariyya when he had been previously nonexistent, and He could bring into existence a new creation just as easily. There was nothing for Zakariyya (as) to do but to lay with his wife, and the Lord Almighty would do the rest. He would heal his wife's infertility and bring him a son in answer to his prayer, a dutiful son, a pious son, a prophet. **We answered him. We gave him Yahya, and cured his wife of barrenness.** (21:90).

And the Angel informed him that this miracle would be enacted invisibly. Allah would cure his wife for him, and she would conceive a child in the usual way. And Zakariyya (as) asked for a sign that his vision was real, that it was in fact a divine communication not a temptation from the devil, not his imagination. Perhaps, before he approached his frail and elderly wife he needed to be doubly sure. Perhaps the pleasure of being in direct communication with his Lord was so great that he desired simply to continue the conversation, to make it last as long as he possibly could. He said, **"My Lord, give me a sign." "Your sign,"** [the Angel] said, **"is that you will not communicate with anyone for three days, except by gestures. Remember your Lord often, celebrate His glory in the evening and at dawn"** (3:41). Allah Almighty in His immense kindness responded even to this need of His servant Zakariyya (as). He gave him a sign. The Angel said that when Zakariyya (as) left the Temple and tried to address the people as he was accustomed to do, he would open his mouth but no voice would emerge. For three days he would be unable to communicate with anyone except by signs, although he would not be sick or have any injury to account for it.

He said, "Give me a sign, Lord." He said, "Your sign is that you will not [be able to] speak to anyone for three full [days and] nights." He went out of the sanctuary to his people and signaled to them to praise God morning and evening. (19:10-11). Morning and night were the main times of prayer for the Banu Isra'il, but it also implies that he should pray then and at all times in between. When Zakariyya (as) exited the Temple he found himself truly without a voice. His tongue formed the words, his breath exited smoothly from his throat, but no sound emerged. He could speak to no one except his Lord. So for three days and three nights he stood humbly before Allah and thanked Him, and worshipped Him in the inner silence of his heart in the manner of the girl child, Maryam (ahs). Then he lay with his wife and conceived a son.

Zakariyya (as) on the right being addressed by the angel on the left. From an Ethiopian Bible circa 1700.

The Dome of the Rock at sunrise, facing east.

12.
Eastward Bound

It is thought that within a few months of Zakariyya's (as) prayer, Maryam (ahs) left her *mihrab* and went somewhere to the east of where she was. **And remember Maryam in the Book when she withdrew from her people to an eastern place.** (19:16). The commentators have found differing ways to understand this verse. Some give the simple explanation that she went to collect water from a spring in a grotto to the east of the Temple enclosure. There is a hadith that says she menstruated for the first time and had to leave the Temple grounds, so she went to stay with her aunt 'Ashya (rah) whose house was to the east of the Temple. But others leave aside the details of her actual physical movement and understand the east as a symbol indicating that she retreated inwardly to a higher spiritual place.

The east is where the sun rises each day. It is the place where light originates in this world, and so it indicates the place where the Creator of light is to be found. It symbolizes the world of the sacred and the unseen. In saying that Maryam (ahs) went east, The Qur'an is telling us that she went towards the light and towards the Creator of the light whose symbolic home is east. The garden of Eden is described in Genesis as being on the eastern side of Paradise. It could, in fact, be a semblance of this protected garden to which Maryam (ahs) retreated.

The logic of orientation (which itself means east, orient) is not universally the same. The ancient Egyptians oriented themselves southward to the source of the Nile. So south was up, ahead. North was down, the feet. East was to the left where the sun rises. West was on the right where the sun sets. The west bank of the Nile was where all the burial grounds and memorials, pyramids, were located. It was considered the place where the sun and humans disappear into an unseen realm. The east bank of the Nile was where the Egyptians had their houses and farms and carried out their daily affairs. The Hebrew and Arabic speaking peoples, however, place east in front of them and call it *qadam*, in front. North is to the left *shimal*. South is to the right, *yamin*, and west is behind, which in Hebrew is called *yam*, the sea.

The Temple itself, like the original tabernacle of Musa (as), was oriented east in that the only entrance to the inner sanctuaries was in the eastern wall of the rectangular structure. The Holy of Holies was located deep inside at the western end of the enclosure, farthest from, but directly facing, the entrance. So like the journey of the sun, the worshipper entered in the east and traveled west. Ibrahim (as) and Isma'il (as), when they built the House of Allah, placed the Black Stone securely in the corner that faces east and the main door to the north beside it. The ritual of tawaf, circling the Ka'ba, begins at this eastern corner and travels north to the west, seven times around, and finally ends at the place it started. East for the beginning and east for the ending. **Surely your God is One, Lord of the heavens and the earths and of everything between them, Lord of the Easts.** (37:4-5). It is also interesting that at the End of Time, when we are told the sun will rise from the west, it will not set in the east. It will travel backwards to the meridian and then retrace its path to set where it rose, in the west.

The verse, **And remember Maryam in the Book when she withdrew from her people to an eastern place.** (19:16), served as the inspiration for many Sufi meditations and spiritual journeys; an inspiration to men as well as women to withdraw from their people and approach closer to Allah. Al-Kashani (thirteenth century) says in his Tafsir that the east represents the sacred world while the west represents the material world. But the journey of the sun is west, and so the journey to Allah must be in that direction, passing through the material world around and back to the east and the eternal home from where we originally came. In a curved world, if you go far enough west you will reach the east. And it is interesting to note that the Arabic word for the true natural state of belief, *hanif*, comes from the root meaning to bend or incline.

The three religions of the Book, the Jews, the Christians and the Muslims, actually proscribe praying as the pagans did, to either the rising or setting of the sun. Their *qiblas* are the holy places, holy sanctuaries that Allah designated for them. For the Jews and Christians their *qibla* is Jerusalem, and that is why the churches and synagogues in the west are oriented east. The ones to the west, south, and north of Jerusalem should be oriented west, north and south just as the mosques are turned to Mecca wherever in the world they are situated and not to the east in itself. However, the holy sanctuaries that serve as their focus, the *qiblas*, are themselves oriented east.

Then we are told, that Maryam (ahs) **placed a veil (*hijab*) between herself and them and We sent to her Our spirit who presented himself to her as a perfect male human being** (19:17). A barrier separated Maryam (ahs) from her people. Some say that as she reached womanhood she began to cover with a shawl or scarf as the word *hijab* is understood today. Others say she hid behind some sort of barrier or screen in order to immerse herself, as required by Jewish law, in water to get ritual ablution, although it is very unlikely that an angelic being would approach her in that place. It might be that Allah Almighty is continuing to suggest the metaphor of the Holy of Holies in the Jerusalem Temple which was hidden from the people not by a wall of brick or stone but by a veil woven by chaste women and girls (perhaps by Maryam (ahs) herself) of the finest linen and hung from pillar to pillar to demarcate the place where no unconsecrated person could enter.

Maryam (ahs) entered from the east into the most sacred space. Here she was separated from the rest of mankind by a curtain or veil, in a place where no other human being could follow. And in this most sacred of places, alone with her Lord, she was suddenly confronted by the appearance of a man.

Maryam (ahs) being surprised by the angel in the form of a man at the spring when she went to collect water. Rashid ud-Din Hamadan, History 14th century Mongol.

13.
A Sign for Mankind

Twice Allah states in The Qur'an **We made the son of Maryam and his mother a sign**: (23:50) (21:91). Together the two, mother and son, constitute one sign. A sign indicates a miracle, something out of the ordinary that would draw people's attention and point to something else. And in both cases these verses are followed by another proclaiming, **Verily this, your community (*ummah*), is one community, and I am your Lord, so be mindful of Me. (23:52). Truly, this, your community, is one community and I am your Lord, so worship Me. (21:92).**

We are told that Maryam (ahs) was afraid when she saw the spirit in the form of a human man. Her ancestor Ibrahim (as) had also been frightened when the three messengers of Allah descended on his tents in the middle of Canaan to announce the miraculous birth of Ishaq (as). When the angels came to Ibrahim (as) and said, **"Peace,"** he said, **"We are afraid of you."** (15:52). Although, in both cases the angels had taken the form of perfectly ordinary men, *basharan sawiyyan* (19:17), no doubt the aura of their presence was far from ordinary. The word *bashr* comes from a root meaning skin or hide. Its derivatives mean human being, and good news particularly of pregnancy. *Sawiy* means made symmetrical, straight or perfect. It is as if the being of light was wrapped in skin to look perfectly like a human being. It is interesting to note that in the case of the angel guests of Ibrahim (as), Allah uses a word from the same root, saying that they are messengers of *bushra*, good news (15:53). This is understood as being news so good that it makes itself apparent on the skin, bringing color to the cheeks and light.

Neither Ibrahim (as) nor Maryam (ahs) was unfamiliar with the presence of angels. They knew that something heavy was happening, that they were in the company of something bearing the presence of Allah Himself. Maryam (ahs) did not scream or call for help, she did not turn away or run. She knew from whom to seek shelter and to whom to run for refuge. She sought the protection of *Ar-Rahman*, the aspect of Allah that is mercy and compassion. This was perhaps His aspect with which she was most familiar and also the one of His majestic qualities most connected to women since from the same root comes the word for womb, *rahm*. She held her ground and spoke to the intruder quietly but firmly: **"I seek refuge from you in *Ar-Rahman*, the Compassionate, if you are God-fearing."** (19:18). In that moment, it is said, Maryam (ahs) achieved perfect connection, union. Her self dissolved and she flew in wholeness to her Lord. Ibn 'Arabi writes that if Jibra'il (as) had blown the spirit into Maryam (ahs) at that time, 'Isa (as) would have had such a formidable disposition that no one would have been able to be anywhere near him.

When she called on Allah Almighty to rescue her from the one she perceived as an assailant, the spirit, who is usually identified as Jibra'il (as), was perhaps a little alarmed. He replied quickly to assure her that he intended no harm. He said, **"I am only a messenger from your Lord, to bestow on you a pure son."** (19:19). In that moment, he let go his hold on his assumed shape, on his covering of skin. As he assured her he was an angel, a messenger from her Lord, he briefly or partially reassumed his real form and appeared to Maryam (ahs) in his luminous magnificence. Far from being terrified at this alteration, she relaxed. The company of angels was not new to Maryam (ahs). She was now sure of his identity, sure that she was being asked to accept a trust from her Lord. She accepted and opened completely to whatever it was that her Lord was sending. And so, says Ibn 'Arabi, 'Isa (as) was conceived with the most receptive and responsive of dispositions.

When Jibra'il (as) came to the Prophet Muhammad (sas) on Mount Hira with the first revelation and ordered him to **Read, read in the name of your Lord who created.** (96:1) he answered with an excuse that amounted to almost an apology. He said, "But I am not one of those who read." In the same vein, Maryam (ahs) replied to the angel **"How can I have a son when no man has touched me and I have not been unchaste?"** (19:20). She was willing, but she asked to know how it would come about since she knew she did not meet the requirements needed to make it happen herself. She could not have a child since she had never had contact with a man. This is similar to Sayyiduna Ibrahim (as) asking how he could have a child when he and his wife were significantly past the age of having children. It is similar to Zakariyya (as) asking how he would have a son when he was old, and his wife was barren.

Maryam (ahs) veiled from the world meeting Jibra'il (as). From Al-Biruni, Persia 16th century.

Maryam (ahs) was answered, **"So said your Lord, 'It is easy for Me. We shall make him a sign for all people and a mercy from Us. It is a thing decreed.'"** (19:21). Maryam (ahs) was not required to do anything. Allah just has to say "Be" and it becomes. There is no obstacle. Allah does not need causes in order to create. Allah is the Creator, and **He does what He wants.** (85:16). He gave miraculous children to many of the Banu Isra'il in the past. This time, however, He was not proposing to heal a man and woman of infertility or to return their youth and strength. He was choosing to create a child in a womb that had never been opened or penetrated, a virgin womb and to create His prophet directly from Spirit, Word, and woman.

We are told, however, that this was no more miraculous than to have created the prophet Adam (as), the first man, with neither father nor mother. **The likeness of 'Isa to Allah is as Adam. He created him of dust and said to him "Be" and he became.** (3:59). It was no more miraculous than to have created our mother Hawwa (rah) from a man without the agency of a mother. So it is seen that Allah can create mankind in at least four different ways. He can create using a man and woman as a means which is the manner in which most people come into the world. He can create without the agency of either a man or a woman in the manner of Adam (as). He can create using only a man as in the case of Adam's (as) wife, Hawwa (rah). And lastly, He can create from only a woman as He did in the creation of 'Isa (as). All of them indisputably His creations, humans not gods.

The physical being of most humans is formed from the pairing of a mother and a father by permission of their Lord and His command "Be". The physical form of Adam (as) was made of molded mud and the command "Be". The physical form of Hawwa (ra) was, as if carved, from the bone of Adam's (as) rib and the command "Be". The bodily form was created first and afterwards enlivened with soul by the divine breath. In the case of Adam (as), Allah breathed into him Himself, **I have shaped him and breathed of My spirit into him.** (38:72). However, in the case of Maryam (ahs) Allah Almighty put the enlivening spirit on the breath of his messenger Jibra'il (as) to both form the body and animate the soul of 'Isa (as) together at the same time. By means of the angel **We breathed into her of Our spirit and made her and her son a sign for all peoples.** (21:19) (66:12). Some attribute to this statement a certain uniqueness, an angelic quality, to 'Isa's actual physical composition. However that may be, he is still a creation like all others, made from the same mix of ingredients, earthly matter, spirit, and the word "Be" even if the proportions and timing differ.

There is some ambiguity due to the Arabic of the second of the verses mentioned above, (66:12). Instead of saying breathed into her (*fiha*) it says breathed into it (*fihi*). This has allowed the commentators to take some liberties in discussing just what it was that the angel blew into. The more decorous say he blew into the opening of her sleeve or the opening of her neckline or even the hem of her robe. Some say he blew into her body or her womb. Some say other things. It seems totally unnecessary, however, for the spirit to need any sort of physical opening. Surely spirit can penetrate and permeate a whole being without a specific point of entry. And does spirit have any destination other than the heart? In addition, it seems inappropriate, to say the least, that a woman, protected by Allah from all manner of sin, especially sexual misconduct and slander, should have her body exposed even to the imagination.

Ibn 'Arabi says that from the fact that Maryam (ahs) was a human being, 'Isa (as) inherited his mortality. From the fact that she was a woman, he inherited his humbleness and softness. His manly physical shape he inherited from the angel spirit in the form of a man. From the Word of Allah, he received life and the power to give life. **Behold! the angels said: "O Maryam, Allah gives you glad tidings of a Word from Him: his name will be *Masih*, 'Isa son of Maryam, held in honor in this world and the Hereafter and of (the company of) those nearest to Allah.** (3:45). **So in time she conceived him, and then she withdrew with him to a distant place.** (19:22).

Spring of Siloam, called Maryam's pool, Jerusalem.

Opening of Surah Maryam 19th century, Dagestan.

14.
The Good News of Yahya (as)

After Zakariyya (as) had witnessed the gifts of fruit out of season that Allah bestowed on Maryam (ahs), he had gone into the sanctuary and prayed for a son to inherit him as a prophet and guide for the Banu Isra'il. The angel Jibra'il (as) had answered immediately on behalf of the Lord that He was sending a boy child who would be conceived and born in the manner common to most human beings. Allah would heal 'Ashya (rah) and remove whatever obstacles there had been that prevented her from conceiving in the past (21:90). **The angels called out to him, while he stood praying in the sanctuary, "Allah gives you news of Yahya, confirming a Word from Allah. He will be noble and chaste, a prophet, one of the righteous." (3:39)**

Zakariyya (as) asked for a sign so he would know that what he heard was the truth from God. **He said, "Give me a sign, Lord." He said, "Your sign is that you will not [be able to] speak to anyone for three full [days and] nights." (19:10). So Zakariya came out to his people from his chamber: He told them by signs to celebrate Allah's praises in the morning and in the evening. (19:11).** Zakariyya (as) found his vision to be true. He was unable to speak except by signs for three days and nights although he was neither sick nor injured. Locked inside himself, he went home and continued to pray and praise Allah for the determined number of days. Then he rose from his chamber and went to his wife.

And so to the disbelief of all her neighbors and relations and to her own tremendous, incredulous joy, 'Ashya (rah) discovered that in her old age she had at last conceived a child and was pregnant. She went to the Temple to give an offering of thanks to Allah and she sought out her little niece Maryam (ahs) to give her the incredible good news. She found Maryam (ahs) in her *mihrab,* and the two embraced. 'Ashya (rah) felt a movement within her, as if the child she was carrying was bowing over. She leaned heavily on Maryam (ahs). As Maryam (ahs) helped her aunt to the ground 'Ashya (rah) confided in her that she was with child. Maryam (ahs) was overjoyed for her aunt for she knew how much she had longed for a child. Hugging her close Maryam (ahs) whispered in her ear that she also was pregnant. 'Ashya (rah) replied that she had wondered at the strange movement of the baby in her womb. Now she understood that her child was bowing low to the child inside of Maryam (ahs). She had no doubt that the baby inside of Maryam (ahs) must be of an even higher station than her own because even the prophets of God are ranked although their ranking is the concern of none but their Maker. He has ordered us to say, **we make no distinction between any of His Messengers.** (2:285).

Yahya (as) inside 'Ashya (rah) bowing before 'Isa (as) inside of Maryam (ahs). Monastic Family of Bethlehem.

Unlike the men in their lives, 'Ashya (rah) did not, even for a minute, think evil of Maryam (ahs) or question the origin of her baby. Maryam (ahs) told her the whole miraculous story, and 'Ashya (rah) accepted it and its truth for she also was the recipient of a miracle. The two women clung to each other in joy and wonder. Two miracles from Allah Almighty, what could it mean? What changes, what events could Allah be planning to send into the world through them? This only increased their humility and the intensity of their worship. They were not proud nor did it occur to them that they might be deserving of these living gifts or the special attention of the Almighty. They knew the responsibility that comes with God's favor, and they accepted it as realistically as they could and with awe. They prayed for the strength to be able to carry what they were given and to bring it to a good conclusion.

About six months later Ashya (rah) was delivered of a baby boy much to her joy, and the astonishment of her family and neighbors because it is said that Zakariyya (as) was one hundred and twenty years old and that 'Ashya (rah) was ninety-eight at the time their son was born to them. Whatever their ages, they were considered much too old to have children. The very existence of the child was a clear miracle. They named him Yahya (as) as they had been ordered to do. **We bring you good news of a son whose name will be Yahya. We have chosen this name for no one before him.** (19:7).

There has been some confusion about the uniqueness of the name. This is mostly due to a mistake in the translation of the name from Greek. In the Greek New Testament, the son of Zakariyya (as) is called John, and he would become the one the Christians call John the Baptist. In the Tawrah, however, there are several men named John mentioned in earlier generations. The name John in Hebrew is Johanan, or Yohanan meaning Jehovah is Gracious. Ye (Je) is Jehovah and *hanan* means compassionate or kind. Yahya is a completely different name that stems from the root *h-y-y* and means he lives. It is interesting to note, however, that one of the adjectives used to describe Yahya (as) in The Qur'an is *hanan* (19:13).

To complicate the matter a little bit more, *Jan* in Persian and Turkish does mean life or soul and is used familiarly as an endearment. The name Yahya would translate into Persian correctly then as *Jan* although not into the Greek Ioannes or the Hebrew Johanan.

Yahya in Arabic means, he lives. There is no consensus as to why Allah chose this name for him. Some say that it had to do with the healing of his mother, that he brought life when before there was none. Some say that he would enliven, revivify the religion. Others say that he would die as a martyr, and we are told not to say that martyrs are dead but that they are ever living. (2:154). It is also said that Yahya (as) confirmed the living Word that Allah Almighty implanted in the form of 'Isa (as). Ibn 'Arabi says it is because, through him, his father Zakariyya (as) continued to live because Yahya (as) inherited him both physically and spiritually. It may be also that Yahya (as) inherited from those who had held this position before him, a living chain of prophets and saints, the *Abdal*, who serve Allah at all times as deputies to His creation. Another understanding of this Qur'anic verse is that the specific quality of life with which Yahya (as) was endowed was unlike that given to any other before him.

Al-Tha'labi writes that according to some accounts, which he leaves unnamed, Yahya (as) was lifted up to heaven as soon as he was born and nursed on the waters of Paradise. Others say that at his birth his parents dedicated him to service in the Temple but that his elderly mother nursed him for the prescribed period of three years, again much to the amazement of everyone. After he was weaned, he was put in service at the Temple where his father could carefully watch over his education and upbringing. It is recounted that their house and every place he went was lit by the radiance of his presence, and all hearts were uplifted and softened by the beauty and kindness of his face.

Yahya (as) being raised by angels. Illustration for the History of Sayyid Luqman, Ottoman 1586.

Birthplace of Yahya (as) Ein Karem, Israel.

Ketuba marriage contract drawn up in 449 BCE between Ananiah and Tapamet who lived in the Jewish settlement on Elephantine Island, Aswan Egypt.

15.
St Josef (ra)

It was the belief of the Banu Isra'il at this time that any girl child below the age of three was for certain a virgin, but after that age they could not guarantee her purity unless she was raised under the eyes of a family known to be strict and pious Jews, or she was raised in the Temple under the eyes of the priests. So it was the custom to engage children at that very young age although they would not actually marry until they reached maturity, much in the manner of 'Aysha (rah) and the Prophet Muhammad (sas).

It is said that the boys who served in the Temple, once they reached maturity at fifteen years, were given the choice whether to remain in service or to rejoin their families and return to secular life. Girls perhaps could choose to marry and leave the Temple or stay on as 'nazirites', men and women who took a vow of celibacy and seclusion and lived in the Temple for however long they vowed, a month or a year or a lifetime.

Rabghuzi says that when it became time to betroth Maryam (ahs), she would not consent. He goes on to explain why it was that she had no interest in a husband and no need for one. He says a woman needs a husband for three reasons. First, she needs someone to work and provide her with food and necessities, but Allah provided Maryam (ahs) with all she needed. Second, she needs a man to partner in the production of sons and daughters, but Allah gave her the best of sons without the need for a man. Thirdly, she needs a husband to enjoy the pleasures of marriage, but the Lord gave Maryam (ahs) more pleasure in obedience and worship than any husband could possibly provide.

According to some there was a young man named Josef (ra) who served with Maryam (ahs) in the Temple. Their chores overlapped and they helped each other to draw water from a source at the foot of the Mount of Olives, Siloam, and carry it back to the Temple. It is even said that as Zakariyya (as) got older he found the care of Maryam (ahs) beyond his capacity and so initiated another casting of lots among the men of the Temple. In this way the younger Josef (ra) was divinely selected to take over her guardianship.

Josef (ra) is not mentioned in The Qur'an or in any of the hadith. Most of the stories that the Muslim authors have told about the prophets who preceded Islam are garnered from Jewish and Christian sources. However, the Muslim scholars have selected the ones they felt expressed the Muslim point of view or, more accurately, the ones that do not express something in contradiction to anything in The Qur'an or hadith. In most of the accounts, Josef (ra) appears briefly at this point in the story. The authors may indicate that they are not sure of the accuracy of the story by predicating it with phrases such as, "it is said" or "some say" or "only Allah knows". However, they still find it acceptable enough to mention Josef (ra) in relation to the story of Maryam (ahs).

Saint Josef (ra), as he is known, is universally recognized among all denominations of Christianity as the husband of Maryam (ahs). Whether or not they ever shared the intimacy of husband and wife differs among the sects, some saying they went on to have children of their own, some saying he was more like a father and protector. Either way, he stood by her, protected and supported her for the birth and the flight from Herod that followed.

In some ways, to Muslim eyes, he seems an unnecessary figure since his presence actually serves to cast suspicion on the virginity of Maryam (ahs). The Christian apologists, strangely, use him to refute the accusation that Maryam (ahs) had a child out of wedlock since they say she was legally, although not actually, married to Josef (ra). In some of the Gospels Jesus (as) is even called the son of Josef the carpenter (ra). The Muslims in general have not adopted this view. The purity and excellence of Maryam (ahs) is believed without question as she was chosen by God and praised most highly by Him in The Qur'an. Josef (ra) is an ancillary personage who is dropped from mention almost immediately after being introduced. However, in all the cultures and religions of the Middle East, a woman must have a male guardian, *mahram* or *wali* – usually her closest male relative. Without a father or brother, and with her uncle too aged, Maryam (ahs) required some male figure to fend for her. Even to stay in the Temple Maryam (ahs) needed a guardian. Certainly for her to have left the Temple, traveled, been accepted anywhere, it is believed that she would have needed to be attached to some man and under his protection. So, whether it was Josef (ra) or not, perhaps it was inconceivable that there was no one.

It was simply the custom that, when a girl servant of the Temple reached a certain age, a husband was chosen for her. Some of the authors explain the second drawing of lots as the way they chose a husband for Maryam (ahs). The lot fell to Josef (ra) who, in this version of the story, was a widower, much older than Maryam (ahs), with children of his own. He at first refused because either he felt too old to take responsibility for such a young girl or he felt he would be ridiculed for having a child as a wife. In the end, he was forced to accept because the throwing of the pens indicated it was a divine order.

So Maryam (ahs) was engaged to Josef (ra), a carpenter who repaired and maintained the Temple as a charity. He was Maryam's (ahs) cousin on either her father's or mother's side. However, even if the engagement had taken place and they were aware of each other and the promise between them, they had never shared intimacy, and they were not yet considered married.

Maryam (ahs) occupied a prominent place in the main Temple of the Banu Isra'il. It is said that she had gained somewhat of a reputation for her piety and holiness among the inhabitants of the Temple and among the faithful at large. She was, therefore, well known and visible. She could not hide or disappear in order to conceal her condition. It was therefore Josef's (ra) responsibility now to protect her and her reputation. He was her guardian and so was legally responsible for her behavior and, as her future husband, he was also under suspicion.

The penalty for unwed pregnancy was not a light one. It was considered adultery, and the punishment could be death by stoning. After the birth of the baby, the sinning couple would be surrounded by men and pelted with rocks until they both were killed. This was the law of the Tawrah and later the law of the Muslims as instituted by Sayyiduna 'Umar (ra). There was another recourse in Judaism called the Ordeal of Bitter Waters. First the woman suspected of adultery was questioned and if she swore that she was innocent, she would be given a drink of the water of Siloam in which the ink of her sworn statement was dissolved. If she lied, she was expected to die a horrible death but if she lived, her innocence was publicly affirmed.

There is in fact some evidence in the Protoevangelium of James, one of the so-called apocryphal gospels, that both Maryam (ahs) and Josef (ra) were forced to undergo just such a test, which of course they passed. But it shows the misunderstanding and injustice these true men and women of God had the capacity to endure. History recounts that a few years later this practice was abolished because adultery had become so common that the priests could not keep up with the demand. This is just another indication of the declining state of the Banu Isra'il during the time of the second temple.

The men in her life were not as happy and sympathetic to the changes in Maryam's (ahs) condition as 'Ashya (rah) had been. They found it difficult to reconcile her purity and piety with the state they saw before them. Whether it was Saint Josef (ra) or the prophet Zakariyya (as), her guardian became very troubled and his heart was torn. It was more likely to have been Josef (ra) because he was neither a prophet, nor had he been acquainted with Maryam (ahs) for long. Zakariyya (as) had known Maryam (ahs) from birth. He was witness to the miracles that Allah Almighty enacted for her sake. He would have had enough trust, hopefully, not to doubt her. He knew that he had kept close watch over her. He knew her habits and her ways. No one could have approached without her guardian knowing, and besides she was not devious or deceitful. She had never exhibited any interest in a relationship with anyone other than God, not even the close friendships of the other girls. She had hardly ever looked up from her prayers and devotions except to give a smile or return a greeting. She did her chores and her work cheerfully, she gave advice or helped when she was asked, but everyone could see that she was anxious to return to her prayers. It was a mystery that filled his heart with doubt and apprehension.

It is said the guardian of Maryam (ahs) at this time, whether Zakariyya (as) or Saint Josef (ra), approached his young charge unable to bear any longer the suspicion that was darkening his heart. According to Wahb ibn Munabbih (ra) he asked Maryam's (ahs) permission to speak personally. Delicately skirting at the outset the real object of his questioning, he said, "O Maryam does a plant grow without a seed?" To which she answered, "Yes". "O Maryam" he continued "does a tree grow without rain?" Again she answered, "Yes". Finally reaching the object of his questioning he said, "Can there be a child without a father?" And she looked at him, meeting his eyes with her own unwavering gaze, and she said "On the day they were created did not the plants and the trees appear full grown without seeds or water? Or do you think that Allah cannot create a tree without the help of water, or a plant without the help of seed?" He was ashamed and hung his head. She continued, "Did not Allah create both Adam (as) and Hawwa (rah) without a mother and father?" Her guardian said no more. Maryam (ahs) had made her point clear. Allah can do anything He pleases, and there is no asking why or how.

And from her transparent sincerity and her steady gaze he knew that she spoke the truth, and his heart regained its customary composure. From that point on he became her noble guardian and protector. He took over whatever heavy chores she might have had in the Temple, and he shielded her as best he could from the eyes of the people. But it became clear that Maryam (ahs) could not remain in the seclusion of her *mihrab* much longer.

The Prophet Muhammad (sas) receiving revelation, in a state of *fana fi-Llah*. Ottoman illustration for a Life of the Prophet (Siyer-i Nebi) 1595.

16.
A Thing Forgotten

She conceived him and withdrew with him to a distant place. (19:22). As she became more pregnant she knew she would have to leave the only home she had ever known and go somewhere private and secure to deliver her child. Perhaps she went first to 'Ashya (as), her sympathetic aunt. She might have gone in order to be of help to her after the delivery of Yahya (as). But it also could have been that her presence there resulted in trouble rather than help. There were so many political factions surrounding the Temple at that time that most likely her situation was being used by some for their own agenda: to disparage the priests, or Zakariyya (as) in particular, or even to discredit the religion as a whole. So The Qur'an tells us that Maryam (ahs) withdrew to a distant place. Somewhere far from the scandalmongers and troublemakers of the Temple.

It has also been reported by the Muslim writers that while Maryam (ahs) was pregnant with 'Isa (as) she could hear him praising Allah from inside her. When it was quiet and there were no people around, she would talk to him and they would worship Allah together. So there were also positive reasons for her to seek solitude in some distant place, far away

The Prophet (sas) setting off on the Night Journey, from Nazami's Khamseh 1492.

from the presence of others.

Although some say she went to Nazareth, which might have been the ancestral home of her parents, and why Christians in Arabic are called *Nasara*, most say she went ten miles south of Jerusalem to a small village called Bethlehem. The Christians say that because the Emperor in Rome had ordered a census, every man had to return to the city of his tribal origin. Josef (ra) was of the family of Dawud (as) and so had to return to Bethlehem, the city where Dawud (as) was born, to be counted along with his new wife, Maryam (ahs), and their unborn child. It was actually God's plan, however, because the prophet Micah, eight hundred years earlier, had predicted that one day a messiah would be born in Bethlehem who would right all wrongs, destroy the idols and those who worship them, restore rule to the Banu Isra'il and vanquish their enemies. (Micah 5:2). And the followers of 'Isa (as) believed that he was indeed that foretold messiah (Matthew 2:1-6).

The Muslims agree that Maryam (ahs) fled to Bethlehem to deliver her baby because, one starry night in the noble city of Mecca, the Prophet Muhammad (sas) was woken by the archangel Jibra'il (as) and mounted on the celestial steed called the Buraq (as). He was taken on a heavenly journey, first to lead all the prophets in prayer on the holy mount in Jerusalem, then to ascend to visit each of the seven heavens and finally into the presence of Allah Almighty. In the beginning of their journey, just before reaching Jerusalem, Jibra'il (as) had halted the Buraq (as) and asked the Prophet (sas) to dismount and pray two rakats. He was told that the place they had prayed was Bethlehem, the spot where Sayyida Maryam (ahs) had given birth to the prophet 'Isa (as).

As the scholars say, when the stars had reached their appointed stations in the heavens, Maryam (ahs) felt that her time had arrived. Not knowing what to do or where to go, a young girl with no experience, no family, no friend, she fled into the countryside alone.

Some of the chroniclers say that her pregnancy and delivery were as miraculous, immaculate, and unique as her conception. The most extreme say she was pregnant for an hour (Jalalayn), and her delivery took only another hour. Some say she was pregnant a month; others say perhaps three months. They say she delivered from her navel or even from her mouth so that she maintained an incorruptible virginity and purity, never losing ablution. However, The Qur'an says, **And the pangs of childbirth drove her to the trunk of the palm tree. She said: "Oh, would that I had died before this and had become a thing forgotten!"** (19:23). This does not sound like the description of an angelic delivery, bloodless and painless. This is a succinct but poignant description of a very real birth. This young girl, all by herself in the hills of Judaea, gave birth to a very special and extraordinary prophet in a very ordinary and painful way.

Her wish to be a thing forgotten, to an experienced midwife might indicate the classic signs of the last stage of labor. She was in transition. Like so many tests in life, when you think you have reached your limit, that there is nothing more you can do, nothing more you can bear– it is then that Allah opens the way. Only then can the baby be delivered.

But this is not how this verse has been interpreted by the male scholars. To them Maryam's (ahs) cry sounds like despair and a wish for death, both of which are not strictly permissible for a believer. A Muslim should never despair of Allah's mercy and never hope for death. As a result, many of the discussions of this verse attempt to clear Maryam (ahs) of having actually wished for her own death out of despair. She is said to have wished instead that she had never been born, not to save herself from the pain of childbirth but rather from the dishonor it would bring on her and her family. She was worried for others. She was afraid that her guardians would be blamed and punished. She was concerned that because of her renown as a holy person, people would lose their trust in God and His religion. They recount that the Prophet Muhammad (sas), when Jibra'il (as) delivered the first revelation while he was in seclusion in the cave on Jabal Nur, considered throwing himself off the mountain out of horror that he might be going crazy or even worse, be a poet. Ibn Kathir argues because of these instances, that in certain dire circumstances, it is permissible to wish for death but not, of course, to act on it.

The Sufis, however, have a very different interpretation of this verse. To them it expresses, with heart-rending accuracy, the longing of the seeker to be nothing, a thing forgotten, dissolved within the oceans of the Oneness of the Lord. They see it as an ultimately good thing and encourage all people to be like Sayyida Maryam (ahs), to seek the gaze of Allah rather than the eyes of men, to realize in themselves the true state of nothingness that is *fana fi-Llah*. As Ibn 'Arabi writes in the *Futuhat*, "God wishes you to be with Him as you were when you were not a thing."

Grotto of the Nativity, birthplace of 'Isa (as), in the Orthodox Basilica commissioned by Constantine the Great in 330 CE. Bethlehem West Bank.

Maryam (ahs) shaking the dead palm tree which is coming alive and hung with dates. The baby 'Isa (as) lies on the ground beneath and the stream is pouring out at her feet. Ottoman 16th century.

17.
A Stream Beneath Her

The scholars say that Allah sent His angelic messenger Jibra'il (as) to console the new mother: **he called her from below her (*min tahtiha*), "Do not grieve; your Lord has provided beneath you (*tahtaki*) a stream."** (19:24). The dry river bed at her feet began to run with clear, clean water - water to quench her thirst, water to wash herself and her newborn child. It was heavenly water much like Zamzam, that had welled up out of the sand for Hajar (rah) and her little boy Isma'il (as). From the top of the hill of al-Marwa, Hajar (rah) had heard a voice telling her to look down and there, beneath her, she saw water gushing up under the feet of her infant son (al-Bukhari).

Water from beneath her, the very same words Allah uses in His Book twenty-seven times to describe the gardens of Paradise under which rivers flow (*min tahtiha l-anhar*). In addition, there is a hadith of the Prophet (sas) that says "Heaven lies under the foot of the mother." So after her labor, Maryam (ahs) is consoled with a little bit of Paradise. Her trial ended in rest, her journey brought her to Paradise.

It is interesting also to note that the actual town of Bethlehem sits above a large natural underground aquifer. The springs and rivers around Jerusalem itself were inadequate for the population that gathered there, and so polluted by the refuse of the animal sacrifice that was taking place on the altar in the Temple that the city needed to import clean water by means of underground channels from Bethlehem. The original reason Bethlehem even became a town was to fortify and protect Jerusalem's main water source. So Allah Almighty perhaps is giving us a hint in The Qur'an of where it was that Maryam (ahs) gave birth to 'Isa (as).

But of course this is not the only possible location offered in the Muslim histories. Damascus is also a possibility although technically it is outside of the area where date palms grow. Many early Muslims believed that all of 'Isa's (as) life played out in the precincts of Jerusalem unlike the Gospels that put 'Isa (as) in Jerusalem for only a few short periods of time in his life. He was conceived, born and spent his infancy on the Temple Mount. He taught his disciples, was taken to heaven and will return, all in the confines of the city of Jerusalem. The fifteenth century author of a history of Jerusalem, Mujiru d-Din al-'Ulaymi related a hadith of the Prophet (sas) as saying that the *sakhra* (the rock under the Dome) stands on a palm tree which stands on a river which is one of the rivers of Paradise. This could point to the miraculous birth of 'Isa (as) occurring at least spiritually, if not physically, in this sacred space.

Rabghuzi, in his inimitable way, comments on the perfection of the stream that Allah provided for Maryam (ahs). It was not a fast flowing river that would be too dangerous and deep for her to safely approach and wash. It was not a brook with a trickle of water too shallow and slow to be clean or to bathe in properly. Allah provided a stream, *sariyya*, not too big and not too small, neither dangerous nor dirty but rather the perfect size to be inviting and accessible.

Water of course is the very essence of life. Allah has said that He created all living things from water (21:30). In the desert where most of our prophets lived, water was the difference between life and death. What is dry is dead, and what is wet is living. (6:59). And water is the most obvious symbol of Allah's mercy. It is the sign of *Ar-Rahman*, the aspect of Allah to whom Maryam (ahs) appealed. Rain in Arabic is even called *rahma*, mercy.

For the ancient Banu Isra'il, as for the Muslims, water was required for the major and the minor ablutions, to prepare the worshipper for prayer. For the Christians water became the means of entry into God's kingdom, the ritual of baptism. Water was used to purify the Temple itself at least twice a day, and it had to be 'living' water that is flowing, not water from a cistern or a bucket. Allah provided Maryam (ahs) with living water in which to refresh and clean herself and in which to safely bathe her child.

The angelic messenger went on to instruct Maryam (ahs) to **shake the trunk of the palm-tree towards you: it will drop fresh, ripe dates upon you.** (19:25). The commentators say that the palm tree whose support she sought in labor was a dead tree. Its trunk was still standing, but its fronds were dry and brittle. When Maryam (ahs) was a little girl in her *mihrab*, Allah provided sustenance for her without her having to work or even ask. Now He told her she must do something impossible. She must shake the solid, unbending trunk of a dead palm, to cause the invisible fruit to fall. Allah would enliven the dead tree and hang it with ripe dates, all by His creative power, but Maryam (ahs) had to exert the effort to harvest it.

This is a lesson for us not to expect Allah's mercy without some effort on our own part. Just as Hajar (rah) did not sit in the shade of the thorn tree and wait for help. She exerted herself under the hot desert sun, running between the two hills of as-Safa and al-Marwa, looking for whatever her Lord would send. This ritual, reenacted by those on pilgrimage to the Holy House in Mecca, is called *sa'i* meaning to strive or to work. So the examples of Hajar (rah) and Maryam (ahs) teach us that, as responsible adults, in order to become open to receive the miraculous generosity of our Lord which is hanging like ripe fruit all around us, we must first make an effort and do our part.

Maryam (ahs) shook the physically unshakable trunk of the palm tree, and it returned to life and dropped ripe dates into her lap. **So eat, drink, be consoled,** (19:26) Allah told Maryam (ahs).

The Prophet (sas) used to put a tiny piece of date in the mouth of the newborns who were brought to him for blessing (a practice called *tahnik* in Arabic), and he recommended it as the best of foods for postpartum women and babies, soft, sweet and nutritious. He also called the date palm the brother of mankind because when the Lord molded the shape of Adam (as) with His two hands, He did not use all the clay. From the clay that was left over Allah made the date palm.

It is interesting also that the date palm, like the human being, is created as either male or female. Only the female trees bear fruit, but they need to be fertilized by a male. Although the pit or stone of a date will sprout and grow, just like with a human being there is no guarantee what kind of tree will result, male or female or even what variety. If you want a fruit just like that of the mother tree you need to separate one of the small shoots that grow up from her roots. These shoots are called *batul*, separated off, virgin. Each offshoot, when planted on its own, will produce a tree exactly like the mother. So although the palm reproduces by seed, it also reproduces by an offshoot of the mother tree without the need for a male. And this nicely symbolizes Maryam (ahs) who, by the power of Allah, conceived without the need of a husband. The ancient Greeks named the date palm *phoenix*, a word that is also used for the mythical bird of the Arabian desert who dies and is resurrected.

Our sister the date palm.

The Salus Populi Romani icon first painted in the 5th – 6th century. Perhaps similar in date to the painting that the Prophet (sas) saved from destruction inside the Ka'ba.

18.
Silence Is Golden

Maryam (ahs) might have spent her forty days in the wilderness by the side of the stream with food and water provided by her Lord, or she might have bathed in the stream, wrapped the baby in her shawl, and returned to her people within hours or days. For those who say her pregnancy lasted only an hour and her labor only another hour, she returned immediately to the Temple grounds and laid her infant son in the hollow of a smooth rock beside her *mihrab*. This rock is still in place today.

Allah, the Most Merciful, warned Maryam (ahs) that her people would not be supportive, and He counseled her to remain patient and quietly endure their hurtful and slanderous accusations: **say to anyone you may see: "I have vowed to *Ar-Rahman* to abstain from talk, and I will not speak to anyone today." Then she brought her child to her folk, carrying him and they said, "Maryam you have surely committed a monstrous thing! Sister of Harun, your father was not a wicked man, nor was your mother unchaste."** (19:26-28).

She is told that when they confront her with lies and recriminations she must simply express by signs that she has vowed a fast of silence. In the

Saint Anne (Hana), Nubian fresco, Faras Cathedral, Sudan, 8th century CE.

same way, Zakariyya (as) was not able to speak for three days after receiving his promise of a son from the angel of the Lord. But Zakariyya (as) was prevented from being able to speak. Maryam (ahs) must refrain from speaking on her own accord. Perhaps this is a reflection of the different outward expressions of being either male or female. The command for the highest of male spiritual forms, a prophet, is to speak, to warn, to teach, to interfere. So Zakariyya's (as) silence must be forcefully attained. The command for the highest of female spiritual forms, however, is to voluntarily withhold from interfering, to let others speak for her, to let things manifest organically in accordance with their inherent nature, and so she is simply advised to continue doing what she has already been accustomed to do. These patterns have to do with the highest of spiritual stations and are not necessarily appropriate for lower ones.

As she approached the area where her family lived they came out of their houses, tearing their clothes and throwing dust on their heads, crying. **Then she brought her child to her folk, carrying him: and they said, "Maryam you have surely committed a monstrous thing!"** (19:27). They called her **"O sister of Harun"** (19:28) because they wanted to contrast her apparent sinfulness to the sanctity and purity of her forefather the prophet Harun (as) and because the hope of her mother, Hana (rah) in giving her the name of Harun's (as) sister was that she would be her equal in sanctity. **"Your father was not a bad man, nor your mother unchaste."** (19:28). By saying this they were essentially accusing her of being both. They were shamed by her and ashamed of her. She had seemingly defiled herself and defamed her entire family.

Yet Maryam (ahs) knew that she had done nothing wrong and committed no sin but had, in fact, excelled her mother's expectations and lived up to the legacy of her prophetic forebears. She had submitted herself totally to her Lord and would continue to do so. The ways of the Almighty are not always clear and not always consistent with what seems fair to the human mind. It is a fact that He tests the ones He loves over and above others because they can carry it, and in doing so they become examples of heroic effort and nobility. So although we speak of paradise in relation to Allah's chosen, that paradise is not an earthly one. Their earthly lives were far from smooth or heavenly, but they managed to transform them or transcend them by trusting totally in the goodness of their Lord and keeping their love for Him shining.

Her heart breaking, in silence she stood before her people, judged and condemned. The warm bundle she held closely in her arms seemed to be the clear proof of her guilt. She kept her promise to her Lord not to speak. What could she have said? She didn't cry or complain. To whom and to what purpose would she complain when it was her compassionate Lord who had written for her this trial? She didn't try to explain. How could she explain such an extraordinary thing to ordinary people? Who would believe her? It was just in anticipation of this that she had wished to be a thing forgotten, never to have been born. And if she could bear the false accusations for herself, how much harder was it to think of her beautiful baby having to live among these people, the object of ugly whispers and unspoken judgment.

At the time of the Prophet Muhammad (sas) it is related that he and his companion Abu Bakr (ra) were sitting together when a man came up to them and started to shout at Abu Bakr (ra) and to curse him. The Prophet (sas) didn't move away or speak, and it is said he even smiled at one point. Twice the man spit insults at Abu Bakr (ra), and twice Abu Bakr (ra) held his peace and kept his eyes on the ground. The third time, however, Abu Bakr (ra) lost his patience and shouted back in self-defense. The Prophet (sas) was displeased but, still saying nothing, got up and left. Abu Bakr (ra) followed after him wanting to know the reason for the Prophet's (sas) displeasure. The Prophet (sas) turned and explained that when Abu Bakr (ra) had kept silent, Allah Almighty had sent an angel to defend him.

6th century icon, St. Catherine Monastery, Sinai.

It was the angel's behavior that had caused the Prophet (sas) to smile. But once Abu Bakr (ra) answered the insults for himself, the angel had disappeared. Whenever a person holds his tongue while he is insulted or falsely accused, leaving his case to Allah, then Allah will be his support and his defender (ibn Hanbal). Sometimes the best answer is no answer as the Prophet (sas) said, "Whoever is silent has been saved" (al-Tirmidhi).

And much later Sayyida 'Aysha (rah), another young girl accused of things she did not do, took the same path as Maryam (ahs). Rather than argue with her family who had already appeared to judge her, she turned her face to her Lord to defend her, which He did. Allah Almighty sent His Prophet (sas) verses of The Qur'an explicitly to declare her innocence. (24:11-21).

So Maryam (as), young in years but supported by Allah in wisdom, simply made her people understand, as she had been told to do, that **"I have vowed to the All-Merciful a fast, and today I will not speak to anyone."** (19:26). She then **pointed to the child.** (19:29) They said in outrage and disbelief, **"How shall we speak to one who is still in the cradle, a little boy?"** (19:29).

This was the first miracle of Sayyiduna 'Isa (as). Allah gave him the ability to speak and express the truth clearly in language all could understand. He said, **"Lo, I am the slave of Allah. Allah has given me a Book and made me His prophet. Blessed He has made me wherever I may be; and He has enjoined on me prayer and alms so long as I live, and likewise to cherish my mother. He has not made me arrogant, unblest. Peace be upon me, the day I was born, and the day I die, and the day I am raised up alive."** (19:30-33).

Maryam (ahs), a young girl tested.
Jorge Hernández 1980.

Needless to say, the people who heard him speak were astounded, shocked into a silence of their own. If they did not understand or could not comprehend, they at least were stopped in their tracks, transfixed. By the miraculous testimony of 'Isa (as), it is said that his mother, his uncle Zakariyya (as), and his cousin Josef (ra), were all cleared of any sin or transgression of the law. And his own destiny and rank were foretold and made obvious for those with ears to hear, eyes to see, and hearts to understand.

On the eighth day after his birth, 'Isa (as) was circumcised as prescribed in the Tawrah, privately in a cave in Bethlehem. After forty days, Maryam (ahs), bathed and brought a sacrifice to be a burnt offering on the altar of the Temple in Jerusalem to complete her ritual purification after childbirth. It was perhaps at that time that she had to confront the priests who had been her teachers and companions. These were the very same priests who, not so long ago, had disputed with each other over who would take charge of her; the ones who had witnessed the purity of her character from the time she was a toddler. They should have known her well enough to vouch for her innocence. Instead they judged her as being capable of what they were accusing her. They were unable to believe that a miracle of such magnitude could have taken place in their time and before their very eyes. They might actually have made her undergo the Ordeal of Bitter Waters in order to prove herself innocent of promiscuity.

Maryam (ahs) transcendent. Raphael, 1512, Sistine chapel Vatican.

The Journey of the Magi, James Tissot, 1894.

19.
The Unwise Wise Men

There were three shaykhs, wise men, who were students of the ancient books of wisdom of the early prophets. They lived somewhere in the East, a sign of their being holy and sent from God. They had been watching the stars for they knew how to read their signs, not as fortune tellers do but by means of a science that has since been lost. They had seen a star coming out of the east that indicated the birth of the one they had been waiting for, the one who would be called the heavenly king. They left their homes and set out to look for him following the light of his star.

They carried with them three gifts. The first was a nugget of gold because gold is pure, the king of minerals, just as the newborn would be the king of people. They carried myrrh or aloes because it heals wounds and broken bones just as the newborn king would heal and restore the sick and the dead. They carried frankincense because of all the incense, it is the one that rises quickly and surely to God just as the newborn had been sent from Allah and would return to Him quickly and surely.

On their way they stopped at the palace of a king. Some say he was a king of Syria, but most say he was Herod the Great, the man of the

The Magi by Henry Siddons Mowbray, 1915.

Banu Isra'il whom the Romans had set up as their deputy to rule over Judaea. Herod was old by this time and sick. He felt uneasy on his throne and imagined everyone out to depose him. He felt threatened even by a baby, whom the wise men unwisely told him was the rightful king of the Jews. Misinterpreting the kingdom of heaven for the kingdom of earth, thinking that he could change divine destiny by his own will, he slyly let the three men continue on their journey with the promise that after they had visited the child they would return and tell Herod where to find him. But Herod had no intention of bowing down to a child or anyone else for that matter.

The wise men were wise enough, however, to suspect that Herod's interest in the child was not spiritual or benevolent. After they had visited 'Isa (as) and Maryam (ahs) in Bethlehem and presented their gifts, they returned home by another route. Traveling at night, they avoided being detected by the spies and soldiers Herod had planted along the roads.

When the three men had not returned, Herod became obsessed with finding this baby who might usurp his power. Consulting with his advisors, he decided to kill all the baby boys under the age of two in the vicinity of Bethlehem, just as Namrud had killed the babies at the time of Ibrahim (as), just as Pharaoh had killed the babies at the time of Musa (as). Temporal authority is jealous and afraid to admit or submit to the true authority of God. The baby victims of what is termed the Massacre of the Innocents, are commemorated to this day in the Catholic Church every December twenty-eighth as the first martyrs of Christianity.

Being warned by angels of the coming massacre, Maryam (ahs), 'Isa (as), and perhaps Josef (ra) as well, fled for their lives. **And We made the son of Maryam and his mother as a sign: We gave them both shelter on high ground, affording rest and security and furnished with springs.** (23:50). By using the dual form in this verse, Allah mentions only two people who were given refuge, 'Isa (as) and his mother (ahs). Josef (ra) being the third is not included.

It is said that after Maryam (ahs) left, the priests pursued Zakariyya (as), accusing him of betraying his trust and failing in his guardianship. There was no one left to testify for him, to vouch for his innocence. He had been too outspoken in the past, telling them where they had left the straight path, advising them to return to the law and the spirit of the Tawrah. They would accept his learning and knowledge of the Tawrah, but they would not accept his knowledge of the unseen. They continued to judge by their own minds and missed the benefits of having a living prophet among them. Now they turned on him and evicted him from the Temple. He was not afraid, and he did not change one letter of the message that Allah had charged him with. He decided to follow after Maryam (ahs) and her son and to attach himself to them for as long as he lived. But he did not know where they had gone, and it was not his destiny to join them.

Others say that because he would not tell Herod's soldiers the whereabouts of his own son Yahya (as), they killed him on the steps of the altar, in the place where the sacrifices were offered. Ashya (ra) and Yahya (as) managed to escape

Relics of the gold, frankincense and myrrh presented to the baby 'Isa (as) by the Wise men, preserved in the monastery on Mt. Athos, Greece.

and seek safety on one of the surrounding mountains. When they were unable to climb any higher, they asked for divine help, and the mountain split open and then closed around them until the danger had passed.

Others say Zakariyya (as) escaped from the Temple and managed to warn Maryam (as) and 'Ashya (rah). Only when he knew that they and their children were safe, did he flee into the hills leading the angry mob away from them. He was a very old man and, although spry for his age, he could not run very fast or very far. Some say he only made it as far as a grove of trees just outside the Temple walls. He slid slowly to the ground with his back against one of the trees in order to catch his breath and to focus on asking his Lord for guidance. Before he could do that, a voice issued from deep within the tree itself, inviting him to hide inside. The gracious tree split itself open, and Zakariyya (as) squeezed into the crevice. The tree then gently wrapped its bark around him. But shaytan, the devil, who was leading the murderous mob, came in sight of them just as the tree was closing around the prophet. Quickly stretching out his boney fingers, shaytan was able to grab the corner of Zakariyya's (as) cloak before the tree sealed him safely inside.

When the men arrived a few minutes later, with their knives and their hatchets, they found it hard to believe that Zakariyya (as) was inside the tree. Shaytan had to get up and show them the corner of the cloak pinched between the rough edges of bark where the tree had closed over it. Then the men understood and, directed by shaytan, they began to chop at the tree. Zakariyya (as) heard the voices and felt the shudder of the tree as the axe blades tore into it. He would have cried out, but he was informed that if he uttered even one cry or one complaining groan his name would be erased from the register of prophets. Some say that this was because he had sought refuge with the tree instead of with his Lord. Allah Almighty would have saved him, but since he accepted the offer of the tree first, he must suffer the consequences. But as Maryam (ahs) was advised silence when she was tested and as Zakariyya (as) himself had been silenced earlier when he asked for a sign, silence seems to be one of the themes of this company of prophets and believers. There was silence when it would be natural to speak and speaking when it was most unnatural, by a tree and an infant boy. Now Zakariyya (as) must hold his tongue and his breath and fix his heart patiently on the pleasure of his Lord. The misguided men in their anger proceeded to savagely kill two of

Allah's innocent and obedient servants.

According to Wahb ibn Munabbih (ra), however, it was the prophet Sha'ya (as) (Isaiah) who was chopped down inside a tree. Zakariyya (as) died peacefully much later in his bed, an even older man. This nicer alternative is supported by the fact that many of the stories we have about Yahya (as) as a youth also involve the presence of his father. According to the Christians, Zakariyya (as) may have been martyred in the Temple itself causing some Muslims then to situate the tree just outside the gate of the Temple. He is considered to have died a martyr, but how exactly he died and when, whether when Yahya (as) was still a baby or much later after his son had grown to manhood and was invested with prophethood, Allah knows best.

Allah bless Zakariyya (as) and the tree who tried to shelter him.

The martyrdom of Zakariyya (as), Persian 1550.

Maryam (ahs), 'Isa (as) and Saint Josef (ra) on their flight to Egypt. Eugene Alexis Girardet, 1880.

20.
The Rabwa

It is said that all prophets have had to leave their homeland, fleeing for their lives from their own people who refused to believe them. The Prophet Muhammad (sas) fled from Mecca to Medina, a journey called the *hijra*. Ibrahim (as) fled from Harran to Canaan, Musa (as) from Egypt to Madian, Yusuf (as) from Canaan to Egypt. This is the story of the *hijra* of 'Isa (as).

After the unwise declaration of the wise men about the coming of the King of the Jews, Herod proceeded to kill all the boy babies in the vicinity of Bethlehem. It is said by historians that he did kill several of his own sons and their mother because, in his paranoid senility, he suspected them of treason, but there is no record nor physical evidence of his having killed hundreds of boy babies. It is even related that his friend, the emperor of Rome, Caesar Augustus, commented wryly, "It would be better to be the pig of Herod than to be his son." However it was, the Christians continue to memorialize this act with a day of mourning they call the Massacre of the Innocents. The Byzantine Christians claim 14,000 boys under the age of two were martyred, the Syrian church says 64,000, and the Coptic church says the number was 144,000, probably more than the total population. Modern Catholics have reduced the number to possibly ten or twenty. The splintered bones, supposed to be of these infants, however, are still kept in reliquaries on the altars of churches all over Christendom.

Allah protected the real target of Herod's campaign of murder by sending an angel warning them to leave the area and seek shelter elsewhere. Allah says: **We gave them both shelter on high ground (*rabwa*) affording rest and security (*qararin*) and furnished with springs (*ma'in*).** (23:50)

All the commentators agree on the meaning of this verse but they do not agree on the actual location to which it refers. Al-Tha'labi says that according to 'Abdullah ibn Salam (ra), a companion of the Prophet (sas) who converted from Judaism, Maryam (ahs) and her son (as) took refuge in the vicinity of Damascus. Abu Hurayrah (ra), another close companion, said it was in Ramla. Qatada (ra) and Ka'b (ra) said it was in the place on earth closest to heaven, perhaps Mecca. Abu Zayd (ra) said it was Egypt. Al-Dahhak (ra) said Damascus, and Abu Aliyah (ra) said Jerusalem.

Those who believe that the *rabwa* was in the vicinity of Jerusalem cite a single hadith in which the Prophet (sas) said to one man that he would die in the *rabwa* (Al-Tabari and Ibn Kathir). The man ended up dying in the area of Ramla, about fifty km northwest of Jerusalem. Ramla itself does not fit the description of being a high place, as it lies on the coastal plain, but between it and Jerusalem stand a range of mountains with streams that could have possibly provided security to Maryam (ahs) and her child.

The second possibility is the area around Damascus, approximately two hundred kilometers from Jerusalem, a journey of several days on foot. A mountain called Qasyun rises to the north and looks out over the city proper and the rich agricultural plain of the Barada River called the Ghuta that skirts the city on the east and south. Today at the base of the mountain sits the maqam of Ibn 'Arabi. On its slope is a small cave in which it is said that the first prophet, Adam (as), lived, and that became the site where Qabil killed Habil (as) in the first murder. A large rock bulges from the roof of the cave and seems to have a mouth open in horror. There is a handprint on the rock where Jibra'il (as) steadied the mountain which would have collapsed in sorrow. Red tinged water drips down the rock from above like bloodied tears. The prophet Ibrahim (as) is also said to have prayed in the cave on his way to Canaan. Built above this ancient site there is a small mosque containing forty prayer niches, *mihrab*, where the forty saints known as the *Abdal*, gather to pray their night prayers. The *Abdal*, or substitutes, are hidden saints whose job is to protect and help Allah's creatures. They wander the world during the day witnessing and supporting the believers. When one of them dies another man is appointed to take his place so there are always forty of them. At night they gather to pray high above the city of Damascus. It is here on this ancient chosen spot that some believe Allah Almighty provided shelter to Sayyida Maryam (ahs) and her son 'Isa (as).

Jabal Qasyum in foreground, Damascus Syria.

Imam As-Suyuti reported a hadith in which the Prophet (sas), when asked specifically about Jabal Qasyun, replied that whoever wants to visit the *rabwa* should visit that mountain. As-Suyuti says he should climb Jabal Qasyun to the cave near the top because that is where 'Isa (as) and his mother found refuge from the Jews. As-Suyuti added that whoever visits there should not shorten his prayer or cut short his supplication because it is a place where prayers are answered.

It is interesting to note that there were a few other sacred things indicated by a *rabwa*. When the Holy House in Mecca, given to Adam (as), was taken back to heaven before the flood, the spot where it had rested was marked by a raised area of red earth also called *rabwa* in Arabic. And the spot in the second temple where the lost Ark should have rested was marked in a similar manner by a raised area inside the Holy of Holies.

Egypt as the place to which Maryam (ahs) fled is not mentioned specifically either in The Qur'an or hadith. Egypt, *Misr*, is mentioned as a place of refuge in relation to other prophets however. Yusuf (as) and his eleven brothers and his father Ya'qub (as) found refuge there. It is where Musa (as) was born and raised and out of which he led the Banu Isra'il through the sea. In addition, it is said that Ibrahim (as) sought refuge there during a time of drought. Egypt as the place where Maryam (ahs) and 'Isa (as) took refuge is only specifically mentioned in the Injil and then only in the Gospel of Matthew (2:13-18). It says that Saint Josef (ra) was ordered in a dream to take his family to Egypt to escape the murderous intent of Herod. In Christianity this is a universally accepted fact. The Coptic church has established many holy places from Sinai to Assiut that are associated with the visit of the holy family. Many of these were revealed by Sayyida Maryam (ahs) herself in a vision to Theophilus the Coptic patriarch of the late fourth century. The list was further expanded by a couple of bishops in the eighth century and committed to writing in the eleventh century. Even today new places continue to be revealed or rediscovered and added to the list.

Map of the Journey of Maryam (ahs) and 'Isa (as) according to the Coptic Church.

In recent years the head of Al-Azhar has endorsed this version of the childhood of 'Isa (as). For this reason and because the other two possible locations have been almost forgotten while the Egyptian tradition continues to live on, we will relate a few of the stories of the stay of the holy family in Egypt even though it seems that the earliest Muslims put more credence on the other two possibilities. Only Allah knows the truth.

It is said that Saint Josef (ra) traveled on foot leading a donkey which carried Maryam (ahs) and the two-year-old 'Isa (as). Qadi 'Iyad (twelfth century) says that this donkey was named Ya'fur and was the ancestor of the donkey given to the Prophet Muhammad (sas) by the Muqawqis, the head of the Copts in Egypt at the time. The family crossed out of the Roman territory of Judaea at Al-Arish. As Yusuf (as) said to his brothers **"Enter Egypt, God willing, safe and secure."** (12:99). There

Broken idols, Tell Basta Egypt.

might have been as many as a million Jews living in Egypt at the time of 'Isa (as). Most of them settled in Alexandria on the Mediterranean coast, but there were smaller communities up the Nile, in Memphis (Cairo), Al-Bahnassa, and Elephantine Island near Aswan. However, most of the Egyptian people clung to a version of the polytheism of ancient Egypt that had been adjusted to incorporate the gods of Greece and Rome, their current rulers. In consequence, the holy family did not find such a warm welcome in most of Egypt. This might have been aggravated by the fact that, wherever he went, it seems the young prophet toppled idols and caused general havoc.

In Tell Basta they stopped to seek food and shelter but found only one man who would take them in or even give them water. Known at the time as Bubastis, it had been the capitol under pharaoh Shoshenq around 900 BCE. It was still the thriving center of the cult of Bastet, the cat god and the location of a spring orgy involving alcohol and sex. It has even been suggested that *bastet* is the origin of the English word bastard alluding to the many pregnancies arising from the occasion. The temple there boasted three hundred and sixty towering stone idols, one to be worshipped each day of the year as is said about Mecca before the advent of the Prophet (sas).

'Isa (as) was taken to visit the shrine, perhaps for his entertainment because it was swarming with well-fed temple cats of all sizes and colors. The moment he entered, however, there was a loud rumble, and every idol instantly crashed in pieces to the ground at his feet. It is still to be seen today as it was, a field of broken heads and shattered stone bodies. 'Isa (as) then caused a spring of fresh water to rise out of the ground from which his mother could drink. Because they would not give her water, he made it blessed for all people but cursed it for the inhabitants of Bubastis itself.

Photograph of the miracle at Zeitun, Cairo in 1968.

This well is still the goal of Christian pilgrims. In fact, the trail of the baby 'Isa (as) could actually be said to be a trail of wells. Either due to the nature of the terrain or that of the people, in order to refresh themselves, drink and wash, they had to provide their own sources of water. 'Isa (as) says in The Qur'an, **He [Allah] has made me a blessing wherever I go.** (19:31). The Christians say that, pursued by the soldiers of Herod, they proceeded south creating wells and springs, healing the sick, exorcising devils, leaving handprints and footprints in stone, blessing and destroying. There is even a street in Cairo where, to this day, bread dough will not rise because its inhabitants long ago refused hospitality to Maryam (ahs) and her child. There are Coptic churches built over most of the holy sites and miracles are still said to occur associated with them. One such miracle was the well-documented appearance of Maryam (ahs) herself as a figure of blazing light on top of the dome of the Church of Maryam in Zeitun, Cairo in 1968.

Following a circuitous route around the delta, the holy family stopped in the Cairo area where until recently there was a grove of balsam trees and several caves and wells made holy by their ancient visit. After hiding in a cave beneath a synagogue, they boarded a boat and traveled up the Nile to another large Jewish community in Al-Bahnassa, then known as Oxyrhyncus. Two stories that are almost always repeated by the Muslim historians are said by the Copts to have taken place there. The stories seem to be Muslim in origin without specifying the country in which they took place. The Christians of the seventh or eighth century adopted and adapted them to fit their own scenarios.

One story was related by Muhammad al-Baqir (q), the great grandson of 'Ali ibn Abi Talib (ra) and the father of Ja'far as-Sadiq (q). Staying some time in the area, Maryam (as) decided to send 'Isa (as) to study with one of the rabbis in the synagogue. The teacher asked 'Isa (as) if he knew the alphabet. 'Isa (as) turned the question around and asked his teacher if he knew the inner meaning of the letters. When the teacher was puzzled and did not answer, 'Isa (as) proceeded to explain the esoteric significance of each of the Hebrew letters which in the Muslim stories are represented by Arabic letters. So it is said he explained: the letter *alif* stands for "La ilaha illa Allah – there is no god but the God"; *ba* stands for *baha* the splendor of Allah; *jim* for the majesty of God, *jalala*; *dal* for religion, *din*, and so on. The rabbi sent 'Isa (as) back to his mother refusing to teach someone who knew more than he did. The other event is a detective story involving a theft, a cripple, and a blind man that we will tell in a later chapter. This story comes from Wahb ibn Munabbih (ra) a Jewish convert to Islam in the seventh century.

Stairs leading down to the river where Maryam (ahs) embarked. Cairo, Egypt.

Crossing over the Nile the family disembarked from their boat at Jabal at-Tair. 'Isa (as) left a hand print on a rock that would otherwise have fallen on them. They entered the town and approached the Egyptian temple that lay at its center. All the statues immediately fell on their faces before him, shattered. The holy family had to flee up the mountain to escape the anger of the inhabitants. The mountain split open to protect them in a cave until it was safe to leave. On their way back to their boat, a large acacia tree bowed to the ground to honor the prophet and his mother. This tree was still alive until just twenty years ago when someone chopped it down in an unrelated dispute over land.

At Al-Ashmunayn, more Egyptian temples and their stone gods

crumbled before Allah's messenger. Further south in the vicinity of Assiut, the holy family was able to hide from their pursuers for over six months, their longest stay in any one place. Deir al-Muharriq is the second holiest place on earth to the Coptic Christians, after Jerusalem. Here Saint Josef (ra) built the family a small mud house which the vision of Sayyida Maryam told Pope Theophilus was her favorite house. In it was a stone slab that served 'Isa (as) as a bed or Maryam (ahs) as an offering table. This has become the altar stone of the first church on the face of the earth. The house is gone, replaced by a succession of churches built one above the ruins of the other. It is here that the prophecy of Sha'ya (as) was fulfilled: "In that day there will be an altar to the Lord in the midst of the land of Egypt." (Isaiah 19:19).

It was there that the angel Jibra'il (as) is said to have come to Saint Josef (ra) informing him of the death of Herod the Great and instructing him to take 'Isa (as) and Maryam (ahs) back home to Judaea. On the way, at Al-Qussia, 'Isa (as) again toppled idols and cursed its inhabitants so that today there is a wasteland in the middle of town where the temple ruins still lie.

The Christians say that all this took place in the space of two or three years. Those Muslims, however, who say that 'Isa (as) and his mother traveled far from Jerusalem also say that he did not return until he was twelve years old. Allah knows best.

The oldest Christian altar, Deir al-Muharriq.

A painting of Yahya (as) as a child by Bartolome Esteban Murillo, 1665.

21.
A Wise Child

While Maryam (ahs) and 'Isa (as), with or without Josef (ra), were given shelter by Allah on a high place (*rabwa*) in a distant land, 'Ashya (ra) and Yahya (as) ran for their lives into the hills that surround the city of Jerusalem. It is even said they were chased up one of the mountains and, when their pursuers caught up with them, the mountain opened itself and invited them inside. And so they hid within the heart of the mountain until it was safe for them to return home. It is thought that within a few years Herod died and one of his younger sons, Herod Antipas, took power under the auspices of Rome. Things did not improve for the Banu Isra'il, but at least the execution of baby boys was forgotten. This second Herod was the one with whom 'Isa (as) and Yahya (as) had to deal most of their too short lives.

Yahya (as) as a young child was dedicated by his devout parents to service in the Temple. He grew up, was trained and educated under the eye of his father, who according to this version of things, continued to live and minister as High Priest. **And it was said unto his son: O Yahya! Hold tightly to the Book. And We gave him wisdom when still a child.**

(19:12). This order the young Yahya (as) took very seriously. He held fast to the Book, meaning the authentic Tawrah as it exists with Allah. He is an example of one whose hold was firm and untiring, whose attention was steady and unwavering, whose love was deep and unfaltering - definitely a wise child.

When his friends would ask him to come and play with them, he replied that he had not been created to play. He saw the asceticism of the older men, perhaps of the Nazarites who as adults had taken vows of celibacy and withdrawn from the world to live and worship exclusively in the Temple, and he was drawn to be like them. He asked his mother to give away the fine soft clothing she had made especially for her only child and instead to weave for him a coarse robe out of stiff goat hair. He spent his time inside the Temple compound listening to the talk of the priests and the reading of the holy books, absorbing what wisdom he found there.

It is said that this might indicate that Yahya (as) had taken the vow of the Nazarite himself, a word meaning in Hebrew, to separate or to consecrate. A Nazarite dedicated himself to God. Both men and women could take this vow. They had to refrain from alcohol and any product of the grape, from cutting their hair (except once a year), from sex, and from any contact with the dead. Even if their mother or father should die they would not be able to attend to them (Numbers 6:2-21). The Nazarite vow could be taken for any period of time from thirty days to a lifetime. It is said that there is some evidence of the existence of this practice from before the time of Musa (as). However, according to the Bible, among the prophets only Samuel (as), Samson (as), and Yahya (as) are thought to have taken this vow for life. In some ways it is similar to the Muslim laws that forbid the pilgrim (*hajji*) from cutting their hair or nails, from sex, and from killing anything. Wine is, of course, at all times forbidden. It is as if the Nazarite took a vow to be a pilgrim on the way to God. And in fact, this is just how the Muslims regard both Yahya (as) and 'Isa (as) - as exemplary pilgrims on the path of Allah.

His father Zakariyya (as) pleaded with him "My son, why are you so hard on yourself? You are still only a child. Allah Almighty is Merciful." He even went so far as to say that he had not asked for a son from the Almighty just to worry about him and grieve over him. And Yahya (as) would reply "Isn't it possible that someone my age can die? Wasn't it you who preached in the Temple that the fires of Hell are waiting for those who are heedless? Wasn't it you who said that the bridge over Hell is paved with the tears of the believers?" Zakariyya (as) had to admit that he had said those very words, and that they were true. "Then" said his son, "it is you who should be doing as I do". And Zakariyya (as) could only bow his head in agreement. So the tears of father and son mingled together on the ground. The Prophet (sas) said, "There are two eyes that will not be touched by Hellfire: an eye that cries from fear of Allah and an eye that spent the night as a guard on the path of Allah (*jihad*)." (Tirmidhi).

The Jordan River where Yahya (as) used to wander and where he performed baptisms.

After this, it became the habit of Zakariyya (as), before he began to give a talk in the Temple, to look carefully in all directions to see if his son was among the gathered crowd. If he was not there, Zakariyya (as) would preach on the punishments of Hell. If Yahya (as) was present, however, then Zakariyya (as) would preach on the beauties of Paradise. One day Zakariyya (as) came to the great courtyard within the gates of the Temple where men and women gathered to listen to the Tawrah and words of wisdom. He looked carefully but didn't see Yahya (as) so he began to warn the people of the many acts of heedlessness and selfishness that can lead to divine punishment. Yahya (as), however, was among those in the assembled crowd. He was hunched over in the middle of the people with his big robe covering his head and his face buried in his knees.

Zakariyya (as) began to describe some of the regions of Hell as they had been shown to him by the archangel Jibra'il (as). Suddenly Yahya (as) threw back his hood and rose to his feet. In anguish he cried, "How unaware and how heedless I have been about the wrath of the most merciful God." And he ran headlong out of the Temple into the wilderness beyond the gates of the city.

Zakariyya (as) cut his lecture short and went home to tell 'Ashya (rah). In concern, she hurried in the direction her son had been seen to go, calling his name and asking his whereabouts from all she met. Finally, a shepherd directed her to where Yahya (as) was wandering in distraction through the streams beds, his feet bleeding from the sharp rocks, wet and shivering, pleading with his Lord to forgive him and accept him into His mercy oceans.

'Ashya (ra) took his hand and led him out of the water. She dried his feet and she held him close. His body was so thin that it felt as if she held nothing but empty clothes. His cheeks were red and raw where the tracks of his tears had scoured their way through his flesh. She applied pieces of felt to the wounds to keep them dry. Her heart breaking, she begged him to come home with her.

Yahya (as) loved his elderly parents with all his heart. He was always **kind to his parents, not arrogant or rebellious.** (19:14). He would not ever knowingly disobey or hurt them. He allowed his mother to take his hand and lead him back to the warmth of the family home. There she put him in soft dry clothes and fed him a hot meal and put him to sleep under warm blankets and skins. 'Ashya (rah) and Zakariyya (as) breathed deep sighs of relief, thanked Allah and went to sleep themselves, their hearts at peace and full of gratitude.

However, the warmth, the food, and the soft bed kept Yahya (as) asleep through the morning prayer, and his parents could not bear to wake him. When he did awake and saw the sun already risen, his grief was beyond description. Devastated by remorse and regret, broken hearted, he threw off the soft covers and the clean clothes, drew his rough woven garment over his head and vowed never, for as long as Allah gave him life, to let comfort distract him from worship. As he sobbed ever more bitterly, his mother tried to comfort him, but his father advised her wisely to let him be. Yahya (as), by means of his sorrow, had been brought close to his Lord. He would never find fulfillment or joy in the pleasures, however simple, the world had to offer. This was the way it had to be.

Six hundred years later, it is said that the Prophet Muhammad (sas) had a conversation with shaytan. He asked the devil if ever he had felt remorse for any of the deeds he had done to distract mankind from worshipping their Lord. Shaytan had answered "Yes - but only once". That one time was when he had kept Yahya (as) asleep through the morning prayer. The deep anguish of Yahya's (as) sorrow had brought tears even to the cruel and vengeful eyes of the devil.

The respect due to parents. Anonymous Italian, 1630.

Russian icon of the prophet Yahya (as).

22.
From the Source of Life

Yahya (as) grew up to be a handsome young man. Ka'b al-Ahbar (ra) described him as having a beautiful face with fine features, long nose, and eyebrows that met in the middle. His body was thin with little hair. He had graceful hands with short fingers, and a soft voice. He was a prophet with such *himmah*, religious zeal, that he surpassed all others in worship and obedience to Allah, and his asceticism had a lasting effect on his appearance. He spent long periods of time in the wilderness by himself seeking the pleasure of Allah. He ate only the wild plants and berries he happened to find until he grew as thin as a stick. The New Testament says he ate only locusts and wild honey. It is said that he preferred to eat with the wild animals rather than with men. His compassion for them was such that he would wait for the animals to finish eating before he ate his share of what they had left uneaten. His cheeks were permanently lined with deep grooves made by the streams of tears he cried in penitence and awe of his Lord. He took no joy in the pleasures of the world, but that did not make him either stern or angry. People were not repelled by his gaunt appearance or by his severity. Rather they were drawn to him by the light of his obvious love for Allah, and the consequent concern and kindness he felt for all of creation. They began to seek him out and would gather around him and ask him to tell them about God.

The Qur'an says: **Allah gives you good news of Yahya, testifying to a Word from Allah (*musaddiqan bi kalimatin min Allah*), noble (*sayyidan*), utterly chaste (*hasuran*), a prophet from among the righteous (*nabiyyan min as-salihin*). (3:39). And We gave him tenderness from Us (*hananan min ladunna*), and purity (*zakatan*), and he was devout (*taqiyyan*).** (19:13). These are a lot of descriptive adjectives for one prophet. He would have wisdom while yet a child; he would have compassion (*hanan*) from the divine presence; he would be pure (*zakatan*) and God-fearing (*taqiyyan*) (19:13). He grew up to be **kind to his parents, not arrogant or rebellious** (19:14). He would mature into a noble (*sayyid*), chaste (*hasur*), prophet among the righteous (*salih*) (3:39). He would confirm (*musaddiq*) a Word from his Lord (3:39) and he would be named Yahya (as), a name or attribute that Allah had given to no one before him (19:7).

An oasis looks black against the desert sand.

Sayyid is translated into English in so many different ways - a noble, a lord or master, a prince, eminent, exalted, a leader, slow to anger, one who can rise above being treated badly by those for whom he cares, devout, forbearing, abstaining from unlawful things. How are all these meanings derived from a single word? The root of the word, *s-w-d*, is also the root for *aswad* meaning black or dark. Black in Arabic is used both as a good thing and a not so good thing. For a face to be blackened means shame or punishment, but for the desert dweller black can also mean life. The normal panorama of the desert is bleached and white. Habitations, gardens, trees look black against this white. The dark green of an oasis is often referred to as black, and a valley full of villages and farms is also called black. An abundance of things or people, household possessions, kitchen utensils, is collectively called black. So perhaps *sayyid* can best be understood as someone in whom all the virtues, all the qualities worthy to be followed are collected. He is densely filled, he is black, with princely attributes.

Hasur also is accorded many different translations into English. The most common one is chaste, specifically one who keeps away from sexual relations with women either because he voluntarily restrains his physical desire in order to please God or because some impairment restricts his ability to do so, abstinent. It comes from a root that in general bears the meaning to restrict, to imprison, to besiege. In extension it can even be used to designate one who conceals secrets and one translator of The Qur'an actually uses it to say that Yahya (as) kept the divine secrets that were revealed to him. It can also refer to a king because access to him is restricted. It is said that in the case of Yahya (as) it means that, although manly and capable, he was too concerned with his relationship with his Lord to be interested in any other relationship. He was so immersed in worship and striving that he had no house nor job, no desire nor ability to provide economically or emotionally for a wife or family. It might also be an indication that he had taken the vow, voluntary restriction, of the Nazarite.

Zaki is usually translated as pure. The Prophet (sas) said that on the Day of Judgment everyone will come carrying their sins except for Yahya (as). Yahya (as) not only never sinned, but he never even thought about committing a sin. *Zaki*, however, also can mean to cause to grow by the blessings of God, to increase, to bear fruit. He will grow and live which would tie into the meaning of *yahya*, 'he lives'.

Taqiyyan, often translated as pious, actually stems from a root meaning to fear. God-fearing is the most comprehensive one-word description of Allah's prophet Yahya (as). Since early childhood he remained in continual consciousness of Allah, fearing His displeasure, seeking only His pleasure. At a desperately low point in the prophet Muhammad's (sas) life, after the death of his wife and his protecting uncle, after being ejected from the garden city of Ta'if, he prayed to Allah saying, "If You are not displeased with me, nothing else matters." For Yahya (as) this was the full extent of his intention. Fear of his own inability to appreciate and honor the Creator adequately was what drove his life. However, in the manner of a rightly guided prophet (*salih*) he never judged others as he judged himself. He simply begged them to consider the truth as he knew it to be.

Hanan means forbearing, compassionate, tender-hearted, and kind. We are told that the compassion of Yahya (as) was not an ordinary kindness, but rather it was a part of Allah's divine all encompassing, universally pervasive compassion. It derived from the holy Presence of Allah (*min ladunna*). This made him compassionate to others and they sympathetic and irresistibly drawn to him. He was loving, and people found it easy to respond to him with love. It is interesting because in Hebrew the name John, which is commonly confused for Yahya, is Yohanan (Yo-hanan) which translates as the 'tenderness of God', and means essentially the same as *hananan min ladunna*. Perhaps Allah places these clues or *ayah* in The Qur'an to reference and tie together the former scriptures. When Allah says, **We bring you good news of a son whose name will be Yahya, We have chosen this name for no one before him,** (19:7), what is unique is not so much the name itself but rather the essence of divine compassion with which Yahya (as) was endowed - the divine love and compassion out of which all creation springs, the very source of life itself.

Allah says about Yahya (as) in The Qur'an, **Peace be upon him, the day he was born, the day he dies, and the day he is raised alive.** (19:15).

The mouth of the cave of Yahya (as) in Tzuba, Israel.

The interior pool that he might have used for secret ritual baptisms.

Yahya (as) preaching to the multitudes which include members of every nation, by Pieter Brueghel the Younger, 1

23.
The Teaching of Yahya (as)

Yahya (as) did not stay in the Temple for long after he grew up. Or perhaps the death of his father Zakariyya (as) drove him away. He left the Temple and its politics and went into the wilderness around the Jordan River. Here he lived off the land, sleeping wherever the night found him, eating whatever Allah in His graciousness provided. According to the Injil he ate locusts and honey, wild food that conformed to kosher law. Whenever people found him they asked for his guidance, and crowds began to be drawn to this thin, quiet boy who spoke with such passion about the kingdom of Allah.

According to a hadith of the Prophet (sas) (ibn Hanbal, Tirmidhi), Yahya (as) was ordered to deliver a message to the Banu Isra'il, but he was reluctant to do it. This could be because another possible derivation of the name Yahya might be from the word *haya'* meaning shy or reserved. 'Isa (as) scolded him and threatened to do it himself if Yahya (as) refused. So Yahya (as) finally went up to the Temple in Jerusalem and called all the people to gather. There was such a crowd that they were crouching on the walls and hanging over the sides. Then he reminded them of what he called the five virtues, the duties that all people owe their Creator.

1. He said, there is no god but God so do not associate anything with Him. If you do it is as if you were the slave of a kind man who paid for you, fed and clothed you, taught you a trade. Then when you became successful, you gave all your love and thanks to some other man.

2. He said, focus on your prayers. To be distracted during prayer is like asking to see the king but when brought before him, you give your attention to the golden glitter of the throne and the chatter of courtiers, to the decoration on the walls and the bright patterns of the rug at your feet. You cannot pull your eyes away even once to look at or reply to the king. The result is that the king turns his attention away from you and takes care of the needs of someone else.

3. He said, give charity. The one who gives charity is like a man who has been captured and held for ransom by his enemies. Then he convinces his captors to accept all his possessions in return for his freedom.

4. He said, make *dhikr* Allah. Remembrance of God is like a strong fortress. When the enemy approaches, you enter inside the walls, and you are safe. The devil cannot penetrate the fortress of remembrance.

5. He said, observe ritual fasting. To fast is similar to having a container of the best smelling perfume whose scent delights you as well as all the people who come in contact with you.

To this list, according to the hadith, the Prophet Muhammad (sas) added five additional instructions, five things he was ordered to do, and that he was in turn ordering his community to follow.

1. Listen to Allah and His Prophet (sas). *Sami'na wa ata'na* **We hear, and we obey. (Grant us) Thy forgiveness, our Lord. Unto Thee is the journeying.** (2:285).

2. Obey Allah and His Prophet (sas). (4:59) Leave your self and come.

3. Struggle on the way of Allah (*jihad*) by studying, by fighting the ego, by working, by cleanliness, by carrying others without anger or complaint, by accepting with gratitude whatever thing, easy or hard, that Allah sends your way. Fighting in the way of Allah is only one possible form of *jihad*, and it has its own very specific requirements that cannot be determined by any one individual for himself. **Strive hard (*jihad*) for Allah as is His due: He has chosen you and placed no hardship in your religion, the faith of your forefather Ibrahim. Allah has called you**

Muslims—both in the past and in this [message]—so that the Messenger can bear witness about you and so that you can bear witness about other people. So keep up the prayer, give the prescribed alms, and seek refuge in Allah: He is your protector—an excellent protector and an excellent helper. (22:78).

4. Journey, (*hijra*) emigrate to Allah. All the prophets have fled their homelands for at least some period of time. Ibrahim (as) fled from Harran to Canaan, saying **"I will go to my Lord, He will guide me"** (37:99). Ya'qub (as) fled from his brother 'As (ra) in the night journey (*isra*) from which he got his name Isra'il. Yusuf (as) was forced to find refuge in slavery in Egypt from his brothers. Musa (as) fled from Pharaoh to Midian saying, **"My Lord, save me from the people who do wrong. May my Lord guide me to the right way."** (28:21-22). And most famously, the Prophet Muhammad (sas) fled from Mecca to Medina to avoid being murdered by his relatives. Even if you do not actually leave your country, you should consciously decide to migrate from the bad to the good.

5. Jama'a – Be together with other believers, not alone with shaytan. Do not separate yourselves into sects. Do not separate yourself off from the community in your thinking or your practice: **hold firmly to the rope of Allah all together and do not become divided.** (3:103)

The Prophet Muhammad (sas) teaching his companions.
Illustration for Al-Biruni 1489.

'Isa (as) as a young carpenter, 20th century Peruvian artist.

24.
The Hidden Years

Herod the Great sickened and died. He was so afraid his funeral would not be well attended that in his will he ordered that a group of prominent men be executed at the time of his death so that the country would be in a sincere state of mourning. His heirs, fortunately, did not fulfill their father's behest. After the death of Herod the Great, Rome divided his kingdom among four of his remaining children. Herod Antipas became the ruler of Galilee. Herod Achelaus got Judea and Jerusalem until he was deemed too despotic even for Rome and was replaced by a Roman prefect. Herod Philip took the north and east of the Jordan River and a sister Salome I inherited Jamnia (Yavne), a small area on the coast. The incident of the wise men and kingly baby was forgotten by all but the grieving parents. The second generation of Herods continued to maintain a tight hold on the countryside, and so things appeared relatively peaceful but underneath it was seething. At this time, when 'Isa (as) was between five and twelve years old, Maryam (ahs) returned home. But where was home?

Most Muslims say they returned to Jerusalem and continued their life in the vicinity of the Temple. Some say they went to live in Nazareth, a very small village in the north, not far from the Sea of Galilee, which was the Biblical home of 'Imran (ra) and Hana (rah). It is estimated to have been a two week walk from there to Jerusalem due to the nature of the terrain and the political situation at the time. In fact, until quite recently it was thought this must be a mistake in the Gospels because there was no archaeological evidence for a town in that area. But recently they have uncovered some houses indicating that there was indeed a settlement in Nazareth of perhaps as many as four-hundred people and it was a Roman garrison town of mixed population.

Bahira the monk (ra) recognizes Muhammad (sas) even as a young boy. Illustration for Jam'ia l-Tara'ikh, 1307.

The life of 'Isa (as) is a miracle from his conception to his being taken up to heaven alive. And he will continue a miraculous existence until his death in the last days. It does not seem possible that a being of this nature could be hidden for so many years. But most of the prophets were hidden until they reached maturity. The Prophet Muhammad (sas) did not receive his message until he was forty and had lived a seemingly ordinary, uneventful life among his people up to that point. He was remarkable only for the honesty and goodness of his character. But there were a few who, like the wise men who followed the star of 'Isa (as), recognized him and knew immediately for what he was destined.

We can only speculate where 'Isa (as) was living and what he was doing for the eighteen years before his mission began. The Gospels tell us that he spent time in the Temple listening to the teachers and learning the Tawrah. The Muslims have assumed that it was the main Temple in Jerusalem. It could be even that he was dedicated to serve there since it is quite a distance to commute from Nazareth. However, one companion of the Prophet (sas), Wahb ibn Munabbih (ra) says that the Nazareth where 'Isa (as) lived was in the mountains of Hebron much closer to Jerusalem than the one in Galilee.

Twice it is said in The Qur'an that Allah Almighty taught 'Isa (as) **the book and the wisdom, and the Tawrah and the Injil** (3:48, 5:110-113). This is understood as Allah having taught him four separate and different things. Some think that the Book refers to the heavenly Book, the *Ummu l-Kitab*, that is kept with Allah and from which all the other books are drawn. Some say it means simply that 'Isa (as) was able to read and write. Others say that it refers to all the previous revelations except the Tawrah and Injil because they are mentioned separately. What the wisdom is, again the scholars are unsure. Al-Tabari believes that it refers to the books of the earlier prophets. Ibn Kathir believes that it means the deep understanding that would allow him to establish a new interpretation of the old law, the comprehension of the divine purpose behind the divine command. 'Isa (as) was also taught the Tawrah, which means the law, as it was set down by Musa (as) and the earlier prophets. And then finally his own book, the Injil or Gospel, the good news which would be **confirming that which preceded me of the Tawrah and to make permissible to you some of what was (previously) prohibited to you.** (3:50).

Consequently, we can assume that much of his youth was spent learning these things either by being dedicated to the Temple or in some other way. But in the end, his apprenticeship to the priests did not go smoothly as shown by the story related earlier of the rabbi trying to teach him the alphabet. When the teachers tried to get their pupil to focus on the outward reading of the words, 'Isa (as) turned the tables and asked them for the spiritual significance of each letter, a science said by Ibn 'Arabi to be a special gift Allah Almighty gave to 'Isa (as). Being formed from a spirit (*ruh*) from his Lord delivered on the breath of the angel messenger, he embodies the secret of breath. It is the mouth that forms the letters, but it is the breath that manifests them. The secret of the Word, the secret of letters, is his special domain. So 'Isa (as) left the Temple and its scholars.

'Isa teaching at the Temple. Carl Bloch, Danish 1850.

Herod Antipas was busy following the example of his father in building monuments to himself. He was having a city built at Sepphoris not far from Nazareth in Galilee. Since 'Isa (as) is called a carpenter in the Gospel of Matthew, some scholars imagine that Josef (ra) as a skilled carpenter or stone mason worked to help build the city, and perhaps his young stepson was his apprentice. English Christians, on the other hand, say that 'Isa (as) had a wealthy relative known as Josef of Arimathea (ra). He used to sail to the far west of the Roman empire to trade for tin. One year he took his young kinsman along to help him. Together they spent some time in the area of Glastonbury, England before sailing home to Judea. After the passing of 'Isa (as), the elderly Josef (ra) returned to England to preach the Gospel and establish the first church.

'Isa (as) and his relative Josef of Arimathea (ra) visiting England. A banner in the Church of Pilton, England.

There are some stories mentioned in almost all the Muslim histories that must have taken place during this time. 'Isa (as) and his mother were staying in an area under the protection of a kindly shaykh. Maryam (ahs) was very careful to only provide her son with *halal* food, food that is both clean and permitted, food that she either paid for or collected herself. She would gather wild greens and fruit from the hillsides. At harvest time she would follow in the wake of the harvesters in the fields and pick up the grains they had missed or dropped, that they left for the birds and the poor. She supplemented this by spinning yarn from flax or wool and selling it.

The shaykh had a guesthouse in which travelers were welcome to find safety, shelter, and provision. The shaykh had a secret storeroom above the guest quarters in which he kept his stores of food as well as his gold and money. One day he went into his storeroom and found his money missing. Very upset he called everyone in the area to gather in one place to be questioned, but he found his only guests to be a lame man who could not stand unsupported and a man who was blind. Since the door to his treasury was high above the ground only accessible by ladder, he reasoned that the thief could not have been the lame man. Since to have known the location of the storeroom required sight, it could not have been the blind man. The kind and generous shaykh became distraught, with no idea who might have taken his property.

Just then 'Isa (as) and his mother (ahs) came down from where they were living. Maryam (ahs) was particularly concerned for the kind man who had given them protection. She begged 'Isa (as) to help their benefactor. 'Isa (as) proceeded to inform the shaykh that the thieves were in fact the cripple and the blind man. The two protested their innocence, and the shaykh believed them rather than the small son of Maryam (ahs). Only the foolish would accuse a blind or a lame man of being able to carry out such a theft.

However, 'Isa (as) proceeded to show everyone how the crippled man was the one who saw the existence of the storage room. He told the blind man and, guiding him where to stand, he mounted on the blind man's shoulders, pried open the door and swung himself into the storeroom by his strong arms. He looted the treasure and came down the way he went up. The two men divided the money intending to slip away in a few days. Startled and exposed, the two men admitted their guilt and returned the treasure to the kindly shaykh, who was both thankful and impressed. Some time later this same shaykh was celebrating a wedding or hosting some very important guests, when the wine he was serving ran out. 'Isa (as) prayed to Allah to refill the empty wine jars. Miraculously, to the shaykh's relief, all the large vessels became full of the finest wine, enough to serve all the people. In some Muslim accounts the jars were filled with oil rather than wine.

In The Qur'an 'Isa (as) says, **"And I tell you what you eat and what you store up in your houses."** (3:49). It is explained by As-Suddi that when 'Isa (as) was a boy he would know what the people living around him were doing privately in their houses, what they ate and what they stored. Sometimes he would playfully tell his friends what they had had for breakfast, and what their mother was making for dinner, and even what the family was eating when the child was not home. The children reported this to their parents who thought 'Isa (as) must either be sneaky or possessed and, in consequence, forbid their children to play with him.

One day 'Isa (as) was lonely and went to look for his friends. They were all gathered in one house, but when he knocked, the woman who answered the door lied and told him they were not there. 'Isa (as) could hear the sounds of the children playing, and so he asked "Then who do I hear?" Maybe because it sounded like a lot of squealing, the woman answered, "pigs". This would be a strange thing for a Jew to say, but most of country was peopled by a mixture of both Jews and idol worshipers. The young 'Isa (as) replied "So they shall be". And when the woman turned back into the house all the children had been turned into pigs. Muhammad Asad, however, explains this verse in a perhaps more useful way, by saying that 'Isa (as) informed people what things they could do that were good for them in this worldly life, and what things they could do that would be stored for their eternal life.

The most famous story of his childhood is mentioned in The Quran twice, (5:110 and 3:49). It is said that when playing with some children his age, 'Isa (as) formed a simple figure of a bird out of clay. The fact that he was doing this on the Sabbath aroused the anger of the parents. They confronted him about his disobedience of the law. To try and teach them something about the reality behind the law, he took permission from Allah and blew into the clay bird. To the astonishment of the onlookers it became warm and alive. Chirping, it flew away - **how, by My leave, you fashioned the shape of a bird out of clay, breathed into it, and it became, by My leave, a bird;** (5:110). Some commentators have said that he made a bat because it is such an odd monstrosity of a creature, like a mouse with wings, that it could very well be the creation of a child's imagination. Some say, however, that it was a sparrow. Others understand it as a metaphor for his mission as a prophet. He took the clay of the material, lifeless form of the children of Adam (as) and breathed into it faith and love, the spirit of true life.

Because of actions like these, it is said that 'Isa (as) was forced to leave. One wonders anyway what a child like this had to learn among the scholars and scribes, among the priests and politicians. And so 'Isa (as) did not find wisdom in the courtyards of the Temple. He found greed and hypocrisy. He found them worshipping the world and squabbling over its refuse. Most likely, when he was old enough he and his mother joined his cousin Yahya (as) in the deserts and wastelands, eating the fruit of the earth, drinking from the streams, sleeping under the stars, depending on none but Allah, devoting his life to none but Allah.

'Isa (as), by permission of Allah, blows life into clay birds. St. Martin church, Switzerland, 1109.

Ethiopian icon of the twelve disciples, *Hawariyyun*.

25.
Dyers, Bleachers, and Helpers

Perhaps because her son did not benefit from the classes of the priests, Maryam, (ahs) at some point, decided to apprentice him to a bleacher of cloth, *hawari*. One day the man told 'Isa (as) to take care of the clothes the people had brought while he went out to do some errands. When he returned, he found that 'Isa (as) had put all the whitened clothes in the vat of indigo dye instead of dying each of them the color its owner desired. The dyer was very upset, and 'Isa (as) was also upset for his mistake. So 'Isa (as) asked the man to tell him which color each piece of clothing should have been dyed. One by one, he pulled them out of the vat of blue indigo, each in the precise color it was supposed to be. This was a clear miracle.

[We take our] color from Allah, and who is better than Allah at coloring? We are His worshippers/slaves. (2:138). The word for coloring here is *sibgha* meaning, in its primary sense, to dye or to be a dyer. Metaphorically it has come to mean religion, that which penetrates the heart and colors it like a dye. For the Arabic speaking Christians this is the word used for baptism. It has even been said by Yusuf 'Ali, that the early

The fullers field, where the bleachers worked at the time of 'Isa (as), Jerusalem.

Christians actually put dye in the baptismal water in order to lend a physical manifestation to a spiritual transformation. The dyer and all his apprentices fell at 'Isa's (as) feet and testified to their belief in his being a messenger from God. A number of them, how many is not specified in The Qur'an, resolved to apprentice themselves to 'Isa (as) rather than to the dyer.

To clean other people's dirty clothing, pounding it between rocks in the river to whiten them and then dye them anew, was considered a very lowly occupation at that time. It was a dirty job, and only the very poor would have taken it on. 'Isa's (as) path, however, was to keep company with the very poor. They were his people, his nation. It has been the case for all the prophets that the poor were the first to believe and respond to Allah's message. Most of the first believers in the Prophet Muhammad (sas) were also the poor and enslaved. Among the questions asked by Heraclius, the Byzantine ruler, when he received a letter from the Prophet (sas) inviting him to Islam, was: "Who follows him, the rich or the poor?" because the answer would be a clear indication of his sincerity and his disinterest in worldly things.

It is said that Allah gave 'Isa (as) twelve men to be his closest helpers in fulfilling his mission and to give him companionship. In the same way Allah appointed twelve leaders from the twelve tribes to support Musa (as) (5:12) and twelve Helpers (*Ansar*) from Medina at Aqaba to support the Prophet Muhammad (sas). However, there is a hadith of the Prophet (sas) in which he called Zubayr ibn 'Awwam (ra), a companion from Mecca, his *hawari*. In consequence, there are some who reserve the honor of being the *hawari* of the Prophet (sas) for twelve of his companions from Mecca instead: Abu Bakr, 'Umar, 'Uthman, 'Ali, Hamza, Ja'far, Abu 'Ubayda, 'Uthman ibn Madh'un, 'Abdu r-Rahman ibn 'Awf, Sa'd ibn Abi Waqqas, Talhah ibn 'Abdallah, and Zubayr ibn 'Awwam, may Allah be pleased with them all.

The disciples of 'Isa (as) traveled with him and were witness to his words and his miracles. By being in intimate association, observing and absorbing his every word and movement, they were being trained to teach others and to record his Book. These twelve are called *Hawariyyun*, the bleachers or disciples. In Arabic the word is related to *hur* to be white or to whiten. So it is said that they either dressed all in white like the Nazarites, or their hearts were pure, or they had previously worked as bleachers of cloth. However, *Hawari* was in common usage among the Christians of Ethiopia for the disciples of 'Isa (as) and could have been a familiar term among the Arabs as well.

'Isa (as) walking on water to save the fishermen who would later become his companions. 12th century mosaic, Sicily.

More disciples joined them later. Some of them had kept close company with Yahya (as) before his death and afterwards joined 'Isa (as) as his successor. Some were new and had left everything to follow him. They were not educated in the religion. They were laborers, young men without land or property. Ibn Abbas (ra) says, as in the Gospels, that some of them were fishermen on the sea of Galilee. They witnessed 'Isa's (as) miracles and accepted his invitation to become "fishers of men". Most say, however, that they were bleachers of clothes, washermen. Whatever their stations were before, Allah says that He inspired their hearts with the truth of 'Isa's (as) message: **I inspired the disciples: "Believe in Me and in My Messenger." They said, "We have believed, so bear witness that We have submitted (become Muslim)."** (5:111). Allah raised them up to be able to be trained by His prophet, to fulfill the role he needed of them. Perhaps in the same way Allah elevated Harun (as) to accompany and assist his brother Musa (as).

There is a wide spread of opinion about the sanctity of the disciples. Some take them as lesser prophets, who after the death of 'Isa

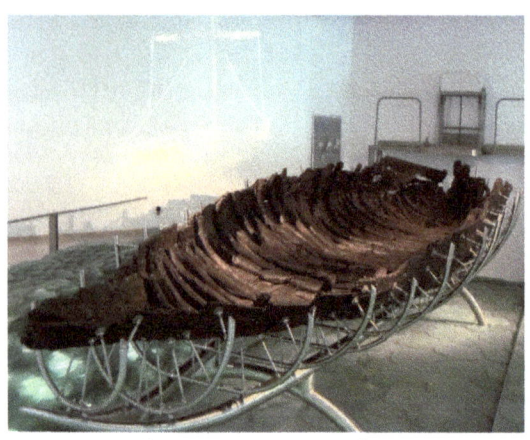

A 1st century boat discovered near the Sea of Galilee similar to the one on which 'Isa (as) fished.

(as) were inspired and performed miracles of healing similar to his own. Some consider them saints and holy men. Some, however, think of them as good intentioned but flawed individuals. They did not manage to keep the purity or truth of their master's message. **Those who say, "Allah is the Messiah, son of Mary," have defied God. The Messiah himself said, "Children of Israel, worship Allah, my Lord and your Lord." If anyone associates others with God, God will forbid him from the Garden, and Hell will be his home. No one will help such evildoers.** (5:72).

In the end there were twelve prominent disciples, whom the Muslim scholars name: Butrus (Simon Peter), Andrawus (Andrew), Mattus (Matthew), Tumus (Thomas), Filibus (Philip), Yuhanna (John), Ya'qub (James), Barthulmawus (Barholomew), and Sham'un (Simon the Zealot). But according to the Arab Gospel there were at least seventy other men who were in close association with 'Isa (as) and, although not of the twelve, they were companions and later were important in spreading his message. They included Lazarus (Al-'Azar) and Barnabas (Bar Nabas), may Allah be pleased with them all. Saint Paul, who became the most successful and prominent proponent of the Christian movement, never actually met 'Isa (as) in person.

Those who became the followers of 'Isa (as) are called *Nasara* in The Qur'an. This is not the only Arabic word used for Christians. Those who follow the Christ, the Messiah are called *Masihiyya* in Arabic. There has been some debate over the meaning of *Nasara*. Many believe it means people who follow the one from Nazareth. But Nazareth plays little part for Muslims in the life of 'Isa (as). Rather they place him in or near Jerusalem for most of his life. Consequently, there are other explanations for the name *Nasara*.

Some say it relates to the word Nazarite, from the Hebrew, meaning to separate, to consecrate. A Nazarite was one who took a vow to make an extra effort to obey the laws of the Tawrah, to pray, and keep away from the distractions of the world. It is thought that the early Christians, the ones who had been raised in Judaism, still followed this practice as did perhaps the early desert fathers, the monks who lived in the caves and isolated places in and around Arabia. And they are thought to have worn all white clothing which ties in with the disciples, the *Hawariyyun* being the bleachers or whiteners.

Others posit that *Nasara* derives from the Arabic root *n-s-r* meaning to help. *Ansar*, which stems from this root, means helpers in general but is usually used in particular to refer to the people of Medina who pledged themselves to the Prophet Muhammad (sas). The *Hawariyyun* were the helpers of 'Isa (as) as the people of Medina were the helpers of Muhammad (sas). As 'Isa (as) son of Maryam (ahs) said to the disciples (*hawariyyun*): **"Who will be my helpers (*ansar*) for God?" The disciples said: "We are the helpers (*ansar*) for God."** (61:14). This name might have then been extended to refer to all those who believed in the message of 'Isa (as).

However, there was a group of early Christians whom Saint Paul and the Roman Christians referred to as Nazareans. They are thought to have been the followers of the apostle James who succeeded 'Isa (as) as the head of the Jewish-Christians in Jerusalem. The Roman church considered them heretics because they held to the laws of the Tawrah. They circumcised, and they did not consider 'Isa (as) to have been either God or His son. Rather, they believed, much as the Muslims continue to believe, that 'Isa (as) was a man anointed by God, the Messiah, to be a prophet in the line of Adam (as), Nuh (as), and Musa (as), and that he came to confirm and to amend the Tawrah rather than to replace it. There might have been some of these who fled persecution to hide in the remote oases of Arabia and were known as *Nasara*. Another distinct possibility is that 'Isa (as) had nothing actually to do with Nazareth. He was said to be a Nazarene because in the Book of Isaiah (11:1) the Messiah is called a branch of the family of Dawud (as) and branch in Hebrew is *nezer*. Allah knows best.

'Isa (as) and Yahya (as) mosaic from the Aya Sofya, Istanbul Turkey, 13th century.

26.
Life and Spirit

The relationship between Yahya (as) and 'Isa (as) began in the world of souls before they were even born into the world. We know this from the story of Yahya (as) greeting his cousin when both were still hidden in the wombs of their mothers. Allah sent them together into the world, and He weaves their stories together in The Qur'an, first one strand then the other, in the beautiful chapter named after Maryam (ahs). The details of their births alternate, and the language of the verses repeat to form one fabric.

When Allah named Yahya (as) He said, **O Zakariyya, We bring you tidings of a son whose name is Yahya; We have given the same name to none before** (19:7). But there is another equally accurate translation of this verse discussed in the Tafsir of as-Suyuti and of Ibn Kathir, **O Zakariyya, We give you good news of a son: His name shall be Yahya: We have made no one of his like before.** Yahya means he lives or, perhaps better, He lives. It is not the actual name that Allah gave exclusively to him but rather the quality, the essence that was conveyed with the name. The only time this same Arabic phrase is used in The Qur'an is in speaking about

Allah Himself, where it is translated either as **Do you know of anyone worthy of the same Name (Allah)?** or as **Do you know of anyone equal to Him?** (19:65)

In some very real way, perhaps as mentioned earlier, from the nature of his overwhelming compassion, Yahya (as) embodies Allah's name *Al-Hayy* and this was never given in the same way to anyone before. 'Isa (as), on the other hand, by the manner of his creation is of the spirit, *Ar-Ruh*. He was formed mostly of an angelic nature and a spirit from Allah. He is, as much as can be, a human embodiment of spirit. Ibn 'Arabi states that life and spirit are inseparable. Even now the two prophets are together in the second heaven as the Prophet Muhammad (sas) witnessed on his Night Journey. They were connected in the world of souls before birth, in life, and now in heaven.

Not caring for the company of people, Yahya (as) attracted crowds of them. Not caring for the world and its doings, he made quite an impact on the world of his time. It is said that even Herod the King considered him a wise and holy man and invited him to the palace to preach. Herod would weep loudly when he listened to Yahya's (as) teaching and then afterwards return happily to his sinful routine. Many people from all walks of life were drawn to this charismatic young man, who spoke with such passion and who was gentle and kind. His sincerity and honesty stood out clearly in contrast to the hypocrisy of the age. He is called *sadiq* in The Qur'an, a man of truth. He was witness to the highest truth and was able to make it clear to others while he himself was steadfast in adhering to it. It is said that he was more famous and universally revered as a holy man than was 'Isa (as) at the time. The injustice of his death is even recounted in the histories of Josephus who was born in Jerusalem at about the time 'Isa (as) left this world but who mentions him only briefly.

From the written record we know nothing about the time 'Isa (as) and Yahya (as) spent in each other's company. It can only be assumed, because of the similarities in belief and practice, that they kept close association. The Muslims recount a few incidents that happened when they were together. The most famous is a conversation between them in which Yahya (as) said to 'Isa (as), "I see you always smiling. Perhaps you think you are exempt from Allah's displeasure?" 'Isa (as) replied, "I see you always in distress. Have you despaired of Allah's Mercy?" After this, a revelation was sent to both prophets informing them that 'Isa's (as) station was more exalted than that of his more somber cousin. Sufis explain that Yahya's (as) state was one of contraction (*qabd*) from fear of God, while 'Isa's (as) was one of expansion (*bast*). Both states normally take their turns in the seeker like breathing in and breathing out.

Interestingly enough, however, this is not the only version of this story. Its opposite also appears in the Islamic literature. In that case it is Yahya (as) who is smiling and 'Isa (as) who is fearful. Either way, Allah Almighty reveals that the one who is closest to Him is the one who thinks best of Him. In fact, although the first version is the most well-known, the earliest written account is the second, and Rumi (q) uses both versions on different occasions.

Allah Almighty sent the two prophets together in time and place. This is not the usual occurrence. If two prophets were sent at the same time, then their missions were usually among different people, as in the case with Sayyiduna Ibrahim (as) and his nephew the prophet Lut (as). If they were sent to the same people then one took up the mission of the other upon his death as with Ya'qub (as) and his son Yusuf (as) or Dawud (as) and his son Sulayman (as), or Ilyas (as) and his inheritor Alyasa' (as). Most prophets were sent alone to a single people with the major exception of the brothers Musa (as) and Harun (as). They worked together as a team, Musa (as) having received prophecy first and Harun (as) later at his brother's request. They complimented each other. Harun (as) contributed both communication skills and compassion that helped to balance the fierceness and zeal of Musa (as). It could be said that Musa (as) represented the written Law while Harun (as) represented the ritual Practice. This is a model, perhaps, of the kind of spiritual relationship that existed between the cousins Yahya (as) and 'Isa (as). Musa (as) and Harun (as) initiated the prophetic inheritance of the Banu Isra'il, and Yahya (as) and 'Isa (as) concluded it. It was as if each pair were one breath emanating from the Almighty, a breathing in and a breathing out.

It could also be said that the path of Yahya (as) took him into the streams and rivers. His was the way of purity by immersion in living water, the water of life. The Arabic verb *hayy* means to live but it also means to flow, as in flowing water because the basic definition of life is movement. As Allah says about Himself, **every day He is busy with something.** (55:29). If it is alive, it moves. So the planets and stars are alive, as are the earth and stones although their movement may be too slow to be seen.

A sailing stone, a desert phenomenon caused by moisture and cold.

The path of 'Isa (as), however, took him to walk on the water, at a spiritual level few could emulate. Mu'adh ibn Jabal (ra), related that the Prophet Muhammad (sas) said, "If only 'Isa (as) had had a little more faith he would have been able to walk on air." His companions said, "We didn't know that prophets could fall short", and he replied, "Allah's standards are too high for anyone to reach." The Prophet (sas), in his modesty did not say it, but of course he was able to walk on air as he did on the Night Journey and his ascent to Heaven (al-Isra' wa l-Mi'raj).

We learn from the Gospels that when 'Isa (as) was thirty years old he was immersed in the river Jordan, baptized at the hand of Yahya (as). This was not a new ritual. It was a traditional Jewish form of ablution. To become ritually pure after being defiled in some way, after having broken a law, having touched the dead or, for a woman, by having given birth or finished menstruation, it was necessary to be immersed completely in water. This water had to be running and clean, called 'living' water. It was the practice of Yahya (as) that when someone rededicated themselves to following and obeying the laws of the Tawrah and repented of their past actions, they needed to become clean in the river. And he ministered to this act of purification, whitening and dying hearts in the color of God.

One day at a spot on the River Jordan, the prophet Yahya (as) delivered this rite of purification to the prophet 'Isa (as). Some think that this elevates Yahya (as) above his cousin, but it was the custom that the disciple poured water for the master. The mission of Yahya (as) was coming to a close, and the mission of 'Isa (as) was just beginning. Although born miraculously of a virgin mother and a spirit from Allah, although manifesting so many miracles - speaking as an infant, destroying idols, and healing the sick – he had not received his order from Allah to begin his mission. And 'Isa (as) in his deep humility put Yahya's (as) station above his own. He is related to have said about himself, **Peace on me the day I was born, the day I will die, and the day I am brought back to life.** (19:33), but he said it was Allah Almighty Himself who said about Yahya (as), **Peace be upon him the day he was born, the day he dies, and the day he will be brought back to life.** (19:15). In the Gospels of both Matthew and Luke he calls Yahya (as) "a prophet and more than a prophet".

This traditional ritual immersion of the Jews, the *ghusl* (total ablution), of the Muslims, has become the once-in-a-lifetime rite of baptism for the Christians. It was a definite turning point in the life of 'Isa (as). The Gospels say that 'Isa (as) saw the Holy Spirit, Jibra'il (as), descend from Heaven in the form of a white dove marking the opening of his mission. After this deep experience, perhaps similar to the Prophet's (sas) first encounter with Jibra'il (as) on Jabal Nur and the beginning of the revelation of The Qur'an, 'Isa (as) retreated into the desert far from people to pray in seclusion for forty days.

Baptism of 'Isa (as) by Yahya (as). Illustration for Al-Biruni, done in Persia, 1750.

During this time, the devil tested him with temptations but he did not succumb. Shaytan offered him all the riches of the world, wealth and fame, but each time 'Isa (as) showed no interest. One night he lay down to sleep for a few hours. He saw a stone nearby and took it to use as a pillow under his head. When he woke, he found shaytan standing over him grinning. "Finally you have accepted my offer" he said. 'Isa (as) in alarm, asked what it was that he had accepted. Shaytan pointed to the stone. 'Isa (as) picked it up and hurled it at shaytan and never again lay his head on anything but the bare ground.

At another time, shaytan tried to put 'Isa (as) under his control. He approached and slyly commanded him to say, "There is no god but Allah, *la ilaha ila Allah*." Sayyiduna 'Isa (as) refused even to repeat these holy words. He said "These are the words of Allah, but still I will never do anything that you might ask of me." Al-Ghazali comments about this story that shaytan lies and misleads mankind even by means of good things.

The tomb over the spot where the head of Yahya (as) is buried. Now inside the 'Umayyad Mosque Damascus, Sy

27.
On a Silver Platter

Meanwhile, the crowds attracted by Yahya (as) did not go unnoticed by those in power. Although Herod was drawn to him personally, he could not ignore the political potential in the ideas and emotions Yahya (as) generated in his followers. It was a period of great political unrest. There were many groups, known collectively as Zealots, who on the basis of religion plotted violent political reform. Josephus claims that Herod's actions were purely political. He was afraid that the passionate crowds that were drawn to the desert ascetic might be turned to political rebellion. But, on the other hand, Herod liked Yahya (as). He reminded the King perhaps of the man he could have been, and he called him often to the palace to speak with him. Yahya (as) was innocent of ambition or contrivance, he was above courting the favor of the king. He always answered his questions truthfully, never trying to please him with the politically correct answer. Yahya (as) stood firm for the truth, and it wasn't in his nature to duck his head.

It is said that one day Herod went to visit his older brother Philip and fell in love with Philip's wife Herodias and she with him. He managed to coerce Philip into divorcing her and then set about getting rid of his own wife, the daughter of the king of Nabataea. Surprisingly, Herod sought the blessing of Yahya (as) in his affair. Not surprisingly, Yahya (as) refused to give it. Not only was this an adulterous act, but it was strictly forbidden in the Law of the Tawrah to marry a brother's wife if the brother was still living. Blessing or no blessing, Herod went ahead with his plans.

His soon to be ex-wife fled to her father Aretus, king of Nabataea, and so began a political disaster that eventually ended in war. Herod married Herodias, and she came to live with him in Galilee bringing with her a daughter by Philip, whose name was Salome. It might have ended there except that Herodias never forgave Yahya (as) for opposing her. She made it her aim to take revenge.

Thought to be the mausoleum of Aretus in the ruins of the Nabataean city of Petra, Jordan.

The daughter of Herodias grew up to be a beautiful woman, and Herod began to notice her in an inappropriate way. Herodias, an ambitious mother, for some reason did not object. In fact, she encouraged her daughter to arouse the king by appearing before him uncovered and displaying her natural attractions. Herod was no match for the conniving of the women. He fell head over heels in love with his niece and stepdaughter. Once more Herod tried to get Yahya (as) to bless and approve his illicit behavior. Yahya (as) again told him frankly that marriage to a niece or to the daughter of his wife was strictly forbidden by God, and it was absolutely unlawful to be married to a mother and daughter at the same time.

The anger of Herodias knew no bounds. The prophet was

challenging her will once more. This was the chance she had been waiting for to turn her husband against Yahya (as). She insisted that Yahya (as) be arrested and thrown into the prison at Machaerus, a palace whose ruins are now in Jordan. The King bowed to the will of his powerful wife, and Yahya (as) was imprisoned. One night Herod gave a banquet for all the notables in the area. Herodias made sure that Herod had his fill of wine, and then she dressed her daughter in diaphanous veils and sent her out to dance for the King. Salome danced, and Herod was entranced. He asked her to dance again, and she demanded a present if she complied with his request. Too drunk to restrain his desire, he wanted her at whatever cost, he promised to give whatever she asked.

When she had danced, she came to sit beside him to claim her reward. All she wanted, she said, was the head of Yahya (as) on a silver platter. Herod, as drunk as he was, was appalled. He had some idea of the spiritual station of Yahya (as), and he knew enough to know that opposing a saint of God is the same as opposing God Himself. He begged her to pick something else, jewels, palaces, gardens. But Salome was well taught by her mother, and she stuck to her choice. He refused, but the whole court had witnessed his promise, and eventually he gave in. Sobered by the weight of what was taking place, he ordered for Yahya (as) to be beheaded.

Some time later the guards brought Yahya's (as) head on a platter to present to the girl. The deed was done. Herod said to the unlucky girl, "You have surely destroyed us." And after that he could no longer bear to look on her. Even the thought of her repelled him.

It is said the blood gushed from the veins of Yahya (as) until it ran like a river out of the palace and through the streets. The palace guards tried to stem the flow by piling mounds of earth over his head, but the blood continued to boil and bubble until, it is said, it was finally avenged by the deaths of thousands of Herod's soldiers at the hands of their enemies.

The first century Jewish historian Josephus wrote that in 36 CE, after the execution of Yahya (as), Aretas, the King of Nabataea, Herod's ex-father-in-law, declared war on Galilee. Although better manned and better armed, Herod lost the war, and thousands of his soldiers were slaughtered. Josephus relates that the people at the time believed this to be divine punishment for the murder of Allah's righteous slave, Yahya (as).

Herod had also become too ambitious for Rome. He was removed from the throne and banished to the outermost rim of the empire. His wife, Herodias, followed him into exile, and they are believed to have died either in northern Spain or in France. They died forgotten by friends and family, alone. The place of their burial is unknown. The Muslim writers say that the earth was commanded to open up and consume them without a trace.

The whereabouts of Yahya's (as) remains are also contested. Muslims believe that his head was buried in Damascus and a church built over the site. With the coming of Islam, the church was replaced with a grand mosque in the center of the city, the 'Umayyad Mosque, which is open to pilgrims from all religions. The mosque has two minarets and, unlike any other mosque in the world, there is a *mu'adhdhan* in each who join together in harmony to make one *adhan* for every prayer. One of these minarets is called the White Minaret, and it is believed to be the place where 'Isa (as) will descend from heaven in the final days.

There is also a holy site in Nablus on the West Bank where it is said Yahya's (as) head was interred until at least the fourth century. The Topkapi in Istanbul has the top of his skull in a crystal box among the prophetic relics taken from the Byzantines. The Catholics have a shriveled head on display in Capite, Rome that they claim is his.

Some believe that the body of Yahya (as) was buried in Machaerus where he was killed. Some say it was taken to Jerusalem or Constantinople, France, Greece, or Egypt. There was a thriving trade in relics during the Middle Ages, and pieces that were claimed to be of Yahya (as) are recorded as having been sold, traded, or given as royal gifts all over Europe by Kings, Popes, and Sultans. However, it is most unlikely that any of these are authentic. We are told that the earth has been forbidden from consuming the flesh of prophets, consequently he would never be a pile of bones to be broken up and distributed around the world. Secondly, it is most unlikely that Allah Almighty would allow the remains of His prophet to be bartered and sold, used as a pawn in political games, or left unburied on display for public viewing, however reverent. But Allah knows best.

It is the practice of the Christians to display the bodily remains of saints, martyrs, and prophets prominently on their altars or in places in full view of the congregants. Perhaps this is the origin and meaning of the hadith of the Prophet (sas) forbidding the making of graves into places of prayer in the manner of the Christians. It is a strange practice to have developed out of Judaism in which contact with a corpse or graveyard is regarded as defiling in and of itself. Jews are not allowed to pray in Christian places of worship partly for this reason and partly because of the presence of statues and icons although the Temple itself had plenty of statues and representative decoration. They are, however, able to pray in mosques.

It is believed that on the Day of Arising, *Yawmu l-Qiyamah*, everything still living will die including even the angels. The very last to die will be 'Azra'il (as), death himself, and he will be killed by Yahya (as) in recompense for the terrible unjust death he suffered, condemned to die by a faithless woman and slaughtered like a sheep. 'Azra'il (as) will take the form of a bird, and Yahya (as) will be given a spiritual knife to perform the last sacrifice. Yahya (as), the living one, will put an end to death forever. Then all souls will be resurrected to eternal life after which there will be no death. Allah Almighty says about Yayha (as), **Peace on him the day be was born, and the day he dies and the day he shall be raised up alive.** (19:15).

Yahya (as) as a heavenly being with wings and carrying his own head. 10th century Bulgaria.

'Isa (as) honoring his mother. Pseudo Arabic on the halos and damask cloth. Allah's name on Maryam's (ahs) robe. Gentile da Fabriano, Italian 1422.

28.
Masih 'Isa ibn Maryam (as)

We have been given several different descriptions of the physical appearance of 'Isa (as) from the Hadith. The Prophet (sas) saw both 'Isa (as) and Yahya (as) in the second heaven on the occasion of his Night Journey. He later described 'Isa (as) as having light skin flushed with red as if he had just emerged from the bath. His hair was straight with a little bit of curl and appeared to be dripping with water. He was a well-built, sturdy man of medium height with broad shoulders. (Bukhari and Muslim). At another time, the Prophet (sas) said he had a vision in which he was sitting at the Ka'ba when he saw a man leaning on the shoulders of two others making the rounds of the Holy House. He was informed that this man was 'Isa (as). He described him as the most handsome of dark men (often said to be the color of wheat) with the most excellent (thick and glossy) dark hair which hung down to between his ears and his shoulders, again dripping with water. (Muwatta).

At the time of his miraculous conception, Allah gave him the name 'Isa (3:45). 'Isa is an Arabic rendition of the Hebrew Yeshua, itself a shortened form of Yehoshua, which is the name of the warrior prophet

Joshua (as) (Yusha in Arabic) who succeeded Musa (as) and finally was able to lead the Banu Isra'il out of the wilderness into the Holy Land. Yehoshua means 'God saves' because, like Joshua (as), the mission of 'Isa (as) was to bring his people in safety into the Kingdom of Heaven. It was quite a common name at the time. Some Arabic scholars, however, relate the name 'Isa instead to the root, '-y-s, which means of a reddish white color and so substantiating the way the Prophet Muhammad (sas) saw him in the second heaven.

Instead of, or in addition to, a last name or family name, most children in the Middle East were, and still are, given a first name followed by the name of their father. The word for son, *ibn*, or daughter, *bint*, connects the two names, as in Maryam bint 'Imran, or Yahya ibn Zakariyya. But sometimes for various reasons, the name of the mother was used instead of the father. Perhaps the father had died or was a foreigner or less prominent or less memorable than the mother. The purpose of a name after all is to distinguish one person from another, to identify them clearly. Even one of the sons of 'Ali ibn Abi Talib (ra) was called by his mother's name in order to distinguish him from other of Sayyiduna 'Ali's (ra) sons with the same first name. It was not an uncommon practice among Muslims and did not necessarily indicate illegitimacy.

'Isa (as) was created without any kind of a father, either biological or spiritual. This was the first of the many signs by which Allah distinguished him. He was a sign to all of mankind, a reminder that their Creator is fully present in the world and all powerful. This sign certainly was not meant to be hidden or disguised. The Qur'an states that because of the unique manner of his conception and the holiness and purity of his mother, he is to be known by her name, 'Isa (as) ibn Maryam (ahs). This honorable title and truthful description is, however, almost exclusive to Islam. In the canonical Gospels of the Christians, the term 'son of Mary' is only used once in the oldest and shortest Gospel of Mark (ra). The other gospels call 'Isa (as) either son of Josef the carpenter (ra), or son of God, titles which he did not use for himself and which are misleading to say the least. To honor him and to honor her, 'Isa (as) is called 'Isa ibn Maryam, Jesus son of Mary, twenty-three out of the twenty-five times he is mentioned in The Qur'an by name.

There is another name by which 'Isa (as) is called in The Qur'an, so often that some Muslim commentators thought it could have actually been his family name - *al-Masih,* the Messiah. There have been multiple explanations of the meaning and derivation of this word. The most common is that it comes from the Hebrew *Meshiach* meaning anointed. It was the ancient Jewish custom to pour or rub some blessed and scented oil on the head or forehead of a king at the time of his coronation or a high priest at the time of his investiture, in imitation of the divine anointing of a prophet at the outset of his mission. This became the custom in Europe among the Christian monarchs and also for their high church officials. To be anointed came to mean chosen by God for a particular role or position. It designates a God-given honor, and there were many kings and prophets of the Banu Isra'il who were called *meshiach.*

However, in the form of a noun accompanied by the definite article, *the* Messiah, it was used after the Babylon exile in 570 BCE for the one who would come to right the wrongs of the Banu Isra'il. According to the Jewish understanding, his signs will be that he will rebuild the Temple in Jerusalem and restore its rituals. He will bring the twelve tribes back to Jerusalem from wherever they have been scattered and lost. He will eliminate belief in other than the One God, and he will rule everyone with justice according to the law of the Tawrah. Texts found in the caves of Qumran indicate that there may be two messiahs. One, *Meshiach ben David,* will be a military commander who will lead the forces of good against the forces of evil. The other, *Meshiach ben Yusuf,* will be a spiritual leader who will rule for forty years after the battle is won. This is very similar to the belief in Islam of the coming of the Mahdi (as) and the return of 'Isa (as).

The Jews have in the past anointed many men with the title *Meshiach* only to take it away when they died without having accomplished what was written. They even gave this title to Sayyiduna 'Umar (ra) and then to the Khalifa Marwan because they ended the Christian exile of the Jews, allowing them to return to Jerusalem and because they made the preparations needed for the rebuilding of the Temple in the form of the Dome of the Rock. The spot where it was thought the original Temple stood had been used by the conquering Christians as a garbage dump. The site was cleared and cleaned by Muslims and Jews working together. The Dome constructed there was not in the form of a mosque but rather a *mashhad* or shrine which was originally open for the worship of Jews as well as Muslims. Most of the calligraphy illuminating the Dome consists of the verses of The Qur'an refuting the divinity of 'Isa (as).

The Jews reject the title of *meshiach* for 'Isa (as) because he died without fulfilling what they required of him. The Christians, however, believe that he fulfilled them but on a spiritual or metaphoric level and he will return at the end of days to complete his mission on earth. "And they will see the Son of Man coming on the clouds of the sky with power and great glory." (Matthew 24:30). Allah called 'Isa (as) the *Masih* at the time of his birth. Muslims believe he was appointed and anointed by God and he will return at the end of days with Sayyid al-Mahdi (as). Sayyid al-Mahdi (as) will be the *khalifa* from the descendants of Muhammad (sas) who will gather the believers under one banner and bring justice to the world. He will prepare the way for 'Isa (as) who will descend from heaven to finally kill the *Masih* ad-Dajjal, the false messiah, and eliminate belief in anything other than Allah. 'Isa (as) will rule all people in peace and justice under the law of The Qur'an for forty years, not as a prophet in his own right but rather as a member of the nation of the Prophet Muhammad (sas).

The Arabic root *m-s-h* has the original meaning, as in Hebrew, of to touch or wipe, from which the concept of anointing with oil is derived. But the Muslim explanation of what was touched and why, has nothing whatsoever to do with investiture or coronation. The Qur'an says, **when Your Lord summoned the descendants of Adam, and made them testify about themselves,** He asked them **"Am I not your Lord?" They said, "Yes, we testify."** (7:172). It is explained in a hadith that after the creation of Adam (as), Allah ordered all of Adam's (as) future children to materialize and acknowledge their Lord. Then He put them back inside Adam (as) all except for 'Isa (as). The seed of 'Isa (as) was kept with Allah until it was time to blow him into Maryam (ahs). Therefore, it is said that 'Isa (as) was touched or held back since the time of the first creation.

In other interpretations he is called *masih* because he was touched by the angel with the spirit from Allah or because he was able to heal people just by touching them or because, before he was born, Allah Almighty wiped away any future sin and any possibility to sin. A hadith of the Prophet (sas) says that shaytan has poked his fingers in the sides of every newborn human and made them cry, except for 'Isa (as) (al-Bukhari). So 'Isa (as) is called the Messiah either because he was touched or he was untouched or because he touched others. Or because of all three.

Another Muslim tradition derives the word *masih* from *siyaha* meaning to travel. 'Isa (as) had no permanent home and never stayed for long in any one place. He had no possessions other than the clothes he wore. He ate from whatever his Lord provided, and if it was nothing, he made do with nothing. He said, "The world is a bridge. Pass over it but do not build upon it" (Hasan al Basri). It was said that for a long time he owned nothing but a comb and a cup. Then one day he saw a man combing his beard with his fingers so he got rid of his comb. Another day he saw a man drinking water from his cupped hands so he got rid of his cup. Then he thanked Allah for providing him with everything of which he was in need. He did not save for the next day or give any thought or attention to his future needs. He left the things of the world for the foolish, and he lived his life as a permanent pilgrim on the path to his Lord. **Unto Allah is the journeying.** (3:28).

The cup that 'Isa (as) is supposed to have used at the last supper, encased in gold, Valencia, Spain.

6th century painting of 'Isa (as) from the monastery of St. Catherine, Sinai that has a letter of protection said to be from the Prophet (sas) himself.

29.
A Prophet and A Slave

In his first miraculous utterance while still a newborn baby, Allah has 'Isa (as) describe himself, "**I am a slave of Allah, *'abdu Llah*. He has given me the Book, made me a prophet (*nabi*), made me blessed wherever I am. He has commanded me to pray, to give alms as long as I live, to cherish my mother. He did not make me domineering (unjust, lordly) or graceless (unblest). Peace was on me the day I was born, and will be on me the day I die and the day I am raised to life again."** (19:30-33).

The first attribute he ascribes to himself is *'abd Allah*, slave of God. To be a slave is the pride of the men of God. This was also the honored attribute by which the Prophet Muhammad (sas) identified himself and was referred to by Allah in The Qur'an, **When the slave of Allah stood up to pray** (72:19). As part of the testimony of Islam, the *shahada*, we call him *'abduhu wa rasuluhu*, His slave and His messenger. The Qur'an states clearly, **There is no one in the heavens or earth who will not come to the Lord of Mercy as a slave.** (19:93). Willing or unwilling, this is the reality.

Today, as in the days of the prophets, freedom is our pride and we believe it is our right and our heritage. Freedom we think is something

Qala inni abdu Llah – He ('Isa) said, "I am a slave of Allah." (19:30).

to fight and die for. To be deprived of freedom is to be deprived of life. For this reason, people do not like to translate the Arabic word *'abd* as slave. The word servant or worshipper is more digestible. The secondary meaning of *'abd* does mean worshipper, and *'ibada*, stemming from the same root, means act of worship. However, a slave is without choice while a servant has a modicum of freedom to choose his master and leave if he wants. In relation to Allah everything in creation is poor, weak, and a beggar. The reality is that there is no other position in which to stand before the Creator than as a slave, either as a disobedient one or as an obedient one totally submitted to His will, and in either case **He does whatever He wills** (85:16). Those who know say that only the perfect man can be the perfect slave. Only the complete man has no pretensions of willfulness or lordliness, qualities that belong uniquely to the Lord. Only the complete servant is dissolved in his Master and no longer possesses an iota of his own will other than perhaps the will to obey.

Allah says **I created jinn and mankind only to serve Me** (*'abiduni*) –as a slave. (51:56). This is the task our Master has given us - to submit, to serve, to worship. And He has said, **those who are too proud to serve Me will enter Hell humiliated.** (40:60). In other words, if you submit to the reality willingly it feels like heaven, but if you have to be subdued and submitted forcefully it feels like hell. Allah has said about 'Isa (as) in particular, **The Messiah would never scorn to be a slave of Allah, nor would the angels who are close to Him.** (4:172). The lowest of human social positions on earth is the highest of angelic stations in the spiritual world. We are truly slaves to Him Almighty. This is the prototype of slavery, for which the slavery of one man to another is merely a poor and degenerate imitation. The first to follow the prophets were always the poor and the slaves because they were not proud.

'Isa (as) was the perfect exemplar of humbleness before his Lord and before the creatures of His Lord. He was certainly aware of his exalted spiritual position but that was a reality that did not need to be flaunted. Often in the Islamic literature he refers to himself as "Allah's slave, son of Allah's slave (Maryam), daughter of Allah's slave ('Imran)." He did not set himself above the people. He explained the correct attitude to his companions when he said, "Why don't I see you performing the best worship?" They asked what is the best worship? "Be humble before Allah." (ibn Hanbal). He also said more clearly, "Do not look at the wrong actions of people as if you were lords over them (judges). Look at your own wrong actions as if you were slaves. Some people are afflicted by wrong action, and some people are protected from it. Be merciful to the people of affliction, and thank Allah for His protection." (Muwatta).

"He has given me the Book, made me a prophet (*nabi*)" (19:30). Allah gave 'Isa (as) a Book which makes him a messenger, *rasul*, and He made him a prophet, *nabi*. There is a difference between these two terms. A prophet is the bearer of warning and good news, the deliverer of information about the future, prophecy and right guidance. A messenger is entrusted with a divine message or Book. According to hadith, Allah has sent to every community a prophet, perhaps as many as one hundred and twenty-four thousand altogether. Of these we only know of a meager forty-eight mentioned in the Books of the Jews and the thirty-one mentioned by name or referred to in The Qur'an.

Of these the Prophet Muhammad (sas) has told us there are three hundred and thirteen who are also messengers. We know only of the thirteen mentioned in The Qur'an. According to a Hadith of the Prophet (sas) four of them are 'Syrian' meaning those who lived before the Flood, (Adam, Seth, Idris, and Nuh), four Arab (Hud, Shu'ayb, Salih, and Muhammad), and the rest are from the descendants of Ibrahim, may Allah's peace be upon them all. 'Isa (as) is among that number, part of a distinguished elite of the truly guided. To be a messenger in theory requires a message, a new scripture. Some of these we know about and some we do not. Adam (as) and Seth (as), Idris (as) and Nuh (as) came with Books which either have been lost or absorbed into the message that Musa (as) brought called the Tawrah. We know that 'Isa (as) is a messenger but we are not sure if what we have today is exactly his Book. The word Gospel is derived from the Greek word, *Evangel*, and from it the Arabs get *Injil* meaning good news. The surviving Gospels are accounts written about 'Isa (as) by men, all of whom never actually met him. They are not precisely the words of God although they may certainly have been inspired by God. They are not exactly the words of 'Isa (as) although they contain some of his words. They could be seen rather as accounts of 'Isa (as) (his *sirah*). He himself was his Book. Or it could be that his Book is what the modern Biblical scholars call Q – the original lost Gospel from which the others were derived.

'Isa (as) exhibited all the qualities of the chosen of Allah and tried to teach, by his words and his example, the mainstays of religion - prayer, fasting, and charity. **He has commanded me to pray, to give alms as long as I live (19: 31).** All the prophets prayed. The manner of their formal prayer may have differed, but all of them made prostration (*sajda*). "Wherever 'Isa (as) found himself at nightfall he would plant his feet and pray until he saw the break of dawn. He would never leave a place without praying two *rak'ahs*." (Samarqandi). It is said that 'Isa (as) spent the whole of every night in prayer.

All of the prophets fasted, and many had favorite fasting rhythms. The fast of Dawud (as) was every other day. The preferred fasts of Muhammad (sas) were the three white days of the full moon and Mondays and Thursdays. It is related that 'Isa (as) fasted every day and lived on nothing but barley bread and water. The fast of his mother Maryam (ahs) was to refrain from food for two days and then eat for two days.

Allah commanded 'Isa (as) to tithe and give charity. However, his charity could not have been in material objects since he had no money or belongings to give. He was as poor as or poorer than any of those he served. What he gave in charity must have been his attention and kindness, his healing hand, and his answered prayers. He represents for the Muslims the prime example of elective poverty and self denial. However, of the many blessings and spiritual gifts Allah had bestowed on him, he freely and generously gave to others.

He had no possessions, no house, no wealth, no wife or children. Not only did he not have these things, but he refused them when they were offered to him. At one point his friends wanted to build him a house and he consented to their kindness jokingly by telling them to build his house

'Isa (as) traveling and teaching. James Tissot, 1886 CE.

on the shore of the sea where it would presumably get washed away by the incoming tide. His companions wanted to buy him a donkey so that he would not have to walk when they went about the small villages visiting the sick and teaching the people. But 'Isa (as) said to them "I have more honor in the eyes of Allah than that He would give me something that might distract me from Him" (by having to look after it). (Ibn Hanbal).

'Isa (as) used "to eat the leaves of trees, dress in robes made of hair, and sleep wherever night found him. He had no child who might die, and no house that might fall into ruin. He did not save his lunch for his dinner or his dinner for his lunch. He said every day brings its own sustenance." (al-Ghazali). 'Isa (as) used to say, "Hunger is my seasoning, fear is my garment, wool is my clothing, the light of dawn is my heat in winter, the moon is my lantern, my feet are my vehicle, what the earth provides is my food. I retire for the night owning nothing, and I awake in the morning owning nothing. There is no one on earth richer than I." (Al-Isbahani). It is said that the description of himself that he most cherished was "that poor man".

He instructed his followers that "if you desire to devote yourselves entirely to God and to be the light of the children of Adam, you must forgive those who do you evil, visit the sick who do not visit you, be kind to those who are unkind to you, and lend to those who do not repay you.

Charity is not to do good to the one who does good to you. For this is returning good for good. Charity is to do good to the ones who do you harm." (Ibn Hanbal). These are the attributes of a prophet. We are familiar with them from the accounts of the Prophet Muhammad (sas) who had a neighbor in Mecca who used to throw garbage on him whenever he passed under her window. When one day he passed by and nothing was thrown he became worried for her. He found that she had gotten sick so he went to see how she was. This kindness opened her heart, and she became a believer. Much later, when Allah rewarded the Muslims with victory, enormous amounts of wealth passed through the Prophet's (sas) hands. His generosity to his former enemies, in gifts and forgiveness is legendary.

'Isa (as) did not retreat from the company of people as did Yahya (as). Instead he traveled continuously, never staying more than a couple of days in each place. He went to visit the poor and the sick wherever they lived, in the small villages, in the hills and valleys of Canaan because they could not come to him. He stayed in their houses and accepted whatever hospitality they could offer. He was engaged directly and passionately with the people in his charge.

Kindness to parents is another important command in The Qur'an. **Your Lord has commanded that you should worship none but Him, and that you be kind to your parents. If either or both of them reach old age with you, say no word that shows impatience with them, and do not be harsh with them, but speak to them respectfully.** (17:23). This is one of the traits of all the prophets if they had parents. Ibrahim (as) is the prime example. He was patient and loving to his unbelieving father until he forced Ibrahim (as) to leave home. He then continued to pray for his father until Allah ordered him to stop. 'Isa (as) never left Maryam (ahs) behind as he strove on the path of Allah even though there are a few incidents in the Gospels that make it appear as if he did (John 2:4). 'Isa (as) says, **Allah made me to cherish my mother. He did not make me domineering or graceless.** (19:32). There was a bond between them and a purpose they shared. Together they were one sign.

The perfect prophet and the perfect slave. Mi'rajnama, Afghanistan, 1436 CE.

Photograph by Kathrin Swoboda.

30.
A Word and A Spirit

All the prophets were created, inspired, and sent by the One God. All of them are His sincere and humble slaves. All of their words originate from the same Book. All of them are loving, truthful, and fierce; perfect in their own way. Believe in all of them and be rightly guided. Make no distinction between them (3:84, 2:136, 2:285, 4:152). They are reaching out to us as one hand to pull us to safety - one God, one message. And yet each prophet had his own particular destiny, nation, and time. Each has his own unique relationship to the One who created him. Adam (as) is called the Pure one of God (*Safi Allah*), Nuh (as) is called the one Saved by God (*Naji Allah*), Ibrahim (as) is called the intimate Friend of God (*Khalil Allah*), Musa (as) is called the Confidant of God (*Kalim Allah*), 'Isa (as) is called both the Spirit of God (*Ruh Allah*) and the Word of God (*Kalimat Allah*), and Muhammad (sas) is known as the Beloved of God (*Habib Allah*).

Allah bestowed two unique titles on His servant 'Isa (as). He is both a word and a spirit. Traditional Muslim commentators have interpreted the meaning of these titles on many levels. Some consider they are two separate qualities while others see them as intertwined: the spirit

Calligraphic exercise attributed to Mir'imad al-Qazvini 1611 CE, Mughal.

is the breath by which 'Isa (as) was made, and the word is what it manifests. This is truly a mystery of Allah's mysteries, and we can only touch lightly on some of the possible ways the rightly guided have understood it.

'Isa (as) is described in The Qur'an as a word of Allah, *Kalimat Allah*. **O Maryam, indeed, Allah gives you good tidings of a word (*kalimat*) from Him, whose name will be al-*Masih* 'Isa ibn Maryam, honored in this world and the next, and among those brought near.** (3:45). Some say that 'Isa (as) is called a word of God because Allah Almighty created him by means of the word *kun*. Allah **is the Originator of the heavens and the earth, and when He decrees something, He says only, "Be"** (*kun*) **and it becomes** (*fa yakun*). (2:117). All of creation has been created with this word. 'Isa (as), however, was created in a different manner and so manifested it differently. The word remained as part of his nature and was expressed on his own breath to enable him to enliven a form of clay and to raise the dead. Others explain his miraculous ability by saying that the word he was given to use was the so-called Hundredth Name of Allah by which whatever he prayed for was granted.

Some claim that by word, is meant his Book or his general literacy and knowledge of all the previous books. Others, including Ibn 'Abbas (ra), say that 'Isa (as) actually is the word given to him from Allah, embodied. He is his Book, the *Injil*, the Good News. That is why the Gospels are other people's memories of his teaching and can be compared more accurately to the books of *Sirah* or perhaps hadith, while 'Isa (as) himself can only be compared to The Qur'an, which is also a word from the Words of God, a Book from the Mother of Books which is with Allah. In a different but similar way, when 'Aysha (rah), was asked to describe the Prophet Muhammad (sas), she replied that he was "The Qur'an walking", the embodiment of his Book; everything he did and everything he said, inward and outward, could be found expressed in the verses of The Qur'an.

The word that 'Isa (as) embodies is a word of ultimate goodness, and it is why he had only good to say in every circumstance whether addressing an ignorant fool or a dead dog or even a pig. One day 'Isa (as) walked past a pig on the road. He gave salaams to the pig saying "Pass in peace." His companions were outraged, but 'Isa (as) explained that his tongue was not accustomed to ugliness.

We are told in The Qur'an that 'Isa (as) was also strengthened and supported by the holy spirit (*ruhu l-quddus*). **We gave Jesus, son of Mary, Our clear signs and strengthened him with the holy spirit.** (2:253). Most understand the clear signs to be his miracles, and the holy spirit to be Jibra'il (as), who is also considered by most Muslim scholars to be the one who blew the spirit of 'Isa (as) into Maryam (ahs). It was Jibra'il (as), in the form of a man, dressed in the skin of a mortal human being, who at some metaphorical level replaced the function of a father, who continued to inspire and support 'Isa (as) throughout his life. The Archangel Jibra'il (as) is the messenger to the angelic world and to all the human messengers. He brought revelation for twenty-two years to the Prophet Muhammad (sas) and supported him with his companionship and, on occasion, with his angelic armies. Sometimes he appeared in his angelic form and sometimes in human form as he did with Maryam (ahs). Sometimes he was hidden from the sight of people, and sometimes he was visible.

However, the Qur'an also says, ***Al-Masih* 'Isa ibn Maryam was but a messenger of Allah and His word, which He bestowed upon Maryam, and a spirit (*ruh*) from Him.** (4:171) indicating that 'Isa (as) was not just supported by the spirit but that he, in some way, was a spirit from his Lord. It is said that the breath of the spirit by which he was created continued to live on in his own breath. By means of it he could heal the sick, restore sight to the congenitally blind, and raise the dead by permission of Allah. He was a manifestation of the living compassion of Allah. Wherever he saw distress or pain he reached out his hand to help and, by the mercy of Allah, his hand was possessed of the power to heal. The spirit of life flowed through his veins and manifested on his breath, his hand, his gaze. By means of him, raw clay took flight.

One of the most important words in both of the phrases used to define 'Isa (as) is the indefinite article that precedes them. He is not *the* spirit of God and he is not *the* word of God. He is a word from among the innumerable, ineffable Words of God, and he is a spirit from the inexhaustible, incomparable, unfathomable Spirit of God. Spirit is the breath of life, and word is what that breath voices. 'Isa (as) is compared in The Qur'an to Adam (as), and Adam (as) was taught all the names, words, of which 'Isa (as) himself is one. It is said that each letter of The Qur'an is an angel, a living, breathing spirit. Words are then formed from these living letters, which become sounds expressed with breath. As Ibn 'Arabi puts it, 'Isa (as) is the condensation of the divine breath. With this mystery he could manifest life, heal the sick, raise the dead – but only with the permission of his Lord.

The healing of Peter's mother-in-law. Rembrandt Von Rijn, 17th century.

Allah says, **It is not conceivable that a human being unto whom God had given the Book and sound judgment, and prophethood, should then have said to people, "Worship me rather than God"; but instead (he told them], "Be godly (*rabbani*) by teaching the Book and studying it."** (3:79). 'Isa (as) and his mother were *rabbani*. They were profoundly pure, untainted, untouched by anything remotely worldly. They had no desire for fame, fortune, or power. They hardly even desired the comfort of a home and a hot meal. They were protected from satan and sin before they were even born. Their energy was concentrated on pleasing their Lord. Their hearts and minds were clean of selfish motives, and so their actions and responses were also clean. 'Isa (as) was approached by a group of Banu Isra'il who began to revile him. To each thing they said he answered with a good word. When his companions asked him why he was returning their evil with goodness, he answered, "Each person can only give of what he has." 'Isa (as) did not have a word of meanness or selfishness.

There is a Hadith *Qudsi*, a saying of the Prophet (sas) considered to be a divine utterance, which best describes what it means to be *rabbani*. Allah says: "My slave continues to draw near to Me ... so that I love him. When I love him I am his hearing with which he hears, his seeing with which he sees, his hand with which he strikes and his foot with which he walks. Were he to ask of Me, I would surely give him, and were he to seek refuge with Me, I would surely grant it. I do not hesitate about anything as much as I hesitate about [seizing] the soul of My faithful slave: he hates death and I hate hurting him." (Al-Bukhari).

However, in trying to talk about the holy spirit itself we cross into the same murky territory in which the Christians lost their way. According to a Hadith recorded in the Sahih of al-Bukhari, a group of Jews approached the Prophet (sas) one day and asked him to tell them about the spirit, *ruh*. He was silent for quite a while as the state of revelation fell over him. Then he answered them with a new verse of The Qur'an, **They ask you about the spirit, *ruh*. Say, the spirit belongs to the domain of my Lord. Of knowledge you have been given only a little.** (17:85). Therefore, the best course is to acknowledge that we have been given very little understanding of this subject and to leave it for those who have been given more.

And among all these many beautiful names and honored titles with which Allah Almighty dresses 'Isa (as) in The Qur'an, not once is he called 'son of God' or 'God' or part of a trinity of God. There is no hint, no whisper, no possibility of equality in their relationship. One is Lord and one is slave. In fact, The Qur'an directly addresses all people who believe in God and follow a scripture: **O People of the Book,** (referring to the Divine Book that rests eternally with Allah and from which all the earthly scriptures are taken) **do not exaggerate in your religion,** (you love your prophet with all your heart, as indeed you should, but do not exaggerate his station) **and do not say anything about God except the truth: the Messiah, 'Isa son of Maryam, was nothing more than a messenger of God,** (which is not a small thing) **His word directed to Maryam,** (a very special gift) **a spirit from Him** (of a very special nature). **So believe in God and His messengers** (all of His messengers) **and do not say 'three'** (trinity) - stop, that is better for you. God is only one God, He is far above having a son. Everything in the heavens and earth belongs to Him and Allah suffices as a guardian. (4:171).

At least fourteen more times, in relation to the prophethood of 'Isa (as), Allah stresses the uniqueness and singularity of His Own Being and strongly condemns the preposterous notion that He would beget a child or have a relationship to a created creature other than that of Beneficent and Loving Creator and Master. The Christian phrases 'son of God', 'mother of God' are shocking and inconceivable. **How terrible is this thing you assert whereby almost the heavens are torn, and the earth is split asunder, and the mountains fall in ruins, that they attribute offspring to the Lord of Mercy.** (19:89-91).

Other than as well-meaning but inappropriate metaphors to express the love, honor, and high rank with which 'Isa (as) and his mother are established in the Divine Presence and consequently among men, they are unthinkable. He is one of the highest ranking prophets whom Allah Almighty calls, *'Ulu l-Azim* (46:35), the patient ones of firm resolve: Nuh (as), Ibrahim (as), Musa (as), 'Isa (as) and Muhammad (sas). But positing kinship with the Creator is crossing a line that should never be crossed by a believer.

Even in the Gospels 'Isa (as) only refers to himself as "the Son of Man" although he seems to accept being called the Messiah. Since we only have the Gospels in Greek, we don't know the original or even if 'Isa (as) spoke in Hebrew or Aramaic. However, in Hebrew son of man is *Ben Adam* and the Aramaic is *Bar Adam*. Both of which are equivalent to *Banu Adam* meaning simply a human being, one of the descendants of the first prophet Adam (as). To be completely accurate there is another term, *Bar Enosh*, that he might possibly have used that refers back to the Book of Daniel where it is thought to indicate all men in general and the Messiah in particular.

The Qur'an relates a conversation between Allah Almighty and His slave 'Isa (as) in which 'Isa (as) is asked if he ever told people that he is the son of God. He replies in anguish, **"May You be exalted! I would never say what I had no right to say. If I had said such a thing You would have known it: You know all that is within me, though I do not know what is within You. You alone have full knowledge of things unseen."** (5:116).

As for the titles that the Christians have bestowed on their prophet, John Crossan, a Christian scholar, has written that there was someone in the first century CE whose titles were, "Son of God", "God", "God from God", "Lord", "Redeemer", "Liberator", "Savior", and "Savior of the World". And that man was Caesar Augustus. So the followers of 'Isa (as) were simply giving to their beloved prophet that which belonged to Caesar.

Statue of Caesar Augustus in victory pose, 1st century, Rome.

The full illustration of the prophecy of Sha'ya (as) showing Sha'ya (as) on the right, Muhammad (sas) on the camel and 'Isa (as) on the donkey. "And he has seen a chariot – a couple of horsemen, the rider of a donkey and the rider of a camel and he has given attention, he has increased attention." (Youngs Literal Bible, Isaiah 21:7). Al-Biruni, 16th century.

31.
His Name Will Be Ahmad (sas)

'Isa, son of Maryam, said, "Children of Israel, I am sent to you by Allah, confirming the Tawrah that came before me and bringing good news of a messenger to follow me whose name will be Ahmad." (61:6). This verse of The Qur'an tells us three things. 'Isa (as) was sent as a prophet to the Banu Isra'il. He was sent to confirm the Tawrah, not to abandon it. And as Yahya (as) was sent to prepare the way for 'Isa (as), **confirming a word from Allah.** (3:39), so 'Isa (as) was sent to prepare the way for Ahmad, Muhammad (sas).

'Isa (as) came to restore the proper understanding of the Tawrah not to replace it. He came to clear away the things that had been added to divine scripture either by the hands of men or those things that Allah had imposed as punishment on the Banu Isra'il after the time of Musa (as). These mainly involved the unreasonably strict laws for keeping the Sabbath, for keeping ritual purity, and the rigid dietary restrictions most of which, The Qur'an tells us, Ya'qub (Isra'il) (as) imposed on himself (3:93). These had become an unnecessary burden on the believers and deterred those who were not born into the Banu Isra'il from accepting the prophets and from joining in the worship of their Creator. 'Isa (as) came to lighten and restore the law as the Jews understood it at that time and to improve their interpretation of the law so that it was more open to gentile conversion and so that it was more compassionate to the poor, the ill, and the penitent sinner.

Allah says that 'Isa (as) brought the same law, the same teaching that all the prophets had brought before him. All scripture descends from the presence of Allah Almighty, from the Mother of Books (*Ummu l-Kitab*) that He keeps with Him. Instead the followers of 'Isa (as) ended up keeping only half of his message. They accepted the spirit but abandoned most of the law. They held on to the Spirit but forgot the Word while the Jews held on to the Word and neglected the Spirit. About the Jews Allah says, **they change the words from their (right) places and forget a good part of the message that was sent them** (5:13). About the Christians Allah says, **We also took a pledge from those who say, 'We are Christians (*nasara*),' but they too forgot some of what they were told to remember** (5:14). The Prophet Muhammad (sas) was sent five hundred years later to remind them and to fuse spirit and word back together again in one complete book, The Qur'an, and in one complete religion, Islam.

There are accounts of 'Isa (as) permitting his disciples to do things on the Sabbath like harvest grain or help people in need. This aroused the anger of the religious authorities who felt that they were in possession of the only right way. He also associated with people considered impure (such as lepers and launderers) and he extended forgiveness to sinners (such as adulterers and thieves) rather than judgment. These were actions that were considered ritually defiling in the understanding of the priests, actions which they avoided at all costs and that made 'Isa (as) and his followers in their view ritually unclean and unfit to be religious leaders.

It is said that 'Isa (as) reintroduced compassion to the divine law and a proper understanding and interpretation of the words. Otherwise Yahya (as) and 'Isa (as) and those who followed them considered the Tawrah as their Book. They did not abandon it. This was something that the gentile followers of 'Isa (as) did later after the third and final destruction of the Temple in Jerusalem in 70 CE and the banishment of all Jews from the city. The Jewish Christians at that point lost their base and were eventually swept away in the rising tide of Roman and Greek Christianity.

But 'Isa (as) did not just come to restore the law of Musa (as). He had another important mission. 'Isa (as) said that he brought the **"good news of a messenger to follow me whose name will be Ahmad."** (61:6). Ahmad is a word derived from the same root as Muhammad, *h-m-d*, meaning praise. There are hadith that the Prophet (sas) said "I have five names. I am Muhammad and Ahmad. I am *al-Mahi* (the destroyer) by means of whom Allah will destroy unbelief. And I am *al-Hashir* (the Gatherer) in whose footsteps people will be gathered. And I am *al-'Aqib* (the last of the prophets)." (Muslim).

This is the great good news with which 'Isa (as) was sent. Muslims have been wondering for fourteen hundred years where to find this good news written in the Book of 'Isa (as). Because if 'Isa (as) was a prophet adhering to the law of the Tawrah, he was still a prophet sent mainly to the Banu Isra'il. In fact, he was the seal of the prophets of the Tawrah which began with Musa (as) and ended with 'Isa (as). Who then did Allah Almighty send to guide humanity into the new united global world of today? The Prophet Muhammad (sas) told us that "Every Prophet was sent to his nation only. However, I have been sent to all mankind" (Al-Bukhari, Muslim), an impressive statement for a poor inhabitant of a desert oasis.

After fourteen hundred years of searching and researching there is still no answer that is completely satisfying and that puts the question to rest. There are three main schools of thought. The first is that the Christians at some point simply expunged the passage referring to Ahmad. The second is that they altered the reference in some way so it was disguised either intentionally or unintentionally as The Qur'an says that the Christians forgot part of what they were told to remember (5:14). The third is that, like most of God's signs, it was never written quite as clearly and obviously as we think we would like. It was always kept veiled by God Himself, visible to those with the eyes to see, the ears to hear, and the hearts to understand. For the wise, the signs of Allah's representatives have always been as clear as day.

The first explanation can only be proven if an old manuscript should be discovered in which the deleted verse is present. Some believe that the so-called Gospel of Barnabas is such a manuscript. It seems to have been sourced from an earlier original gospel whose view of the nature of 'Isa (as) is similar to the one Allah expresses in The Qur'an. Most scholars,

The grave of Barnabas (ra) in Cyprus.

however, think that it is Manichean in origin and has, in addition, been amended by a Muslim hand. It proclaims the name of Muhammad (sas) clearly as the prophet to come rather than Ahmad (sas). It respects 'Isa (as) as a messenger of God but denies his divinity. Some Muslims accept it and some are dubious. Most non-Muslim scholars, at worst, reject it as a forgery of some kind or, at best, as a contaminated text derived from something authentic that has been lost. Either way, it is not conclusive enough to alter anyone's opinion but serves only to convince the already convinced.

The second supposition began with the earliest biographer of the Prophet (sas), Ibn Ishaq. He believed that the corrupted verse is in the Gospel of John (14:15-16). 'Isa (as) prophesies the coming of a *paracletos* translated in English as comforter, counselor, advocate, friend. It is said that this word was originally *pariclytos* meaning the most praised one, a direct translation of *ahmad*. Whether by intention or by scribal error, one word was substituted for the other.

Certainly 'Isa (as) himself knew of the coming of Muhammad (sas). The Qur'an tells us that all the prophets made a covenant with their Lord in the world of souls before the creation of Earth. **Allah took a pledge from the prophets, saying, "If, after I have bestowed Scripture and wisdom upon you, a messenger comes confirming what you have been given, you must believe in him and support him. Do you affirm this and accept My pledge as binding on you?" They said, "We do." He said, "Then bear witness and I too will bear witness."** (3:81). This is understood by Imam as-Suyuti as confirming that all the prophets pledged themselves to accept and support the last prophet, Muhammad (sas).

Allah says, **My mercy encompasses all things. I shall ordain My mercy for those who are God-fearing and pay the prescribed alms; who believe in Our Revelations; those who follow the Messenger, the** unlettered prophet they find described in the Tawrah that is with them and in the Injil; who commands them to do right and forbids them to do wrong; who makes good things lawful to them and bad things unlawful, and relieves them of their burdens and the shackles that were on them. So it is those who believe him, honor and help him, and who follow the light which has been sent down with him, who will succeed. (7:156-157).

The praised one, Ahmad Muhammad (sas), is the one whose attributes are described in these verses. He is known by his character and his deeds, praised by all who knew him even his enemies. It says he is described, literally written about, in the earlier scriptures. He can be recognized by his signs not just by his personal name. He is the one Allah described to Musa (as), "I will raise up for them a prophet from among their brethren, like unto you (Musa) and will put My words in his mouth, and he shall speak unto them all that I shall command him." (Deuteronomy 18:18). He is the answer to the prayer of Ibrahim (as), **"Our Lord, and send among them a messenger from themselves who will recite to them Your verses and teach them the Book and wisdom and purify them. Indeed, You are the Exalted in Might, the Wise."** (2:129). He is the one foretold by many other Old Testament prophets and the one for whom 'Isa (as) was sent to prepare. His attributes and his actions are deserving of praise, clearly exhibiting the signs God prescribes for a prophet. Those who can see this acknowledge him, follow him, and obey him.

We have assigned a law and a path to each of you. If Allah had so willed, He would have made you one community, but He wanted to test you by means of that which He has given you, so race to do good: your return is to Allah and He will make clear to you the matters about which you differed. (5:48). By the mercy of Allah, He has veiled His signs so that we will not be punished for disbelieving them, and so we will tolerate each other's different understandings and use them to spur ourselves to goodness.

At thirty years of age, 'Isa (as) began the last stage of his mission and the public delivery of the message with which he had been charged.

The two graves of Al-'Azar. Top in Al-'Azariyya, Israel. Bottom in Larnaka, Cyprus.

32.
The Man with Two Tombs

It is said that Allah endowed each prophet with mastery over whatever was of most concern or interest to the people at the time. Ibrahim (as) was given phenomenal wealth. His herds filled the hills and valleys. Wherever he settled water flowed. This is what was of predominant concern to his people, and they recognized the abundance granted to him as a clear sign of divine favor. Musa (as) was sent with a magic staff because the Egyptians of his day were adept in magic, and superior magic was an evident sign to them of the divine hand. The Prophet Muhammad (sas) was sent with eloquence and the inimitable Qur'an because the focus of the Arabs at that time was poetry and eloquence. The root of the word Arab itself, '-r-b, actually means to be fluent, eloquent. So it was that 'Isa (as) was sent with the ability to heal because disease and early death were all too common in his day. Archaeologists have noted that two thirds to three quarters of the occupants of the graveyards from this time period are children under the age of fifteen. Medical knowledge was an important pursuit of the classical scholars of the time.

The most amazing sign with which 'Isa (as) was endowed was the ability to heal the sick including the leper, restore sight to the congenitally blind, and bring the dead back to life: **by My leave, you healed the blind and the leper; how, by My leave, you brought the dead back to life**. (5:110). As much as the Injil relates the details of these miraculous events, The Qur'an does not, even though healing the sick by touch or prayer was the main activity of 'Isa (as). That these miracles occurred is mentioned twice in The Qur'an without details probably, it is thought, because it was an accepted fact at the time without need of elaboration. His life was spent among the poor and outcast, healing and giving them health, teaching them about Allah and giving them hope.

Ahmad ibn Hanbal relates that Allah said, "O 'Isa, I have given you love for the poor and compassion for them. You love them and they in return love you. They accept you as their leader and you accept them as your companions. If a person possesses these qualities on Judgment Day, he will come to Me with the things I love best." It is said that people would come out in the thousands to meet 'Isa (as) and receive his blessing. This of course is just what disturbed those in power. The government worried that he might encourage armed insurrection, and the priests worried that he might undermine their authority.

There are many short accounts in the Islamic literature of 'Isa (as) healing the sick and raising the dead. In most of these cases he brought people to life in order to question them about how they died or how they found the grave, in order to bring wisdom to those still living. For example, one day he was passing a cemetery with his disciples. He called on the occupant of one of the graves to arise and appear before them. A man immediately climbed out of the grave, shaking the dirt from his tattered shroud. 'Isa (as) asked him what he had experienced while dead. The man answered that when he was alive, he was a wood carrier. One day he was hired to carry a load of wood, and he broke off a sliver to use as a toothpick. He had been suffering from remorse every day since he died for that small act of taking what did not belong to him.

Another day, they came upon a man crying by the grave of his newly deceased wife. 'Isa (as) in sympathy brought her back to life for him. While the husband was rejoicing, a prince appeared riding a fine horse. His eyes met the eyes of the wife, and she left her husband and climbed onto the horse behind the prince. She had died in goodness and was resurrected only to become a sinner. In another account, 'Isa (as) brought a father back to life for his grieving children only to tell them that it would have been better to have accepted what Allah willed because there was no more provision written for the father in this world. Yet another time 'Isa (as) felt compassion for a man suffering pain, and he prayed for Allah to relieve him of it. Allah replied to him, "How shall I relieve him of what I am relieving him with?" (Al-Qushayri).

There is another story popular in the Muslim literature. One day the religious authorities tried to belittle the miracles of 'Isa (as) by saying he was only able to bring the recently deceased back to life. So 'Isa (as) agreed to resurrect whomever they chose, by permission of Allah. They chose Sam (Shem) (as) the son of Nuh (as). They all proceeded to the grave of Sam (as) who had been dead for four thousand years. 'Isa (as) called him to rise out of the grave and speak to them. To their horror and amazement, climbing out of the earth came a towering figure. The early prophets had a heavenly stature, said to be twenty or thirty feet tall. Each generation after Adam (as) got smaller. As he brushed the dirt off his head and beard, he said, "O Spirit of God," because the prophets all know each other, "why do you call me? Is it the Day of Judgment?"

'Isa (as) was surprised that Sam's (as) hair was white because that sign of aging only occurred for the first time with the prophet Ibrahim (as). Sam (as) was also surprised. When he died his hair was still black. He had heard 'Isa's (as) call and, thinking it was for Judgment, his fear had turned all his hair white. 'Isa (as) asked him what he thought of the world. Sam (as), who had lived for over six hundred years, answered "The world is like a house with two doors. I entered through one and I left through the other." When asked if he would like to remain alive, he said that one death was more than enough for him. He would rather return to his spacious and peaceful grave to await Judgment and immortal life. And so he disappeared back into the earth leaving no trace behind. Most of those who witnessed this miracle called it magic and still refused to believe.

Another famous incident is that of Al-'Azar (ra) (Saint Lazarus) who with his two sisters, Mary (rah) and Martha (rah), was said to be dear friends of 'Isa (as). They lived in a town called Bethany outside of Jerusalem, now a Palestinian town named after him, Al-'Azariyya. One day 'Isa (as) received a message from the sisters begging him to come quickly because Al-'Azar (ra) was very sick. 'Isa (as) set out, but the journey took him over three days. When he arrived he found the girls in tears. Al-'Azar (ra) had been placed in his tomb four days earlier and his body had already started to decay. 'Isa (as) asked to be taken to the gravesite, a cave whose mouth was sealed with a large stone as was the custom in those days. After many objections by the mourning family, they finally rolled back the stone. 'Isa (as) stood at the opening and prayed. Then he called down into the cave for Al-'Azar (ra) to arise and come. The startled family watched as a shadowy figure made its way through the dark opening of the cave into the light. It was Al-'Azar (ra) answering the call of his prophet as best he could. He hobbled out of his grave with his burial shroud still wrapped tightly around him. 'Isa (as) ordered the family to unwrap, bathe, and dress him in clean clothes.

Al-'Azar (ra) was fully restored to life just as he had been before his illness, and he never left the side of 'Isa (as) after that. However, he could not forget what he had witnessed in the grave, seeing all the agonized souls waiting for hellfire, regretting the manner in which they had wasted their lives. He would dedicate his second chance at life to saving himself and as many others as possible. It is said that he went on to live many years, even to marry and have children, but in that time, because of the memory of those four days in the grave, he was only seen to smile once. The site of the first tomb of Al-'Azar (ra) is now part of the Al-'Azar Mosque in the small town of Al-'Azariyya east of Jerusalem.

It is said that after 'Isa (as) was raised to Allah, Al-'Azar (ra) and his sisters found their lives in danger because of the animosity of the Jews and Romans to those who followed his way. They fled by boat across the sea. The girls ended up in Europe, but Al-'Azar (ra) landed on the island of Cyprus. There he began to preach to people about Allah and His prophet 'Isa (as). Also in Cyprus were Saint Barnabas (ra) and his nephew Saint Mark (ra), originally Cypriot Jews who had met 'Isa (as) in Jerusalem and later kept company with Saint Paul for many years preaching near Antioch. Barnabas (ra) had split with Paul and returned to Cyprus to preach where he was eventually martyred by Jews at the Greek port of Salamis. Saint Paul and Saint Barnabas (ra) together are said to have appointed Al-'Azar (ra) to be the first bishop of Larnaka (known then as Kition).

For thirty years Al-'Azar (ra) guided the people of Kition, and in all that time he was only known to smile once. When he saw a thief stealing a clay jar from a market stall, he remarked, "Clay stealing clay", and he smiled.

At one point, lonely for the company of 'Isa (as) and his companions, Al-'Azar (ra) wrote to Sayyida Maryam (ahs) inviting her to visit him in Cyprus. She was pleased and desired also to visit the friend of her son. She set out to sea but got swept off course. It is unclear if she eventually made it to Larnaka or not. It is said, however, that she either sent, or personally gave, Al-'Azar (ra) a bishop's vestment called an *omophorion* which she had sewn and embroidered especially for him with her own hands.

After thirty years, Al-'Azar (ra) died for a second time and was buried for the final time, in Larnaka. In 890 CE this second tomb of Al-'Azar (ra) was rediscovered. The Byzantine Emperor bartered to have Al-'Azar's (ra) remains shipped to Istanbul (Constantinople) in exchange for building the Saint Lazarus church at the site of the empty tomb in Cyprus. After the destruction of Constantinople by their fellow Christians in the fourth Crusade in 1204, the remains were dispersed throughout Europe. The major portion of them ended up in Marseille, France. The church in Cyprus was briefly converted into a mosque after the Ottoman conquest in 1571 but given back eighteen years later out of respect for the Christian cemetery next to it. In 1972, while repairing it, human remains were found under the altar. It is surmised that the Cypriot church did not, in fact, send all the sacred bones to Constantinople but had secretly kept some of them. The tomb and church remain in the possession of the Cypriot Orthodox Church and a place of pilgrimage for all believers.

The site of his first tomb near Jerusalem is also considered a holy place of pilgrimage by both Muslims and Christians. The Ottomans built a mosque on the site which was intended to be open to all, but the Christians of Europe refused to worship there, saying they preferred to keep the two religions separate. It is the sad custom of the Holy Land for each religion and religious sect to build its own place of worship, one shouldered against the other, around a spot equally holy to them all.

'Isa (as) receives a table spread with food to feed his companions. Persian 1580 CE.

33.
The Table Spread

The miracle for which 'Isa (as) is best known among Muslims is the only one recounted in some detail in The Qur'an. It appears in the fifth chapter named *al-Ma'ida*, commonly translated as The Table because there is no current English word that quite conveys the right meaning. The point is not a physical table with four legs, but rather the feast laid out on it. It is the custom in Muslim lands to present a meal heaped or spread on a large circular platter or tray, around which family and guests gather to eat. The idea of a meal presented as a whole, laid out on top of a table or tray is the image intended, a spread of food.

On the orders of 'Isa (as) the *Hawariyyun* fasted for thirty days in the manner of Ramadan. When it became time to break their fast, they asked their prophet to show them a miracle, **"can your Lord send down a table of food for us from heaven?"** (5:112). 'Isa (as) was concerned about the state of their faith not the state of their stomachs. It was unclear if they were asking because they doubted that the Almighty God, the Creator of everything, was able to send them something to eat or if they were asking because they doubted the ability of 'Isa (as) himself to successfully petition his Lord or if they were of such a low spiritual station that they

Feeding the multitudes. James Tissot 1886 CE.

just wanted food. They certainly did not know the right way to ask. 'Isa (as) answered them sternly, **"Fear God if you are true believers."** (5:112).

Quickly they explained, **"We wish to eat from it; to put our hearts at rest; to know that you have told us the truth; and to be witnesses of it."** (5:113). Some say this shows the weakness of their faith, that they needed physical proof. The Qur'an tells us that Ibrahim (as) asked Allah in much the same way to show him how the dead can be resurrected. Allah asked him in turn, **"Do you not believe then?"** (2:260). Ibrahim (as) answered as the disciples answered, **"Yes," said Abraham, "but just to put my heart at rest."** (2:260). Believing without seeing is one thing. Believing as well as seeing is another. The *Hawariyyun*, like Ibrahim (as), were asking for certainty on all levels. Ibrahim (as) asked clearly for knowledge and understanding, the food of the heart. The disciples of 'Isa (as), however, were asking for a meal. 'Isa (as) accepted their request and turning inwardly to his Lord he rephrased it. He said, **"Lord, send down to us a table of food from heaven so that we can have a festival (*'Id*) - the first and last of us - and a sign from You. Provide for us: You are the best of providers."** (5:114).

Allah replied, **"I will send it down to you, but anyone who disbelieves after this will be punished with a punishment that I will not inflict on anyone else in the world."** (5:115). With this very severe warning, Allah promised to send what they asked; to send them a break fast (*iftar*) after their month of fasting, to send them a table laden with actual food (*ma'ida*) to steady their hearts. They watched in amazement as a table appeared above them in the sky.

Salman al-Farsi (ra) said that the table was of gold, covered with a red cloth. It descended between two wisps of cloud, one above it and one under, hiding the angels who were bearing it. 'Isa (as) prayed for a long time, his eyes flowing with tears, before he finally unveiled the table. When he did, they saw a broiled fish with its scales removed, dripping with fat. There was salt at its head and vinegar at its tail and it was set in a bed of greens. There were five loaves of bread, one with olives, one with honey, one with ghee, one with cheese, and one with meat.

Ka'b al-Ahbar (ra) said that the table was carried by angels, upside down with the food, for all to see, facing the earth. It righted itself as it landed. On it were six fish and six loaves of bread. 'Isa (as) broke everything into small pieces with his hands and distributed it among the waiting people. Because of his touch, it increased to such an extent that soon they found themselves standing up to their knees in food. There are also many accounts of the Prophet Muhammad (sas) satisfying the needs of a multitude of people on a handful of dates or a few pieces of meat or a single skin of water.

There is a difference of opinion about what happened after the table was uncovered. One Tafsir says that as Allah Almighty sent down the table He also sent the message, "I have bestowed My bounty on those who wish to eat, but I have friends who go hungry and endure patiently. They seek nothing from Me other than Myself, find their hearts' rest in nothing but remembrance of Me, forget themselves in My compassion and do not even look at anything else because of their love for Me." (Kwaja Ansari). 'Isa (as) was ashamed before his Lord and would not eat of the feast.

Some say that the disciples asked him if this was the food of Paradise. 'Isa (as) told them that it was not but was instead a special food created by Allah just for this occasion. So the disciples would not eat of it either. They decided to give the food to the poor and the sick and anyone who wanted. Thousands of people gathered to feast on the miraculous food after being warned of the consequences and accepting. The poor were satisfied and enriched. The sick became well. The rich became richer. Then it is said the disciples regretted not having eaten.

But others say that everyone ate from the table as much as they could hold after which the table was raised up to heaven. The next day it returned, and again everyone ate to their satisfaction. This happened every day for three days or for forty days, and then it was raised to heaven and did not return.

They swear by God with their most solemn oaths that if a miraculous sign were to come to them they would believe in it. Say, "Signs are in the power of God alone." What will make you realize that even if a sign came to them they still would not believe? (6:109). The people had been warned. If Allah sends a miracle, and still they do not believe, then the punishment is great. Many of the people who had eaten the heavenly food were only seeking to fill their stomachs or to find amusement. Some say that 'Isa (as) told them to eat as much as they could but not to take any of it home for the next day. This was the case also with the *manna* and *salwa* (20:80) that Allah provided the Banu Isra'il in the desert of Sinai at the time of Musa (as). They were given only enough for each day. If they tried to store some for the next day it turned to dust and Allah told them **Eat from the good things We have provided for you but do not overstep the bounds or My wrath will descend on you. Anyone on whom My wrath descends has truly fallen.** (21:81). This is also considered another explanation of the verse where 'Isa (as) says, **"And I tell you what you eat and what you store up in your houses."** (3:49). They were warned that if they disobeyed, they would be punished.

The people did not believe in the warning, and they did not believe in Allah and His prophet. They hoarded the food and took it home. They called it a magic trick and did not believe. After eating the last heavenly meal, they went to their beds to sleep as usual. When the morning sun rose, three hundred and thirty of them woke to find they had been transformed into pigs. They tried to explain to their families but nothing came out of their snub pig snouts but squealing and snorting. Their children in horror and disgust chased them out of their houses with sticks and brooms. Nobody noticed the tears of regret welling up in their small pig eyes. After three days of this agony, Allah relieved them with death.

Greece 5th century BCE, one of Odysseus' men turning into a pig.

As for the *Hawariyyun*, they said to their master 'Isa (as), "Who is better off then we? You feed us when we are hungry and give us water when we are thirsty?" And he answered them by saying, "The one who works for his own bread and water is better off than you." And so, after that, they began to make clothes to sell and support themselves.

The story does not appear exactly like this in the Gospels. Some Muslims believe it refers to the verse in what the Christians call the Lord's Prayer: "Give us this day our daily bread." Some say it retells the Gospel story of the feeding of the five thousand on five loaves of bread and two fish that is reported in all four Gospels, or of the feeding of the four thousand on two fish and seven loaves of bread related in only two Gospels (Matthew and Mark). Some others think that it is a reference to the Last Supper, when 'Isa (as) ate a Passover meal with his disciples the night before he was taken from them. The salt, greens and herbs, oil, and bread (if it was unleavened) resembles the Passover *seder*. Others believe that, by the saying for **the first and last of us** (5:114) and, because it is called an *'Id*, this was not an event that happened once and finished. The word *'Id* implies both a festival that causes joy and one that returns periodically. It might also indicate the Eucharist, the symbolic consumption of the flesh and blood of 'Isa (as), the Christian ritual of communion that was developed out of the occasion of the Last Supper. Perhaps it is a synthesis of all these Gospel events, painting a picture in one stroke of the spiritual and physical nourishment and healing that so clearly characterizes the message of 'Isa (as).

Once while the Prophet Muhammad (sas) slept he said he heard a conversation between Jibra'il (as) and Mika'il (as). One stood at his head and one at his feet. Knowing that his heart was awake and he could hear, they said, "The reality of your situation is like that of a king who had some land on which he built a palace. He had a banquet prepared, and he sent out his messenger to invite all the people to feast. Some people accepted the invitation, and some did not. Allah is the King. Islam [submission to God] is the land. The house is Paradise, and Muhammad (sas) is the messenger [before him, Isa (as) was the messenger]. Whoever accepts the messenger, accepts Islam. Whoever enters Islam, enters Paradise. Whoever enters Paradise, is filled with what is there." (Tirmidhi).

'Isa (as) admiring the white teeth of a dead dog. Illustration for Nizami's Khamsa, Persia, 1488 CE.

34.
'Isa's (as) Invitation

'Isa (as), however, was not happy with people who asked for marvelous signs but did not listen to the words he was teaching. In the Gospel of Luke (6:46) he sadly rebukes them saying, "And why call me Lord, Lord, and do not the things I say?"

It is thought by Christian scholars that the original Gospel of 'Isa (as), called Q, was composed just of his teachings and sayings. This ancient text, whether written or oral, is lost. All that survives are the Gospels that are believed to be derived from it. They mostly relate his spiritual story as it developed after his passing rather than his actual words. What the Muslims relate, on the other hand, is made up only of 'Isa's (as) words and teaching in the form of short pithy sayings and aphorisms, with a few short stories. Many of these are similar to those found in the Gospels, and many others bear a striking similarity to the sayings of the Prophet Muhammad (sas) found in the collections of Hadith. Neither of which should be surprising. These teachings were not gathered from one source. Rather they are scattered over a broad field of Islamic texts, mostly used to illustrate the path of asceticism and renunciation of the world (*zuhd*).

It is thought that they might actually be another trace of Q, recording the teachings familiar to the Christian and Muslim communities of the seventh and eighth centuries in and around Arabia.

What follows is a small selection of sayings taken mostly from a volume in which professor Tarif Khalidi assiduously collected all the teachings attributed to 'Isa (as) by the early classic Islamic scholars. He calls it the Gospel (good news) of 'Isa (as), but perhaps it could be better described as the *Adab* of 'Isa (as).

Calligraphy, *Adab ya Hu*, Ottoman.

Adab is an Arabic word that has no adequate English equivalent. Usually translated as good behavior, manners, or morals, its root meaning is to invite, as to a feast. It is not the feast itself, however, that is important but rather the act of inviting, making it possible for everyone to accept because you asked properly and served what they can digest – a very appropriate metaphor for 'Isa (as). Rather than etiquette or manners, *adab* indicates a proper relationship to everything; knowing its worth, respecting its goodness while also being appropriately aware of its dangers or weaknesses. Every enterprise, every course of action has its *adab*, a right way to do it, with respect for the rights of God being first and foremost. There is even an *adab* for war. The Prophet (sas) of course had the best *adab*, and he said, "The best among you are those with the best *adab*." To have *adab* is more important than to have knowledge because without *adab* knowledge can be misused. To act with *adab* is, first and foremost, to accept with proper gratitude and humility Allah's invitation to partake of His bounty and approach closer to Him by giving everything in creation its proper due and doing it with grace. Then it is to teach others to do the same.

Adab towards Allah

They asked 'Isa (as) to tell them the best of all actions. He said, "Being content with Allah and loving Him." (Al-Ghazali 1111 CE).

'Isa (as) said: "Not as I will but as You will. Not as I desire but as You desire." (Ibn Hanbal 855 CE).

'Isa said to his companions "Leave yourselves to hunger and thirst, go naked, and exhaust yourselves that your hearts might come to know Allah Almighty." (Al-Ghazali 1111 CE).

'Isa (as) said, "If you are really my brothers and friends, accustom yourselves to the enmity of men. For you shall not obtain what you seek except by abandoning what you desire. You shall not possess what you love except by tolerating what you hate." (Ibn Abi l-Dunya 894 CE).

The Disciples asked 'Isa (as) to tell them of an action by which they would gain Paradise. He said, "Do not speak." They said "This is too hard for us." He answered, "Then speak only good." (Al-Ghazali 1111 CE).

The Prophet Muhammad (sas) related that 'Isa (as) said, "Do not speak much without the mention of Allah for you will harden your hearts. A hard heart is far from Allah." (Imam Malik 795 CE).

'Isa (as) said, "Talk much to God, talk little to people." They asked, "How do we talk to God?" 'Isa (as) answered, "Converse with Him in solitude and pray to Him in solitude." (Al-Isbahani 1038 CE).

'Isa (as) said, "Piety is nine-tenths silence and one-tenth avoidance of society." (Al-Ghazali 1111 CE).

'Isa (as) said, "He who speaks without mentioning God is merely babbling. He who reflects without self criticism is merely heedless. He who is silent without reflection is merely wasting time." (Ibn Qutayba 884 CE).

'Isa (as) said, "Allah hates the man who laughs much without cause, who walks much without purpose, and who mentions Allah's Books in the middle of pleasantries and jesting." (Al-Suhrawardi 1234 CE).

When he was asked which of his deeds was the best, 'Isa (as) answered, "Leaving what does not concern me." (Al-Jahiz 868 CE).

'Isa (as) said, "Be in the middle but walk to the side." (Ibn Qutayba 884 CE). **I have made you a nation of the middle way.** (Al-Qur'an 2:143)

Adab towards the World

'Isa (as) said, "I looked at creation and found that he who has not been created is happier, in my view, than he who has." (Ibn Abi l-Dunya 894 CE).

'Isa (as) said, "The heart of a believer cannot hold both love of this world and love of the next, just as a container cannot hold both fire and water." (Ibn Abi l-Dunya 894 CE).

'Isa (as) said, "I have two loves in this world, poverty and jihad (struggle on the path to Allah). He who loves them loves me. He who hates them hates me." (Al-Ghazali 1111 CE).

'Isa (as) said, "He who seeks the world is like the man who drinks sea water: the more he drinks the thirstier he becomes until it kills him." (Ibn Abi l-Dunya 894 CE).

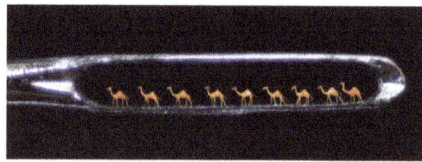

Camels in the eye of a needle. Miniature art work by Willard Wigan.

'Isa (as) said, "Love of the world is the root of all sin. Worldly wealth is a great sickness. The folds of heaven are devoid of the rich. It is easier for a camel to pass through the eye of a needle than for a rich man to enter heaven." (Ibn Hanbal 855 CE).

'Isa (as) said, "Just as kings have left wisdom to you, you should leave the world to them." (Ibn Hanbal 855 CE).

'Isa (as) said, "Blessed is the man who sees with his heart but whose heart is not in what he sees." (Ibn Qutayba 884 CE).

'Isa (as) said: "There are four things which are not found in one man without causing wonder: silence which is the beginning of worship, humility before God, renunciation of the world, and poverty." (Ibn Abi l-Dunya 894 CE).

'Isa (as) said, "You work for this world where you are provided for without working. Whereas you do not work for the next world where you will not be provided for without working." (Ibn Abi l-Dunya 894 CE).

One day his disciples found 'Isa (as) walking across the surface of the water. They asked if they should try to follow him but when they tried, they sank down into the sea. He said to them, "O men of little faith. If the son of Adam (as) had even one grain of faith, he would walk over the water." His disciples protested that they did have faith so he asked them, "When you see rocks and mud and gold, do they all look the same to you?" "No" they answered honestly. "They look all the same to me" he replied. (Ibn Hanbal 855 CE).

Adab towards Creatures

'Isa (as) said, "Be in gentleness to the people like the earth beneath their feet, in generosity like the flowing water, and in mercy like the sun and the moon for they rise upon the good and the bad equally." (Ibn Abi Firas 1208 CE).

'Isa (as) counseled, "Son of Adam, as you have mercy so shall Allah have mercy on you. How do you hope for Allah's mercy if you do not have mercy on His servants?" (Al-Samarqandi 983 CE).

'Isa (as) said, "You must truly love God in your heart and work in His service. Be as merciful to the people of your tribe as you are to yourself." "What is our tribe?" the disciples asked. "The children of Adam" he replied "and what you do not wish to be done to you, do not do to others." (Ibn Hanbal 855 CE).

'Isa (as) said: "If you are fasting put oil on your lips so no one will know. If you give charity with the right hand, hide it from the left. If you pray, close the door so no one sees." (Al-Ghazali 1111 CE).

'Isa (as) and his companions passed by the rotting body of a dead dog. The companions complained of the terrible stench and 'Isa (as) remarked only on the gleaming whiteness of the dog's teeth. (Al-Ghazali 1111 CE).

'Isa (as) said, "No one knows what true faith is until they despise being praised for what they do in obedience to Allah." (Ibn 'Asakir 1175 CE).

'Isa (as) said, "No one comes to true belief until he no longer cares to be praised for his worship of Allah Almighty and no longer cares to partake of the things of this world." (Al-Ghazali 1111 CE).

'Isa (as) was seen leaving the house of a prostitute. When questioned about why he was there, he answered, "A doctor visits the ones who are sick." (Ibn Qutayba 884 CE).

'Isa (as) used to prepare food for his disciples and then call them

'Isa (as) washing the feet of his disciples, Rembrandt von Rijn 1655 CE.

to eat and serve them. He said, "This is what you must do for the poor." (Ibn Hanbal 855 CE).

They asked 'Isa (as) who is the most treacherous of men? He said "The scholar who is wrong. If a scholar errs, all of the people who follow him will fall into error because of him." (Ibn Al-Mubarak 797 CE).

'Isa (as) said, "I treated the blind and the leper and I cured them both. I treated the fool and he made me despair." (Al-Ghazali 1111 CE).

'Isa (as) related that one day he passed by a garden and saw a young man watering. The man asked 'Isa (as) to ask Allah to give him an atom's weight of love for Him. 'Isa (as) warned him that he could not carry it, so the man asked for half that amount. 'Isa (as) prayed to Allah to give the farmer half an atom's weight of love for Him, and then he went on his way. A long time later 'Isa (as) passed by that garden again and looked for the gardener but didn't find him. He asked Allah to show him where the young man had gone. He found him high in the mountains, standing on a rock staring up at the sky. He gave him salams but the man did not answer or even turn his head. Then Allah revealed to 'Isa (as) "How can one who has even half an atom's weight of love for Me listen to the words of a human being? By My Glory and My Might, if you were to saw him in half he would not even notice." (Al-Ghazali 1111 CE). Now we can understand the true state of Zakariyya (as).

A dervish humble before a cat. Persia, 1550.

12th century Syrian image of 'Isa (as) with his disciples at the Last Supper.

35.
The Last Supper

It was the time of Passover, the celebration in remembrance of the deliverance of the Banu 'Isra'il from the tyranny of Pharaoh; a holy occasion established by Allah to reflect on both His mercy and His wrath. He had opened a path through the sea for Musa (as) and Harun (as) to lead the believers out of oppression. He had sustained them in the wilderness until they were ready to enter the promised land. He had destroyed their enemies and punished the unbelievers. It was the custom on this sacred occasion for all who were able of the Banu Isra'il to gather at the Temple in Jerusalem to offer sacrifice and pray. It was a time of thankfulness and joy, but also a time of penitence and humbleness before God. And at the time of 'Isa (as) it served as a stark reminder that although the Banu Isra'il still occupied the promised land, they were once more in bondage to foreign tyrants and in need of deliverance. And so even though it was essentially a religious occasion, it had deep political ramifications and the authorities had reason to be on guard.

'Isa (as) and his followers set out on foot from Galilee weeks in advance, making their way slowly to Jerusalem. They stopped in all the villages and hamlets, healing the sick, exorcising devils, bringing blessing and remembrance to all the forgotten corners of Judaea. One of their last stops was in Bethany at the house of Al-'Azar (ra). After bringing him back to life, they proceeded into the city. Word of the miracles of the man from Nazareth had spread ahead of them. Now when 'Isa (as) traveled, hundreds of people came out to greet him. They brought their crippled children, their sick and wounded. They brought their insane and troubled to see this man whom they had heard could heal every ailment even death; one who just might be the awaited messiah who would heal all of 'Isra'il. Raising his hands and beseeching the Lord, 'Isa (as) performed miracles and opened hearts all along the road leading to the holy center of Jerusalem. It was not a quiet and humble entry.

Of course this emotional procession did not go unnoticed by the soldiers of King Herod and the Roman governor of Judaea, Pontius Pilate. The commanders of the army were alarmed. They knew the state of unrest in the countryside. Herod and his son Herod Antipas were prolific builders. Their aim was to impress Rome with their palaces and temples, their government buildings and fortress walls. Herod had built at least two new capitol cities from the ground up. Formidable stone walls had almost doubled the size of the Temple mount, and the Temple itself was aggrandized and adorned with precious metals and gems. This had been accomplished only by laying the burden of cost on the poor man, the farmer, and the small shop owner. There was deep resentment. 'Isa (as) himself was unimpressed by the splendor of the mosque on the Temple Mount. He said, "Truly I say to you, Allah will not leave one stone of this mosque standing upon the other but will destroy it utterly because of the sins of its people. Allah has no interest in gold, silver, or stones. More dear to Him than all these stones are the pure of heart. Because of them He builds up the earth or destroys it." (Ibn Hanbal). Within fifty years of saying this, the Temple was gone, leveled almost to the ground. It was only rebuilt in the form it stands today by the Muslims around 685 CE. The Jews at the time even called the Khalifa Abdul Malik ibn Marwan a messiah, the title they had denied to 'Isa (as). Abdul Malik had rebuilt the Temple and allowed the Jews to return to Jerusalem after they had been exiled by the Christians. At that time the Muslims were seen as liberators, and the Christians as oppressors.

The political situation had gotten more unstable since the brutal execution of Yahya (as), and now Herod seemed to see his nightmare recur. One very similar to Yahya (as) was marching in triumph through the gates of the city, one who just might have the power to foment rebellion. They watched carefully as the crowds accumulated around this holy man, and the excitement increased in a city already packed with pilgrims for the holy days. The priests in the Temple watched too. Who was this man claiming the right to speak for God, to change their laws, to challenge their authority?

Ibn Abbas (ra) says that someone came out of the crowd and confronted 'Isa (as) with ugly words, slandering his mother, Maryam (ahs). 'Isa (as) was not affected by the words against himself but those defaming his pure mother he would not tolerate. He prayed to Allah to punish the one who dared to utter such things. Allah also has said that He has no patience with those who **disbelieved and uttered a terrible slander against Maryam** (4:156). In full sight of the people, the man was transformed into a pig. This worried Herod and the priests equally. They began to fear this sorcerer who could turn people into the animals they most resembled. And 'Isa (as) did not try to hide himself or conceal his contempt for their authority. He went directly to the Temple and threw out the money changers and merchants who had converted sacred space to a market and were cheating the people. He condemned the hypocrisy of the priests who were living off the donations of the poor. The authorities felt they had to act quickly to protect themselves. It never occurred to them to listen to him because perhaps he spoke the truth. It never occurred to them that if he was, indeed, a messenger from Allah, opposing him could only seal their fate.

'Isa (as) and the *Hawariyyun* entered the city and found a safe place to stay on the second floor of a building near the Temple Mount. It was the day of the feast, and they asked him how they would observe it. It is said that he brought a lamb to the Temple to be sacrificed, and he had the ritual meal prepared for them. Before they sat to eat he poured water for them to wash their hands and feet in the way that was required by Jewish law. They felt shy that their teacher and master was serving them in this way. He told them that he was doing it so they would learn humility and to be an example for them on how to treat the people they would teach after he was gone. He said "Unless one does what I have done, he is not mine and I am not his." (Al-Thalabi).

They ate their meal together, not realizing that it would be their last in his loving company. Then 'Isa (as) asked them to do something for him. He knew that his time with them was short. The thought of death lay heavy on him. He seemed to have always been aware and preoccupied with death. He had resurrected so many from the grave and heard of their agony and remorse, of the regrets that kept them from rest, of the constriction of the grave. Even as a prophet of Allah he did not know in what things he had fallen short, in what ways he had been heedless or distracted or mistaken. It is said that because 'Isa (as) derived his human character from his mother, he was exceptionally tenderhearted and compassionate. He healed and gave life. He never caused harm or killed anything, even an insect. Violence was abhorrent to him, and the anger and cruelty of what was to come was difficult for him to carry. It is said that fear of what the next day would bring made him sweat drops of blood. But he did not run away or try to avoid what his Lord had ordained, instead he turned to Him in prayer.

'Isa (as) asked his companions to keep vigil by his side and to pray that he meet his destiny with strength, although some say to pray it might be averted. He said, "Pray God to make this agony" – meaning death – "easy for me. For I fear death so much that it has become my companion." (Al-Ghazali). They all consented with good intention, but try as they might they could not stay awake. Allah, it is said, made sleep fall heavily on them. When 'Isa (as) looked around he saw not one of his companions awake. He spent that night in solitary devotion. In the morning they felt ashamed and without an excuse. 'Isa (as), in sadness told them that, in addition, on that very day one of them would deny him and another would betray him. They were horrified and could not imagine how any one of them would do any such thing.

But it happened just as he said it would. The police stopped Sham'un (Simon Peter) (ra) in the street and accused him of being a follower of 'Isa (as). Sham'un (ra), in order to save himself, protested that he had no knowledge or connection with anyone by the name of 'Isa (as). The police arrested another of the companions, commonly said to be Judas but possibly another. To free himself, he accepted to betray the whereabouts of 'Isa (as) for the sum of thirty silver coins. The *Hawariyun* had had only three years of training and preparation, their biggest test was yet to come.

The upper room above an ancient synagogue which is also believed to be the *maqam* of prophet Dawud (as). Believed to be the location of the last supper. Jerusalem.

'Isa (as) being raised to heaven by angels. Illustration for Zubdat al-Tawarikh by Seyyid Lokman, Ottoman 1583.

36.
The Substitution

The one thing The Qur'an tells us for certain is that they did not kill or crucify 'Isa (as) as the Christians believe. This is the one fact of which Muslims can be sure. How he escaped or what it was that actually happened, even if he died or not, has been left open to interpretation. And there are prominent Muslims who have held and defended every possible position. The mainstream opinion is, however, that 'Isa (as) did not die on the cross or anywhere else. He was taken by Allah to Himself and will return to complete his life and die in the last days. Since we are promised only one death (37:58, 44:56), he could not have already died and still return to die again. Some hold to a spiritual understanding in which they assert that The Qur'an is only telling us that even if his body did die, what is more important is that his eternal nature as word and spirit of Allah cannot die. No earthly tyrant unbeliever can wipe out or even touch the ever-living word of God.

The pertinent verse is understood in two ways. In one understanding it reads: **they said (in boast), "We killed the *Masih* 'Isa the son of Maryam, the Messenger of Allah"- but they killed him not,**

'Isa's (as) footprint in rock on the Mount of Olives where the Christians believe he ascended. The picture shows the *mihrab* built by the Salahu d-Din in 1187 and maintained as a *waqf* today open for all religions.

nor crucified him, <u>but it was made to appear so to them.</u> And those who differ about it are [also] full of doubts, with no (certain) knowledge, but only follow conjecture, for of a surety they killed him not. Allah raised him up to Himself. (4:157-158). In a variant understanding it reads that they said, "**Indeed, we have killed the Messiah, 'Isa the son of Maryam, the messenger of Allah.**" And they did not kill him, nor did they crucify him; <u>but [another] was made to resemble him to them.</u> And indeed, those who differ over it are themselves in doubt about it. They have no knowledge except the following of an assumption. And they did not kill him, that is certain. Allah raised him up to Himself. (4:157-158). So either all the people were veiled and saw something other than what really was happening or someone else took the appearance of 'Isa (as) and was killed in his place. Either way, the witnesses at the scene were deluded and saw only what Allah chose for them to see, and it was not the reality. That his followers truly believed he was crucified is certain because they proceeded to give up their own lives in defense of their belief.

Some say that when Judas led the soldiers to where 'Isa (as) was staying, a darkness fell over the room. In this thick gloom, 'Isa (as) slipped away through a window. When the darkness lifted, Judas himself had been made to look like 'Isa (as), and the police took him into custody despite his protestations. Even the other disciples and Maryam (ahs) herself were under the mistaken impression that it was 'Isa (as) who had been arrested.

Others say that the guards found the place where 'Isa (as) and his disciples were staying on their own and sent one of their number in to arrest him. Jibra'il (as) descended and took 'Isa (as) away through an opening in the roof. When the officer exited, his appearance had been altered by Allah to look like 'Isa (as). He was bound and dragged off, all the while protesting that they had made a mistake.

Others say that the night before, 'Isa (as) offered his companions the certainty of paradise and an eternity by his side if one of them would take on his identity and be sacrificed in his place. The youngest of the disciples offered himself, but 'Isa (as) did not accept until he had asked three times, and no one else had volunteered. This disciple is variously named Ashyu ibn Qandayra or Sergius, or Simon of Cyrene. The likeness of 'Isa (as) was dressed on him, and he was arrested. However, others say that it is not possible that a prophet of God, especially 'Isa (as), would let an innocent man take his punishment in this world in order to save himself. Either it was 'Isa (as) who was actually taken into custody or it was Allah who removed His prophet from the scene and then appointed a substitute Himself.

The guards took 'Isa (as), or the one resembling him, to prison. The priestly court tried him but could not determine in what way he had transgressed the law so they handed him over to the Roman court which also was not sure on what grounds to prosecute him. However, they both determined that it was safest to be rid of him. So he was condemned to be hung in public view on a cross pole, as was the customary punishment for criminals of the lower classes. As they dragged him through the streets they taunted him saying, "If you are the savior of the people, save yourself. If you can raise the dead, raise yourself." But he did not answer them. According to the Gospel account, a couple of his disciples pulled out swords to try to defend him, but he told them to put the swords away, it was not the time yet for swords (Luke 22:49-51). It is not the way of prophets to ask Allah to change their destiny. Whatever miraculous powers are put in the hands of Allah's prophets, they never use them for their own advantage, and they would never think of defending themselves from Him.

When they approached the place of crucifixion, as Ibn Abbas (ra) tells the story, the sun was eclipsed and darkness fell over the earth like a thick pall. No one could see his hand before his face, and the deadly procession came to a standstill. There was complete confusion. In this heavy darkness Allah took His prophet to Himself and substituted someone or something else. This would imply that 'Isa (as) suffered through the imprisonment, the trial, the humiliation and torment of the slow procession to the place of execution but at the last moment was taken away. When the darkness lifted everyone was confused and no one noticed that the man they had in custody was someone else. He had been beaten and disfigured, perhaps they could not tell. They proceeded to nail him to the cross and to witness his agony. It was naturally assumed that they had killed him. The deception was so thorough that it is said even Maryam (ahs) was not sure if it was her son or not, and she mourned in silent grief in the arms of another Maryam (rah) at some distance from the cross.

There are a few other marginal explanations of how to understand what it means when The Qur'an says that **they did not kill him, that is certain**. (4:157). Perhaps he only appeared to be dead but when taken down from the cross he revived. This is an extremist view adopted by the Ahmadiyya who then say 'Isa (as) left Palestine for Kashmir where he continued to preach for another ninety years and then died and was buried in Srinagar. There are those who even claim he revived and went to live in a Jewish community in the south of France.

A more philosophical view is that it is only Allah who can give or take life. Without it being the will of God, they could not have crucified 'Isa (as). So although he might have died, the Jews and Romans cannot claim it was as a result of their actions. However, one wonders then how the Jews are accorded responsibility for the deaths of any of the other prophets they are accused of martyring, Yahya (as), Zakariyya (as), Alyasa (as) among others. **Whenever a messenger brought them anything they did not like, they accused some of lying and others they put to death** (5:70). It is always and in all cases, Allah who gives and takes life. The fact remains that men bear the responsibility if only because they wanted it and, if they had been able, they would certainly have done it. The case of 'Isa (as), however, is different. At the end of the verses describing the event, it says, **Allah is Almighty ('azizan), Wise (hakiman)**. (4:158). The use of these particular attributes of Allah indicate, the scholars say, that something out of the ordinary has transpired, something that clearly manifests Allah's power. Although they did their best to physically kill 'Isa (as), they were prevented by divine intervention from accomplishing what they set out to do.

There is evidence in the Gospels themselves that supports the theory of some kind of substitution (Zahniser). Three of the canonical Gospels (Matthew 17:1-8, Mark 9:2-8, Luke 9:28-36) relate that at some point 'Isa (as) took three of his closest disciples, Simon Peter (ra), James (ra), and John (ra), up a high mountain to pray. His companions were heavy with sleep. Late in the night they woke, still groggy, to witness the heavenly descent of the prophets Musa (as) and Ilyas (as), representing, they say, the Law and the Spirit. Through bewildered eyes, Peter saw 'Isa (as) become infused with a bright light, his face and form transformed. In the Latin church this is celebrated as the Transfiguration, in the Greek church as the Metamorphosis.

Russian Orthodox icon of the Transfiguration by Theophanes the Greek circa 1408.

Some Muslims think that this is an eyewitness account of the raising of 'Isa (as) to Allah. What was left behind was only a semblance or a shell. And so for the rest of his time among men he was not himself. On the occasion of his arrest, the Jews called for him and, even though he answered them, they continued to ask and not recognize him (John 19). In the events that followed, imprisonment, trial, and punishment, 'Isa (as) acted strangely unlike his former self. He neither claimed nor denied who he was but replied evasively saying only "You have said" (Luke 22:70). In addition, some say that his last words on the cross, "Lord, Lord, why have You forsaken me?" were inappropriate for a prophet of his station and so point to being uttered by a substitute.

However, 'Isa (as) was quoting from the twenty-second Psalm, an earlier prayer very similar to the prayer of the Prophet Muhammad (sas) at his lowest moment after being rejected by Ta'if. "O Allah to You do I complain of my weakness, of my helplessness, of my want of resources, and of my lowliness before men. O Most Merciful of the merciful, You are Lord of the weak and You are my Lord. Into whose hands will You entrust me? To some far-off stranger who will ill-treat me? Or to a foe whom You have empowered against me? I care not, so long as You are not angry with me..." Although it might sound as if he is despairing of the mercy of Allah, he is actually only acknowledging his weakness before the power of the All-Mighty. It is the honest cry of the one who truly knows and accepts his position of slave before the Majesty of his Lord. The result of both prayers was to be taken physically into the presence of Allah Almighty: 'Isa's (as) transfiguration and Muhammad's (sas) Night Journey. And the place from which both of them ascended was the sacred precinct in Jerusalem.

In a more mystical way Ibn 'Arabi says that 'Isa (as), unlike most humans, was only partially created with a physical human body, the part of him that he inherited from his mother Maryam (ahs). The other portion of his bodily substance was angelic, inherited from Jibra'il (as) in the form of a man. 'Isa (as) therefore, consisted partially of an immaterial body of light that could not be killed with knives or nails. It was this innate reality, or this transformed reality, that the disciples witnessed on the mountain. So it is as if on the cross 'Isa (as) may have hung his material body, like a suit of cast-off clothing or a chrysalis, and emerged in his angelic form which continued to be visible to those who had always been able to see it - his disciples and his mother. With this body he can choose to be seen or not and can still work in the world or ascend to heavenly realms. Allah knows best.

This is the totality of what The Qur'an tells us about the matter of the disappearance of 'Isa (as) from Jerusalem on that fateful Friday. Many more verses and much more detail and attention are devoted to his coming into the world than to his leaving it. The manner of his passing belongs appropriately to the unseen, and the whole truth is known to Allah alone.

Only thirty-three years after he was born, only three years after he began delivering the Injil, he was gone. The day 'Isa (as) was raised to heaven it is said that he left nothing behind but a "woolen shirt and a pair of sandals" - and the lasting example of his love and devotion to his Creator.

Peace on me the day I was born, and the day I die, and the day I shall be raised alive. (19:33).

The seamless robe of 'Isa (as) held in the Cathedral of Trier, Germany.

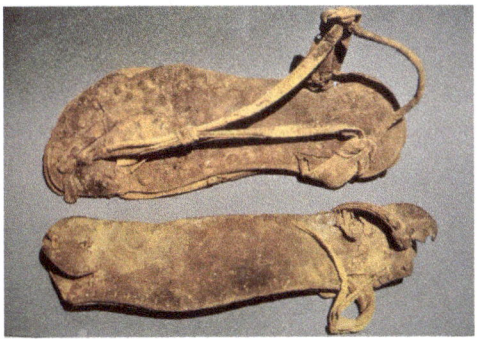

1st century sandals found in the ruins of Masada, Israel. Probably very similar to the ones worn by 'Isa (as).

Woman in mourning. Michelangelo, 16th century Italian.

37.
After Seven Days

Allah raised him ('Isa) up to Himself. Allah is Almighty, Wise. (4:158). For perhaps seven days, 'Isa (as) remained in heaven where Allah had taken him. His apparent death and disappearance confused his family and companions. How could it be, they wondered, that this messenger from God would be taken from them so abruptly and in such a violent anguished way, even though he had told them continually that this would happen, and even though Yahya (as) had been killed in a similar fashion just a few short years previously. Maryam (ahs) herself is said to have been unsure if the body they laid in the tomb was really her son. They were depressed, confused, and disconsolate. They separated and each left to his own home. Passover was over but the Kidron river was still tinged with the blood of the thousands of lambs that had been sacrificed to God in atonement for the sins of men. The image must have struck them, the association between their master and the lambs of God. With this metaphor they bandaged their broken hearts.

Perhaps the most sorrowful of all was said to be a young woman known as Maryam al-Majdalaniyyah (rah). She was a noble woman said to be from the village of Majdalan near Antioch rather than the one we know today on the Sea of Galilee. On reaching adulthood she had never been able to maintain a state of ritual purity. When she heard of the healing powers of 'Isa (as), she had traveled to see him, hoping that he could help her. But on finally meeting him she was too shy to explain her condition, so she slipped back into the crowd to let him pass. As he moved ahead, she shyly wove her hand through the throng of people and lightly touched 'Isa (as) on the shoulder. He sensed her touch and pronounced her healed. From then on she devoted herself to him and his mother Maryam (ahs), accompanying them wherever they went.

Either on the night of the supposed crucifixion, or on the eighth day after his being raised to heaven, Allah commanded 'Isa (as) to return to earth. He found his mother (ahs) and Maryam al-Majdalaniyya (rah) weeping together and asked them the reason for their grief. Looking up they replied in astonishment that they were weeping for him. He told them to dry their eyes for Allah had raised him on high, and nothing but goodness had befallen him. Then he asked them to assemble the *Hawariyyun* in their house to receive instructions on what their duties were to be now that he was no longer among them. Everyone's joy and relief knew no bounds. Their faith in him was confirmed, and the claims of the Romans and of the Pharisees that there was no life after death was clearly disproven.

'Isa (as) looked over the group and noticed the absence of Judas. Asking for him, he was told that, in grief over his act of betrayal, Judas had hanged himself on the very day that they thought 'Isa (as) had died. 'Isa (as) expressed great sadness at this news and said that if Judas had only asked forgiveness, Allah would have granted it. **Do not despair of the Mercy of Allah. Allah forgives all sins. He is truly the Most Forgiving, the Most Merciful** (39:53).

He gave to each of the disciples their assigned mission. Simon Peter (ra) was sent to Rome; Andrew (ra) and Matthew (ra) to the land where 'people eat other people', Ethiopia; Thomas (ra) to the Eastern lands, Babylonia and maybe as far as India; Philip (ra) to Carthage; John (ra) to Ephesus; James (ra) to Jerusalem; Bartholomew (ra) to Arabia; and Simon (ra) to the Berbers, North Africa. The disciples were worried because they didn't know how to get to the places to which they were assigned, and if they got there they would be unable to speak the language of the

The Glastonbury Tor, Somerset England, associated with both 'Isa (as) and the Holy Grail legend.

residents. But Allah put them into a deep sleep and transported them to where He wanted them. They woke in the morning deeply astonished to find themselves no longer under the roofs of their homes but in the open countryside outside foreign cities. To their greater amazement they found that the All-Merciful had instilled on their tongues the ability to speak whatever language it was that they needed to preach to their chosen people. Each of them proceeded to invite the people with zeal to worship the one God and to hear the word of His prophet 'Isa (as) until they met their deaths, almost all of them as martyrs. Some believe that another companion, perhaps a relative, Joseph of Arimathea, was also sent with twelve others to the western limits of the Roman world where they successfully preached the Gospel and established a church in Somerset England.

Ibn Abbas (ra), as related by Ibn Kathir, described concisely what happened to the religion of 'Isa (as) after he ascended to heaven. He says that the followers of 'Isa (as) "divided into many bitterly opposing sects, of which there were three main groups. One group said, 'God was among us as long as He willed, and then He rose up to heaven.' One group said, 'The son of God was among us as long as God desired him to be, and then God raised him up to Himself.' The third group said, 'A slave of God and His messenger was among us as long He wished, and then God raised him to Himself.' This last group were the Muslims. The first two groups overpowered the Muslims and killed them all. Islam remained absent until Allah sent the Prophet Muhammad (sas)."

Perhaps this last group were the ones referred to today as the Judeo-Christians under the leadership of James the Just (ra). They continued to hold to the Tawrah and its laws as it was revived by 'Isa (as). They remained in the vicinity of Jerusalem until the Romans destroyed the Temple, and the Jews were exiled. They held views of the nature and mission of 'Isa (as) that were very similar to Muslim understanding. They were known as Nazarenes, and they were declared a heresy by the Roman church for being too Jewish. Especially hated was the fact that they continued to circumcise and shun the swine. Slowly they disappeared or perhaps found hidden places in the desert of Arabia or Ethiopia where they continued to practice as they believed. It was only with the coming of The Qur'an that the truth about 'Isa (as) was once more clarified. Some say that the verses in The Qur'an that talk about the Christians as *"Nasara"* are only referring to this group. Allah knows best.

Sometime after this had taken place, it is related in The Qur'an that Allah questioned 'Isa (as). **"'Isa, son of Maryam, did you say to people, 'Take me and my mother as two gods alongside God'?" He ('Isa) said, "May You be exalted! I would never say what I had no right to say."** (5:116). And 'Isa (as) felt great sadness and shame because, if his followers had not misrepresented his teaching, his Lord would not have reproached him in this way. But it was a mistake for which he was held somewhat responsible and which he would be given another chance to correct.

Before returning to his heavenly station, 'Isa (as) commended his gentle mother (ahs) into the care of one of his companions. Maryam (ahs) had continued to support and follow her son throughout his life. As he was the seal of sainthood, Maryam (ahs) was the seal of motherhood. She carried her responsibility full circle to completion. As she labored and suffered to bring her child into the world so she served and suffered to witness his leaving it. Although she knew the truth, that his ascension to Allah was not a death, still she was bereft of his company and had to live

The House in which Maryam (ahs) lived in Ephesus, Turkey.

on for many years without him. The prophet Ya'qub (as) became blind from the tears he shed mourning the loss of Yusuf (as) even though he knew in his heart that he was not dead. The prophet Muhammad (sas) wept at the passing of his baby son because it was the last he would see of him in this world.

The Gospels suggest that Maryam (ahs) had a husband and other children. But for the Muslims, Maryam (ahs) had nothing other than 'Isa (as), no family or place where she belonged. She accompanied him as a pilgrim on the path of God among his other disciples. Since they were mostly young men, she probably watched over and cared for them all, and they grew to love her as their own mother. Al-'Azar (ra) missed her so much that after 'Isa (as) had been taken away and the disciples dispersed, he wrote begging her to come visit him in Cyprus. It is said that she tried to go, although no one knows for sure if she made it.

Some say she lived another six years with John (ra) outside of the ancient city of Ephesus where he had been sent. He built her a small house on a quiet hillside where she lived out the rest of her days in peace. If she died there, no tomb has been found. Others say she stayed with James (ra) in Jerusalem and died and was buried there. Churches in all denominations have been built over the spot of the empty tomb where Christians say Maryam (ahs) was buried and then, like her son, rose from the dead after three days and ascended into heaven. Muslims say that she will be raised with her son on Qiyama and then, according to hadith, she will become the heavenly bride of the Prophet Muhammad (sas) - the best of men and the best of women united for eternity. May Allah bless them both and give them peace.

Al-Thalabi says 'Isa (as) was taken back up to heaven where Allah "clad him with feathers, dressed him in light, removed the desire for food and drink, and he flies around the Throne with the angels, though he is human, angelic, earthly, heavenly." **Allah said: O 'Isa, I am gathering you and causing you to ascend to Me, and am cleansing you of those who disbelieve and am setting those who follow you above those who disbelieve until the Day of Resurrection. Then unto Me you will (all)**

The ascension of 'Isa (as), from a French prayer book circa 1511.

return, and I shall judge between you as to that wherein you used to differ. (3:55).

There is a hadith, narrated by Ibn Ishaq in the oldest biography of the Prophet (sas), in which Salman al-Farsi (ra) recounts his life story. He was born a Zoroastrian in a town outside of Isfahan in Persia. One day, hearing the worship inside a church, he accepted Christianity and left his father and his home to dedicate himself in service to a succession of bishops and holy men in Syria. Before each one died, he recommended Salman (ra) to another holy man until the last one said there were no more that he knew of but that a prophet was coming soon in Arabia. So Salman (ra) headed south with a caravan whose leaders betrayed him and sold him into slavery. He ended up in Medina at just about the time the Prophet Muhammad (sas) emigrated there. Salman (ra) recognized him immediately by his signs, which were, in this case, not taking any portion of something given as charity but taking freely from anything given as a gift. Salman (ra) did not need his name written down on a piece of paper to know who he was.

In addition, Salman (ra) told the Prophet (sas) that while he was in Syria he had gone to see a man who once a year was to be found walking on a road between two thick groves of trees. It was the custom of the people at that time to line the path on either side seeking his blessing. As he walked he would heal the sick, cure the cripple, give sight to the blind. The Prophet (sas) listened attentively to the whole story of Salman (ra) and commented that, if what he said was true, then the man he saw was the prophet 'Isa (as).

The Prophet (sas) on the Buraq (as) with Jibra'il (as) meeting Nuh (as) and Idris (as) in Heaven. Illustration from Mir Maydar, Mi'rajnameh, Timurid Afghanistan, 1436.

38.
Hierarchies

The raising of 'Isa (as) into heaven alive, as amazing as it is, is not unique among the prophets. There are at least three other prophets we know of, in addition to 'Isa (as), for whom Allah has expanded or redefined the boundaries of human life: Idris (Enoch) (as), Ilyas (Elijah) (as), and al-Khidr (the Green man) (as).

Idris (as) was a prophet between Adam (as) and Nuh (as). He is credited with teaching mankind much of the basic knowledge that defines what it means to be human: reading, writing, the domestication of animals, tools and weapons, weaving, sewing, and medicine. While on a visit to the angelic realms, he died. At the request of the angels he was restored to life by Allah Almighty and allowed to remain bodily in heaven thereafter. **And mention in the Book, Idris. Indeed, he was a man of truth (*sadiq*) and a prophet. We raised him to a high place.** (19:56-7).

The prophet Ilyas (as) had a long difficult life exhorting the Banu Isra'il to be true to their covenant with Allah when they had strayed far off the path of righteousness and began to worship other gods. His people rejected his teaching and sought to kill him. He was finally saved

The forty *mihrabs* of the Awtad on Mount Qasyun, Damascus Syria.

from their treachery and miraculously relieved of his earthly mission by being taken up to heaven on a horse of fire. He has yet to experience a physical death. **And We left with him for later generations.** (37:129).

Al-Khidr (as) is mentioned, although not named, as the teacher of Musa (as) in Suratu l-Kahf. **Then they found a slave from among Our slaves to whom We had given mercy and knowledge from Our presence.** (18:65). Some say he was among the companions of Ibrahim (as). Some say he was a warrior in the army of Dhul Qarnayn (as) who found the water of life and has yet to die. He has been a teacher and guide to many prophets and saints. He is even believed to have been among the mourners at the passing of the Prophet Muhammad (sas). He is called the green man because whatever he touches turns green with new life. These four immortal figures play a major role in supporting the spiritual life of the planet by maintaining firm and continuous worship.

Saints in Arabic are called *Awliya* Allah, which means friends of Allah and each one is also a protecting friend (*wali*) to His creation. They are arranged in a hierarchy, a Greek word which in its origin refers specifically to the ordered ranks of heavenly beings. The saints and wise men, to whom Allah has revealed knowledge about these ranks of the unseen, differ slightly in how they describe them to us but most agree that there are forty chosen to be the *Abdal*, substitutes, the ones transformed. These are men and women who have persevered on the path of Allah until their bodies of clay have been transformed into light, and they travel the whole world every day in service to the believers. Among this number are four *Awtad*, supports or stakes, who stabilize the spiritual world in much the same way as The Qur'an says that the mountains were created as stakes to stabilize the physical world (78:6-7), in the same way that a tent cloth is staked down at its four corners. Each saint has a realm of responsibility. Ilyas (as) watches over those on the sea perhaps because one of the miracles with which he was blessed was the withholding and granting of rain. Al-Khidr (as) watches over those on land as his touch enlivens the earth. 'Isa (as) and Idris (as) have heavenly positions. 'Isa (as) serves a priestly function as an intermediary between God and man, and Idris (as) functions as a wise and beneficent overlord.

Of these four, Idris (as) is called the *Qutb*, the Pole. The word *Qutb* itself

The Pole Star is at the center and the others stars circle around.

designates the center pole of a tent, or the axis around which everything turns as the stars turn around the Pole Star or, alternatively, the central point towards which everything is gathered. These spiritual posts are filled by prophets but their worldly functions are fulfilled by living men and women in every age. When one of them dies, they are immediately replaced by another from the ranks below. The Qur'an says, **"Peace be upon Il-yasin"** (37:130), which is the plural of Ilyas (as) and is interpreted to mean both him and those like him – the Ilyases. These men and women take on the special character of the prophet they represent and carry out his duties among the living.

The Prophet Muhammad (sas) has told us: "The prophets were the supports (*awtad*) of the earth but when prophethood ended, Allah substituted in their places forty men from the nation of Muhammad (sas), the *Abdal*. Not one of them dies except Allah replaces him with another. Now they are the supports of the earth. The hearts of thirty of these are like Sayyiduna Ibrahim (as). They did not succeed or rise above other people by means of much fasting or prayer…but rather by being truthful in their diligence, having noble intentions, sound wholesome hearts, and giving all the Muslims sincere counsel. Their desire is only the pleasure of Allah. They are patient and forbearing, merciful through and through, and humble without being meek. They do not curse anyone, or harm anyone. They do not see themselves as being higher or nobler than anyone under them, nor do they envy those above them. Their humility is not faked. They do not pretend to be dead to the world and they do not attract attention to themselves. They neither love the world, nor do they love anything else for its sake..." (Ibn Hanbal).

The hierarchy of saints might be envisioned as a great dome or tent within which human beings find sacred space and shelter and, by means of which the material and spiritual worlds are joined, like the Tabernacle at the time Musa (as), like the Ka'ba today. Each corner points in one of the cardinal directions and represents one of the *Awtad*. The *Qutb* is the Black Stone which, although not central in physical position, is still the pivot around which everything turns, the center towards which everything is gathered, the beginning and end of the sacred circling. Idris (as) is said to be the *Qutb* represented by the eastern, heavenward corner.

Knowledge of this hierarchy is not unique to Islam. After defeating a tyrant in battle, according to the Tawrah, Ibrahim (as) passed by the city of Salem to receive the blessings of a mysterious figure called Melchizedek (as), *Maliki Sadiq*, the truthful king and "priest of God Most High" (Genesis 14:18), which is his title rather than his name. This eternally recurrent figure is most commonly thought to be Idris (as) who is also called *sadiq* by Allah in the quote mentioned above (19:86). His position is such that one of the greatest prophets of all time, Ibrahim (as), sought and received his blessing.

Ilyas (as) saving a man from the sea. Hamzanama, 1550.

It is also stated in the Gospels that Yahya (as) "came in the spirit and power of Ilyas (as)" (Luke 1:17), as one of the **Il-yasin**. This was verified by 'Isa (as) himself (Matthew 11:14). After the death of Yahya (as) the people believed that 'Isa (as) inherited his position as representative of Ilyas (as). Melchizedek (as) also appears in the New Testament where he is described: "without father or mother, without genealogy, without beginning of days or end of life, like the son of God, he (Melchizedek) remains a priest forever." (Hebrews 7:3). 'Isa (as) is told that he also belongs to this fraternity and is "a priest forever after the order of Melchizedek" (Hebrews

8:1). Neither 'Isa (as) nor Melchizedek (as) are ritual priests by descent from the prophet Harun (as), but rather they are priests by membership in the eternal brotherhood of hidden servants of Allah. 'Isa (as) also, as recorded in the Gospels of Matthew, Mark, and Luke was transformed into a body of light in the presence of Musa (as) and Ilyas (as).

This points to the possibility that Musa (as) is also still alive in heaven. He has no *maqam*, no place on earth designated as the place of his mortal remains. He disappeared from his people and either died and was buried by angels or was taken up into Heaven alive. The Prophet Muhammad (sas) said that although his own soul will be the first to return to its body on the Day of Resurrection, when he opens his eyes he will see Musa (as) clinging to the Throne of the Almighty. He will not know if Musa (as) was resurrected before him or if Musa (as) had died rather than fainted, and then been returned to life at the time Allah revealed Himself to the mountain in the wilderness of Sinai.

These men of God, the *Awtad*, are always concerned with the state of the world. They have communicated and communed with all the prophets and have guided the saints and the righteous. Sometimes they materialize under different names to act as guides or teachers. Al Khidr (as) appears in the lineages, *silsila*, of the shaykhs of many Sufi orders. Sometimes they appear out of nowhere to enact a miraculous rescue of ordinary people. Seen or unseen they are helping us all, appearing when necessary in obedience to the orders of their Lord. They are not bound by the Law as we know it, by the Tawrah or Injil. They are obedient to a higher law as the account in The Qur'an of Musa (as) and al-Khidr (as) demonstrates.

Al-Khidr (as) turning the desert green. 18th century mughul.

The four *Awtad* can also

be said to represent certain stations, posts or outposts as it were, on the spiritual path. They have also become the model for a level of sainthood filled by men in every age, who by their love for Allah and dedication to His creatures, have been elevated to fill these positions. Ibn 'Arabi, one of the few to relate specific information of this saintly hierarchy, began his spiritual journey under the loving guidance of 'Isa (as) who appeared to him and was his teacher.

This may help to explain how a prophet named specifically by Allah as Yahya (as), 'he lives', did not die but took his place among the ever-living. **And say not of those who are slain in God's cause, "They are dead": nay, they are alive, but you perceive it not.** (2:154). The Prophet Muhammad (sas) has told us that he is alive in his grave and responds to us when we greet him. These things are among the mysteries of Allah, revealed only to those He chooses. However, we are informed of their existence because we need to keep respect for them and reserve a place for them in our lives. In this way the Jewish people set a place for Ilyas (as) at their Passover table to acknowledge and welcome his unseen presence. We need to be aware that there are realms of knowledge beyond our vision or understanding that may sometimes appear in the interstices of our daily lives and in which we must be ready to believe (2:2-3).

The Prophet (sas), represented by the golden flames, visiting the hierarchy of the seven heavens.
Illustration for The History of the Prophet, Persia, 1030.

The Prophet (sas) leading the angels and prophets in prayer. Siyer-i Nebi, Istanbul 1594.

39.
The Three Righteous Men of the Last Days

Less than six hundred years after 'Isa (as) was taken up to heaven, the Prophet Muhammad (sas) was woken from sleep where he lay in the *hijr* of the Ka'ba. Accompanied by Jibra'il (as) he traveled to Jerusalem, and from there he made his own ascent up through the seven heavens all the way to the Divine Presence. As they approached each heaven Jibra'il (as) knocked on its magnificent gate and was asked by the angel on guard 'Who is there?" His answer for each was, "It is I, Jibra'il, and with me is the Prophet Muhammad." Again the obedient gatekeeper asked, not who is Muhammad because of course he knew and had been awaiting this moment for as long as he could remember, but rather he asked "Has his time indeed come?" "Yes" said Jibra'il (as) to the joy of the angelic guardian who then opened his gate wide in welcome.

At each heaven, the Prophet (sas) greeted and received the blessings of one of his brother prophets. In the first he met Adam (as) who welcomed him as a son. In the third heaven he met Yusuf (as), radiant like the moon. In the fourth he met Idris (as). In the fifth he saw the one he called the most handsome of men, Harun (as). In the sixth heaven he met Musa (as) who was the only one to give him advice and insist that he return to Allah three times to ask that the number of prayers prescribed for his nation be reduced. In the seventh, and last heaven, he was greeted by Ibrahim (as) whose appearance most resembled his own. In the second heaven he met Yahya (as) and 'Isa (as) who occupy that level together. 'Isa (as) he described as being tall and well built with reddish skin and long straight hair that glistened as though wet. They spoke briefly about the coming of the Hour of the Last Day, and neither of them knew more than the other about when it will dawn, even though 'Isa (as) will be a major participant in the actions that precede its advent.

We have been told that both 'Isa (as) and Idris (as) are still alive although in heaven. They continue to have a role to play in the life of this world, their destiny is not yet finished. As the world runs its course towards its last day, we see some of the signs the Prophet (sas) foretold happening around us. The beginning of the end as he told us was his own death, and that is now more than fourteen hundred years ago. He is the last messenger. His book, The Generous Qur'an, is the last holy scripture. It is meant for all the people of a global world to cling to and be guided. His death was the first sign. The other signs we are told will follow like beads of a necklace when the string breaks. The hadith about these signs have been gathered together in one volume, from all the collections of hadith, by Ibn Kathir. And it is from this that most of the following has been gleaned. Although the beads have been described, no one knows for sure their order or their pattern on the string, how and when they will fall. Many have already fallen, and others could be falling now.

The Prophet said, according to 'Ali ibn Abi Talib (ra), "The Hour will come when leaders are oppressors, when people believe in the stars and reject *al-qadar* (the Divine Decree of destiny), when a trust becomes a way of making a profit, when people give charity (*sadaqah*) reluctantly, when adultery becomes widespread. When these things happen, then your people will perish." Or, putting it another way, he said, when there is widespread sexual immorality and it is accepted as normal, people will be afflicted with diseases that were unknown before. When there is pervasive commercial dishonesty, famine and tyranny will descend on the people. When charity is considered a burden, Allah will not send rain except a little out of mercy for the wild animals. When the Muslims renege on their covenant with Allah to uphold His religion, an outside force will subjugate them. When they divide into sects they will fight among themselves.

There will be many smaller signs to warn that the Hour is approaching. The barefoot herders of black camels will vie with each other to build high buildings. Every household will be infected with dissention. Adultery, homosexuality, drunkenness, music and female singers will be widespread. Arabia will be green and well watered. Men will obey their wives and disobey their mothers; they will treat their friends well and ignore their fathers. People will compete in decorating mosques. Senseless murder will increase. The slave woman will give birth to her master. There will be many earthquakes. Women will outnumber men fifty to one. A mountain of gold will be found under the Euphrates and men will fight to possess it. People will talk into something like their shoe or their riding crop to find out what is happening with their families at home. Truth will be called a lie, and a lie will be seen as truth. The leaders will be the worst of their nation, and war and murder will be rampant.

Dubai.

The Prophet (sas) said, "Islam began as something strange, and it will revert to being strange as it was in the beginning, so good tidings to the strangers." Someone asked, 'Who are the strangers?' He said, "The ones who break away from their people (literally tribes) for the sake of Islam." And 'Isa (as) said the same, "The ones whom Allah loves best are the strangers." "Who are the strangers?" his companions asked. "He who flees the world with his faith intact" he replied.

When things on earth have reached this point, the Mahdi (as), the Guided one, will be revealed. Preparations for him will be accomplished in one day, so quickly that there is no forewarning. The reigning Muslim khalifa will die and there will be disagreement over his successor. Men of truth will go to Medina and force the Mahdi (as) to take his place even though he is reluctant to do so. He will be a descendant of the Prophet (sas) through his daughter Fatima (rah) and will bear his name, Muhammad ibn Abdullah. He will be born in Medina. He will have a broad forehead, large eyes, and a prominent nose. Although not resembling the Prophet (sas) in appearance, he will be like him in behavior. Ibn 'Arabi says, "he walks in the footsteps of the Messenger of God, and makes no mistakes. He is guided by an unseen angel." The men of knowledge will recognize him immediately, but to others it might not be clear. It is not his lineage that identifies him or his name, but rather the clarity of his vision. **This is my Way. I call to Allah with sure knowledge, I and whoever follows me.** (12:108). He will be a true follower of the Prophet Muhammad (sas).

He is called "the Guided" because it is said he will take counsel with men of high spiritual knowledge. These men, according to Ibn 'Arabi, will be Arabic speakers of non-Arab descent. It is said that, as the Prophet (sas) was the brother of The Qur'an, the Mahdi (as) will be the brother of the Sword, the Sword of Truth and Justice. He will establish justice where before there was only injustice and oppression. He will establish the divine sultanate on earth in the manner of the prophet Sulayman (as), and like him he will be able to understand the language of animals and Jinn. His law will revive and restore the Shari'a of Islam replacing all the various schools of Law, *madhahib*. All men will be judged fairly without prejudice, all wealth will be distributed in equity and in abundance. After judgment is pronounced both the judge and the judged will embrace knowing that Allah's justice was established. For some seven or nine years he will rule the world in goodness.

However, first he will have to fight the *Masihu l-Dajjal*, the false messiah, the one-eyed deceiver, who will appear along with many smaller *dajjals*, his deputies, in every corner of the earth. He will deceive the people by saying that he is a prophet, and then he will say he is God. In the beginning he will speak truly and appear to lead people on the right way, so he will be followed. He will work real miracles even though he is a liar, by permission of Allah in order to test the faith of people. All who are not prepared by belief in the Prophet's (sas) words will follow him. He will be young with white skin and curly hair. His imbalance will be seen in that one of his eyes will be missing or like a floating grape, and his other eye will be like a star. Protection against him will be to hold fast to the words of the Prophet Muhammad (sas), who warned us specifically that there will be no prophet after him, and we will not see God until after we die.

The Mahdi (as) will set out with his army to fight an enemy

variously called Romans or Yellow ones presumably under the control of the Dajjal. They will fight the biggest battle the world has ever known on the plain of Amuq or Dabiq near Aleppo on the Syrian/Turkish border. The Muslims will fight many indecisive battles, and the loss of life will be heavy. When finally they are victorious, they will learn that the Dajjal has slipped through their hands by hiding among the women. Although they fight valiantly, the forces of the Mahdi (as) will not be able to kill the Dajjal. Four out of five will die trying. The Prophet (sas) said, "My community is like the rain. It is not known whether the best of it falls at the beginning or at the end."

At this time Allah Almighty will send His servant 'Isa (as) to help in the fight. Sayyiduna 'Isa (as) will descend from where he is waiting in heaven. **And indeed, 'Isa will be [a sign for] knowledge of the Hour, so be not in doubt about it, and follow Me. This is a straight path.** (43:61). The Prophet (sas) said, "Of all men, I have the most rightful claim to 'Isa ibn Maryam because there was no prophet between him and me. He will be my successor – *khalifati* – over my community. He will surely descend. When you see him, you will recognize him. He shall be a man of medium height, of reddish white color, with straight hair, shining as if dripping with water, although no water has touched it." Some hadith say, however, that water will be dripping from his hair in drops like pearls. He will descend, with his hands on the wings of two angels. He will be wearing two garments of a yellow color. Most

'Isa (as) descending onto the White Minaret of the 'Ummayad Mosque, Damascus Syria. Ottoman 1650.

say he will descend over the white minaret of the Ummayyid Mosque in Damascus, the place where the remains of Yahya (as) are buried. His coming will be signaled by a loud noise and a bright light, so that all the people of the world will be alerted to his presence. The scent of his breath will spread as far as the eye can see, and the hearts of the believers will fill with love for him.

When he descends, the Mahdi (as) will be waiting to welcome him. It will be the time of the morning prayer, and the Mahdi (as) will ask 'Isa (as) to lead the believers. But 'Isa (as) will step aside, insisting that al-Mahdi (as) leads because the time still belongs to him, and he is the appointed deputy of God, *khalifat Allah*. Imam al-Mahdi (as) will lead the prayers from then on with 'Isa (as) following, not as a prophet, but as a Muslim in the nation of Muhammad (sas).

The Dajjal will try to destroy Mecca and Medina, but will be driven from the gates by angel warriors. When he is outside of Medina, a righteous man, whom the Prophet (sas) called the "highest martyr or witness", will come forward and announce to the people that this is the Dajjal about whom the Prophet (sas) warned. The Dajjal will capture him and torture him by having him sawn in half. Then he will bring him back to life in order to try to prove he is God. When the man is revived, he will again fearlessly denounce the Dajjal, and Allah will not allow him to be killed a second time. Ibn Kathir says that some believe that man will be al-Khidr (as). Then the Dajjal will attack Jerusalem. 'Isa (as) will confront him at the gate of Ludd, which is where the main airport in the state of Israel is now situated. 'Isa (as) will kill the Dajjal with his spear and will show the people his blood on its tip. Then the one-eyed Deceiver will dissolve like salt in water, like melted lead, like a slug in the sun.

From there al-Mahdi (as) and 'Isa (as) will wage war on the followers of evil wherever they find them. Having lost their commander, the smaller dajjals will be defeated one after the other. The Prophet (sas) said "'Isa will break the cross and kill the swine, abolish the *jizya* tax, and distribute wealth until there is no one wanting for anything." Breaking the cross means that he will show those who think he died on the cross or that he is God, that they are mistaken. He will kill the pigs, meaning he will abolish the practices that Allah has forbidden. He will win over those who oppose him so that there is no more need for the *jizya*, a tax imposed on those who live under the protection of an Islamic state but, as non-

Muslims, are not required to defend it. Since all people will have come to believe in Allah and all of His prophets there will be no one left to tax.

'Isa (as) will then make the pilgrimage, the Hajj and the 'Umra, in Mecca and go to Medina to live. The Mahdi (as) will continue to rule in absolute justice and then, having accomplished his task, will die. May Allah bless him and raise him close.

The White Minaret of the 'Ummayad Mosque Damascus, Syria.

Israfil (as) blowing the trumpet to signal the End of Days. Ottoman, early 1400's.

40.
The End

At the passing of Imam al-Mahdi (as), 'Isa (as) will take over as the *khalifa* of the Prophet (sas). "Security will cover the earth, so that lions will graze with camels, tigers with cattle, and wolves with sheep. Children will play with snakes, and neither will harm the other." (Muslim).

In his second coming 'Isa (as) will manifest all the qualities of perfection with which he was not dressed in his first. He will accomplish the things that were written for him and complete his own spiritual journey. Since Sayyiduna Muhammad (sas) is the Seal of Prophets (*khatmu l-anbiya*) and there will be no prophet after him, 'Isa (as) will descend at the end of days in the capacity of a saint. Ibn 'Arabi says that he is, in fact, the Seal of Universal Sainthood (*khatmu l-awliya l-mutlaqa*) of whom the prophet Adam (as) is the first and Sayyiduna 'Isa (as) is the completion. He will descend with a sword and destroy evil. He will live a settled life in Medina and marry an Arab girl. He will father children with her and grow to old age. The statement in The Qur'an will be fulfilled that says 'Isa (as) **will speak to the people in the cradle and in maturity, and he will be one of the righteous** (3:46). When he first left the world he was only thirty-three and had not yet reached the age of maturity, *kahla*, someone in the prime of life.

7th century Byzantine icon from Mount Sinai monastery showing 'Isa (as) as an old man.

After years of peaceful rule, in which he will be both spiritual and political leader, trouble will suddenly appear again to everyone's surprise. Two tribes, the Ya'juj and Ma'juj (Gog and Magog), will break through the wall of iron covered with copper that Dhul Qarnain (as) (18:94-97) built to contain them and will overrun the land (21:96). They will be rapacious and voracious and eat everything in sight and drink up all the water. 'Isa (as) will pray to Allah to destroy them, and his prayers will be answered. Allah will send a small insect to bite their necks, and the next morning the Ya'juj and Ma'juj will all be dead. The stench of their rotting carcasses will fill every corner of the earth. Then Allah will send heavy rains to clean the earth and wash their bodies into the sea. Afterwards the earth will shine brightly like a mirror and produce fruit overflowing with blessing as it did in the time of Adam (as). A group of people will be able to feast on the seeds of one pomegranate and take shelter under its empty shell.

Peace will be restored for a short time, and then 'Isa (as) will finally taste of death, hopefully no longer afraid to face his Lord because he has finally delivered his message and cleared his name. The Prophet (sas) said, 'Isa (as) will die in Medina, and the Muslims will pray his funeral prayer. They will bury him next to the Prophet (sas) in a space reserved for him on the other side of 'Umar (ra). Allah tells us **There is not one of the People of the Book who will not believe in ['Isa] before his death, and on the Day of Resurrection he will be a witness over them.** (4:159).

After 'Isa (as) completes his mission on earth, the greatest signs of the end will start to appear. The Ka'ba will be destroyed stone by stone and its treasure uncovered. Yathrib (the original name of Medina) will be deserted and destroyed. The Beast of the Earth (27:82) will emerge out of the sand near Mecca or from the side of As-Safa. An enormous monster unlike anything else, he will hold the staff of Musa (as) in one hand and the ring of Sulayman (as) in the other, and he will brand each person according to their belief or lack of it. Overnight The Qur'an will disappear off the pages of the books and from the memories of those who know it by heart. Dark thick smoke will blanket the earth for forty days. Then a cool wind will arise and gently take all the souls of all the believers until there is no one left on earth who remembers Allah or His Books or His Prophets.

The sun will not rise for three days. No one will know if it is night or day. Only those who were accustomed to praying will be able to awake to pray. On the third day the sun will rise on the western horizon instead of in the east. It will climb to the middle of the sky and then return to set in the west. Everyone who did not believe before will believe then, but it will no longer be accepted. There will be three earthquakes, one in the west, one in the east, and one in Arabia. A fire will burst out of the Yemen and drive all the people to the place of Judgment, the *Mahshar*.

16th century Ottoman miniature showing the sun rising from the west and the resurrection.

Then and only then will the Archangel 'Israfil (as) be commanded by Allah Almighty to unhook the Trumpet from where it is hanging on the divine Throne and put his mouth to the cavernous mouthpiece and blow a mighty breath. All the living will be paralyzed in terror. He will sound the trumpet a second time, and everyone, who has never tasted death before, will die. Then Allah will send a special rain that will cause all the bodies of all living things that were ever created to sprout from the earth like plants. Israfil (as) will be ordered to blow a third time calling each soul by name to enter his new body through the nose and assemble before his Lord to await Judgment. Mankind was created on a Friday and will be taken away on a Friday and brought back to life on a Friday, Jumu'ah, the day of gathering.

16th century Ottoman miniature showing the resurrection and distribution of books of good and bad deeds.

We will stand before the blazing glory of the Throne, barefoot, naked, and uncircumcised. Sayyida 'Aysha (rah) asked if everyone will be able to see us naked. The Prophet (sas) answered her that everyone will be too preoccupied to even look. We will be given the books that the angels wrote containing a record of all our good deeds and intentions, of all our bad deeds and intentions, and we will be feeling terrified and ashamed. We did not serve or obey or love our Beautiful Creator as He deserves. We will look to our prophets. "Adam (as) our father, can you save us?" "No", he will say, "I am worried about myself because I disobeyed my Lord." "Nuh (as) our savior, can you save us?" "No, I am worried about myself because I cursed my own people." "Ibrahim (as) the soft hearted, can you shelter us?" "No. I am worried about myself because I told three small lies." "Musa (as) our leader, can you speak for us?" "No, I am worried about myself because I killed a man in anger." "Dawud (as) our sultan, can you protect us?" "No, I am worried about myself because I took what belonged to another." "Yunus (as) the survivor, can you rescue us?" No, I am worried about myself because I tried to escape from my Lord." "'Isa (as) the gentle, can you save us?" "No, I am worried about myself because my people took me for a god." Only Muhammad (sas) will answer with compassion and without guilt, and he will ask Allah to have mercy and to forgive all of us.

The prophets will be the first to be called to their Lord. We do not know the order of their arising other than that the Prophet Muhammad (sas) said he will be the first but that on opening his eyes he will see Musa (as) clinging to the Throne and not know who was resurrected before the other. Then all the prophets will arise. The Prophet (sas) said that Ibrahim (as), Isma'il (as), Ishaq, (as), Ya'qub (as) and his sons, as well as Musa (as), 'Isa (as), Maryam (ahs), and the earliest companions of the Prophet (sas), will be among the first few to enter Paradise. Ibrahim Khalil Allah (as) will be the first to be dressed in the soft garments of Paradise and then Muhammad (sas), who will stand to his right on a high place of special honor from where he will look out for all of his Nation. Then the martyrs, the saints, and the righteous will enter paradise also without questioning.

Even the plants and animals will bring their grievances before their Creator. The Prophet (sas) said that the hornless sheep will complain about being gored by the sheep with horns, and he will be recompensed. The camel will recount the beatings of his master. Even the plants and the insects will tell their stories of injustice and abuse. Each will take from the good deeds of the ones who hurt them. That day all wrongs will be rectified, and all claims will be satisfied.

Then the people will be called one by one. We will have to read every line and review every word that is written in our books. Even our hands and feet will testify for and against us. It will be a terrible day of reckoning down to the smallest kindness and the slightest lie. The scale will weigh the worth of each soul in perfect fairness. Who will not be found wanting? Then we will face the *sirat*, the razor thin bridge that passes high above the blazing fires of hell reaching finally to the shores of Paradise. Will we cross it, or will we fall? There are just two things we can hold on to tightly, the love of our Prophet (sas) and the Mercy of our Lord.

No one knows when the Hour will dawn except Allah Almighty, but when it happens it will come as a shock. The one holding a piece of bread will not have time to eat. The one milking his camel will not have time to drink. There is no way to prepare for the Hour other than to be prepared at all times. Once, a man asked the Prophet (sas) when the Hour would come, and the Prophet (sas) answered with the verse from The Qur'an, **Verily the knowledge of the Hour is with Allah (alone)** (31:34). He asked the man in return, "What have you done in preparation for that day?" "Nothing," the man answered, "but I love Allah and His Messenger." The Prophet (sas) then gave him, and all of us, the best of news, "You will be with the ones you love" he said.

He is the one who sends down rain after they have given up hope and spreads His Mercy far and wide. He is the Protector (Al-Wali), the One to whom all praise is due (Al-Hamid). (42:28)

O Lord of Mercy, immerse us.

The golden rain gutter of the Ka'ba during a rare downpour.

Glossary

Abdal – a high order of saint, called the substitutes.
Abu Bakr (ra) – The father-in-law and close companion of the Prophet Muhammad (sas) and the first rightly guided khalif in Islam.
Al-'Azar (ra) – Lazarus, a companion and apostle of 'Isa (as) who was raised from the dead.
Ahmadiyya – an offshoot of Islam founded in 1889 in India by a man calling himself a prophet.
'Ali ibn Abi Talib (ra) – the fourth rightly guided khalif and the cousin of the Prophet (sas) and his son-in-law.
Alyasa' (as) – the Prophet Elisha.
'Aqida – creed.
Arhamu r-Rahimin – Epithet for Allah, the Most Merciful of the merciful.
'As - Esau – the son of Isaac (as), twin brother of Jacob (as).
Asiya (rah) – the wife of Pharaoh and the adopted mother of Musa (as).
Ash-Sham – all the land within a radius of 6 days by camel from Damascus:

Canaan, Palestine, Mesopotamia.
'Ashya – Elisabeth (rah) the wife of 'Imran (ra), the mother of the prophet Yahya (as).
Awliya – the plural of wali.
Awtad – a classification of saint called the stakes or supports.
'Aysha (rah) – the wife of the Prophet (sas) and daughter of Abu Bakr (ra).
'Azra'il (as) – pronounced Azra-eel. One of the four Archangels called in The Qur'an the Angel of Death, Maliku l-mawt.
Banu Isra'il – the Children of Isra'il (as) or Jacob, the tribes descending from the 12 sons of Jacob (as).
Barnabas (ra) – a Cypriot Jew who became a disciple of 'Isa (as) and wrote an account of his life called the Gospel of Barnabas. He was martyred in 61 CE at Salamis.
Barzakh – the place where the souls reside after death and before Judgment Day, a kind of limbo.
Bastet – the cat god of the ancient Egyptians.
Al-Bukhari – His collection of Hadith of the Prophet (sas) is one of the most authoritative. He died in 810 CE in Bukhara.
Buraq – the heavenly steed which carried the Prophet Muhammad (sas) on the Night Journey.
Caesar – the ruler of Rome.
Canaan – Palestine, the Holy Land, Bilad ash-Sham.
Cicero – Roman philosopher and statesman. Died 43 BCE.
Dawud (as) – the prophet David.
Dhikr – meaning to remember, also the ritual remembrance of Allah.
Dhu l-Qarnain (as) – A prophet mentioned in the The Qur'an, "the Possessor of the Two Horns", usually identified with Alexander the Great.
Du'a – prayer in the sense of asking for something, making a plea.
Fatwa – judicial ruling
Fitra – the natural state in which Allah made us, submitted to Him.
Al-Ghazali - scholar and sufi. Died 1111 CE in Iran.
Habib Allah – the Beloved of Allah – an honorific of the Prophet Muhammad (sas).
Habil (as) – pronounced Habeel – Abel, the son of Adam (as).
Hadith – the transmitted and recorded words and actions of the Prophet Muhammad (sas) that have been ranked and rated by the

scholars according to their veracity.
Hajar (rah) – the second wife of Ibrahim (as) and the mother of Isam'il (as).
Hajj – the annual pilgrimage to Mecca.
Hana (rah) – the wife of 'Imran (as) and the mother of Maryam (ahs).
Hanif – pronounce haneef from the root h-n-f – to incline towards. One inclining to truth, a true believer.
Harun (as) – pronounced Haroon, the prophet Aaron.
Hasan al-Basri (q) – sufi and scholar tabi'in born in Medina in 642 CE.
Hawari – disciple or bleacher, pl. Hawariyyun.
Hawwa (rah) – Eve, the first woman.
Hijab – veil, or curtain, scarf.
Hijra – emigration, journey, flight.
Holy of Holies – a term referring to the inner sanctum of the Temple which held the Ark of the Covenant.
Hud (as) – pronounce Hood, an Arab prophet not mentioned in the Books of the Jews.
Ibrahim (as) – pronounced Ibraheem. The prophet Abraham (as).
Iblis – pronounced Iblees, The name of shaytan, the devil.
Ibn Abbas (ra) – the cousin of the Prophet (sas) responsible for the transmission of many hadith.
Ibn Abi l-Dunya – Born 823 CE and died 894 CE in Baghdad. Scholar, and tutor to the Abbasid khalifs.
Ibn Abi Firas – Died 1208. Shi'a scholar and author.
Ibn Al-Mubarak - 726-797 CE Iraq. Ascetic and muhaddith.
Ibn 'Asakir – 1106–1175 CE Damascus. Scholar and historian. Murid of Suhrawardi.
Ibn Hanbal – scholar and jurist; founder of the Hanbali Madhhab. Died 855 in Baghdad.
Ibn Ishaq – Born in Medina in 704 CE. Died in Baghdad 768 CE. Historian and writer of the earliest biography of the Prophet (sas).
Ibn Kathir – 1301–1373 CE Syria. Scholar and historian, student of Ibn Taymiyya.
Ibn Qutayba – 828–884 CE. Baghdad. Scholar and judge.
Idris (as) – the prophet Enoch.
Ilyas (as) – the prophet Elijah.
Imam – one who stands in front, a leader, specifically the leader of prayer.
Imam Malik – 711–795 CE Medina. Muhaddith, scholar and jurist.

Collected one of the earliest, most respected collections of hadith, the Muwatta.

Imam Muslim – Scholar and muhaddith, who composed one of the 6 major collections of verified hadith, Sahih Muslim. Died 876 CE Iran.

Iman – meaning faith.

'Imran (ra) – the father of Maryam (ahs) and the grandfather of 'Isa (as).

Injil – pronounce injeel, the Book of 'Isa (as), the Gospel.

'Isa (as) – pronounced Eesa, the prophet Jesus.

Al-Isbahani – Shafi'i scholar and muhaddith. Died 1038 CE Isfahan.

Ishaq (as) – pronounced Is-haq. The prophet Isaac.

Isma'il (as) – pronounced Isma-eel. The prophet Ishmael.

'Isra – a night journey, specifically the miraculous journey of the Prophet Muhammad (sas) from Mecca to Jerusalem.

Isra'il (as) – pronounced Isra-eel. Israel, another name for the prophet Ya'qub, Jacob (as).

Israfil (as) – pronounced Israfeel. The Archangel who will blow the trumpet at the end of time.

Al-Jahiz – 776 – 868 CE Iraq. Scholar and theologian.

Jamarat – pronounced jamaraat. The three pillars representing the devil towards which the pilgrims throw pebbles during the Hajj.

James the Just (ra) – called the brother of 'Isa (as) in the New Testament and a leader of the early church. Died as a martyr 62 or 69 CE in Jerusalem.

Jew – a name derived from Judah (as) the oldest son of Jacob (as).

Jibra'il (as) – pronounced Jibra-eel. The Archangel Gabriel who delivers God's words. Kaffir – one who denies the truth – an unbeliever.

Jizya – a tax on non-Muslims living in a Muslim state that replaces the need for military service.

Joseph of Arimathea (ra) – responsible for burying the body of 'Isa (as) according to the Christians. Born in Jerusalem, died in Glastonbury England.

Josephus – Roman-Jewish historian of the first century CE.

Judaea – the southern kingdom of Israel containing Jerusalem.

Judah (ra) – the oldest of the twelve sons of Ya'qub (as), of the Bani Isra'il.

Jumu'ah – Juma', Friday, the Sabbath of the Muslims.

Ka'b al-Ahbar – 7th century Yemani Jew who converted to Islam and served under the Khalifs 'Umar ibnu l-Khattab (ra) and 'Uthman ibn 'Affan (ra).
Khadija bint Khuwaylid (rah) –the Prophet Muhammad's (sas) first wife and the mother of his children.
Khalifa – deputy, successor, ruler.
Khalil – pronounced khaleel. Meaning intimate friend from the root kh-l-l meaning to penetrate, permeate.
Khalilu r-Rahman – pronounced khaleelu r-Rahmaan meaning friend of the All-Merciful.
Khatm – the seal, the final one, the one who seals up, completes the category or the position.
Khidr (as) – a saint and prophet mentioned in The Qur'an in relation to Musa (as). Also known as the Green Man said to have been given eternal life. Sometimes associated with Ilyas (as) Elias.
Kwaja Ansari – a sufi saint of the 11th century lived and died 1088 in Herat Afghanistan.
La'iqa (rah) – pronounced Laa-ika, Leah wife of Jacob (as).
Lawi (ra) – Levi, the son of Jacob (as), founder of the tribe of Levites.
Lut (as) – pronounced Loot. The prophet Lot.
Luqman – a prophet or saint mentioned in The Qur'an sometimes identified with Aesop.
Madhhab – pl. madhahib. School of Law. There are now only four accepted Sunni schools – Hanifi, Shafi'I, Maliki, and Hanbali. There used to be hundreds of others but they have no more followers. The Shi'a also have their own school. They come to different conclusions on matters of Shari'ah all based on The Qur'an and Hadith.
Mahdi (as) – a member of the Prophet's (sas) family who will fight the antichrist at Armageddon.
Mahshar – the place of gathering for judgment on Yawmu l-Qiyama.
Manna and salwa – some kind of grain and quails with which Allah Almighty provided the Banu Isra'il in the desert.
Maqam – place, station, shrine.
Marwa – one of two small hills in Mecca, as-Safa and al-Marwa, between which pilgrims run, sa'i, in memory of Hajar (rah).
Maryam (ahs) – the Virgin Mary, mother of 'Isa (as).

Masih – Messiah.

Masih ad-Dajjal – the Anti-Christ, the false messiah.

Midrash – Commentary on the Torah and stories of the Rabbis collected in the first ten centuries CE.

Mihrab – a niche indicating the direction of prayer in a mosque, or a small secluded place of prayer.

Mika'il (as) – pronounced Mika-eel. The Archangel Michael who is responsible for the vegetation of the world and justice.

Mikva – the ritual bath where the Jews get *ghusl*, full ablution.

Mi'raj – the ascent to Heaven of the Prophet Muhammad (sas).

Mishna – called the Oral Torah, it is like a tafsir of the Torah by Rabbis.

Muhammad Mustafa (sas) – Muhammad the Chosen one (sas).

Muqawqis – the head of the Coptic Christian state in Egypt at the time of the Prophet (sas).

Musa (as) – pronounced Moosa – The prophet Moses (as).

Mushrik – meaning idolater, one practices shirk, to worship other than Allah.

Muslim – from the root *s-l-m* meaning peace, submission.

Al-Muwatta – the 8th century collection of hadith of Imam Malik.

Nabataea – an ancient Arab kingdom stretching from the Red Sea as far as Damascus across Northern Arabia from the 4th century until annexed by the Romans in 106 CE.

Nabi – meaning prophet. pl. anbiya.

Nabiyya – prophetess.

Nazarite – a Jewish person who has taken a vow to withdraw from the world and dedicate themselves to worship.

New Testament – composed of 27 books that tell the story of 'Isa (as) and the first century Christians. The New Testament and the Old Testament combined are the holy scripture of the Christians, The Bible.

Nuh (as) – pronounced Nooh, the prophet Noah.

Old Testament – it is divided into 39 Books which are a different ordering of including the Torah and the books of Prophets and Wisdoms called the Tanakh by the Jews.

Palestine – Canaan, Ash-Sham. The land promised Ibrahim (as), Mesopotamia.

Pharaoh – King of Ancient Egypt.

Qabil – pronounced Qabeel – Cain the son of Adam (as).
Qarin – pronounced qareen, meaning a companion but usually interpreted as a personal devil who encourages men to sin.
Qibla – the direction faced in prayer.
Qira'a – the seven authentic ways the Prophet (sas) used to recite The Qur'an. They entail some variation in pronunciation but not in meaning.
Qirba – a whole goat skin that is prepared to serve as a bag to hold water.
Al-Qushayri – born 986 and died 1074 CE Khorasan. Scholar and sufi.
Quraysh – the tribe to which the Prophet (sas) belonged, descendants of Isma'il (as).
Qutb – meaning pole or pivot. The head of the hierarchy of saints.
Rabb – meaning Lord, Sustainer, the One who nourishes.
Rabwa – a safe place on high ground.
Rahila (rah) – pronounced Raheela, Rachel wife of Jacob (as).
Rahm – the womb.
Rahma – compassion.
Rasul – pronounced rasool, meaning messenger.
Rifqa (rah) – Rebecca wife of Isaac (as).
Ruku' – the act of bowing in the Muslim prayer. Raka'in, those who bow in prayer.
Sadaqa – charity
Safa – one of two small hills in Mecca, Safa and Marwa, between which pilgrims run, sa'i, in memory of Hajar (rah).
Sajda – the act of prostration in the Muslim prayer.
Sakhra – rock, particularly the rock under the Dome of the Rock in Jerusalem.
Salah – prayer
Salam – pronounced salaam. Meaning peace and also to be submitted to God.
Salih (as) – an Arabian prophet only mentioned in The Qur'an, whose people, the Thamud, may have lived north of Mecca in Mada'in Salih.
Salman al-Farsi (ra) – one of the close companions of the Prophet Muhammad (sas) of Persian Zoroastrian origin who searching for the true religion was enslaved and brought to Medina where he met the Prophet (sas)

and became Muslim.

Al-Samarqandi – Abu l-Layth, 944- 983 CE Uzbekistan, scholar and author of a respected Tafsir.

Sanhedrin – the main judicial and law making court in Jerusalem during Roman times.

Sarah (rah) – the wife of Ibrahim (as), mother of Ishaq (as).

Sayyid – master, lord.

Sayyida – mistress, lady.

Sayyiduna – pronounced sayyidina, our master.

Sayyidatuna – pronounced sayyidaatina, our lady.

Seder – the traditional Passover meal of the Jews consisting of: unleavened bread, lamb, salt, sweet and bitter herbs, greens and egg.

Shamwil (as) – pronounced Shamweel, the prophet Samuel.

Shari'ah – Islamic Law derived from The Qur'an and Hadith by exceptional men of great learning and understanding.

Shaytan – satan, the devil. Shem (as) – son of Noah (as) ancestor of the Semites.

Shu'ayb (as) – an Arabian prophet to the people of Madyan whose daughter became the wife of the prophet Moses (as). He is sometimes identified as Jethro.

Siddiq – a man of truth.

Siddiqah – a woman of truth.

Simon of Cyrene – a man related by the Christians to have been present at the crucifixion and who helped carry the cross of 'Isa (as).

Sirah – meaning life or journey, it refers to a history or biography.

Sirat – the razor thin bridge over Hell that must be crossed safely in order to reach Paradise.

Al-Suhrawardi – Shihab ud-Din, scholar and sufi. Born 1154 in Iran, died 1234 in Syria.

Sulayman ibn Dawud (as) – the prophet Solomon son of the prophet David.

Sunnah – the practices and example of the Prophet Muhammad (sas) as recorded in the Hadith.

As-Suyuti – Egyptian scholar, jurist, historian, 1445 – 1505 Cairo.

Surah – chapter of The Qur'an.

Ta'if – a mountain city near Mecca.

Tabut – the Ark of the Covenant.
Tacitus – Roman politician and historian 56-120 CE.
Tafsir – explanation, interpretation, exegesis of The Qur'an.
Tahnik – the practice of the Prophet (sas) of feeding a newborn a small piece of date.
Talmud – Rabbinical commentaries on Jewish the law and tradition written after the Babylonian exile.
Talut – King Saul.
Tanakh – what the Christians call the Old Testament consisting of the Torah, History, Prophets, and Wisdoms.
Tawaf – circumambulation around the Ka'ba.
Tawrah – Torah – the Law as revealed to Moses in the 5 books of Moses – Genesis, Exodus, Leviticus, Numbers, and Deuteronomy called by Christians the Pentateuch, part of the Old Testament.
Tirmidhi – scholar and muhaddith, 824–892 CE Uzbekistan. He compiled one of the 6 canonical collections of Hadith.
'Umar (ra) – Sayyiduna 'Umar ibnu l-Khattab (ra) a close companion of the Prophet (sas) and the second rightly guided khalif of Islam.
Ummah – nation, community.
'Umra – the ritual visit to Mecca that can be accomplished at any time of the year.
Uways al-Qarani (ra) – a companion of the Prophet (sas) who never physically met him but with whom he had a spiritual connection.
'Uzayr (as) – pronounced Oozayr, the prophet Ezra.
Wahb ibn Munabbih (ra) – a Yemeni convert to Islam, 655–738 CE. Some say of Jewish origin. He collected many of the stories of the prophets.
Wali – a protector, a saint, a friend of Allah.
Walid – pronounced waleed – birth parent.
Wudu' – ablution, ritual washing in preparation for prayer.
Ya'juj and Ma'juj – Gog and Magog. Two tribes of ravenous creatures who will appear at the end of time and devour everything.
Yahya (as) – the prophet John the Baptist.
Ya'qub (as) – pronounced Ya-coob, the prophet Jacob.

Yawmu l-Qiyama – the Day of Arising, the Resurrection.

Yuchabad (rah) – the mother of Moses (as).

Yunus (as) – the prophet Jonah.

Yusha (as)– the prophet Joshua.

Yusuf (as) – the prophet Joseph.

Zakah – tithe, tax, giving a prescribed amount of your wealth once a year to be used for those in need. Derived from the root meaning 'to grow'.

Zakariyya (as) – the prophet Zachariah, father of Yahya (as).

Zoroastrianism – the major religion in Iran before the coming of Islam. Considered a monotheistic religion having temples where fires must be kept burning.

Zuhd – asceticism, renunciation of the world. Sayyiduna Ali (ra) said "a zahid is not one who owns nothing but rather one who is owned by nothing."

Qur'an Translations

I have used all the following translations interchangeably throughout the text, sometimes one, sometimes another depending on which seems most appropriate or most graceful. Where it occurs I have taken the liberty to change archaic vocabulary, such as thou to you etc.

Abdel Haleem, M.A.S. trans. *The Qur'an*. Oxford: Oxford University Press, 2004.
Ali, A. Yusuf. trans. *The Holy Qur'an*. NY: Aftner Publication, 1946.
Asad, Muhammad trans. *The Message of the Qur'an*. Gibraltar: Dar al-Andalus, 1980.
Nasr, Seyyed Hussein editor. *The Study Quran*. New York: Harper Collins, 2015.
Pickthall, Marmaduke trans. *The Meaning of the Glorious Qur'an*. London: Allen & Unwin Ltd., 1930.
Islamicity Qur'an Search provides 10 different English translations of each ayah. https://www.islamicity.org/quransearch/

Bibliography

Abboud, Hosn. *Mary in the Qur'an*. London: Routledge, 2014.
Abu Dawud. *Sunan Abi Dawud*. Accessed from: https://www.searchtruth.com/searchHadith.php
Adil, Hajjah Amina. *Lore of Light*. MI: Institute for Spiritual and Cultural Advancement, 2009
Adil, Hajjah Amina. *Muhammad – Messenger of Islam*. Washington D.C.: ISCA, 2002
Adil, Hajjah Amina. *Forty Questions*. Washington D.C.: ISCA, 2013.
Armstrong, Karen. *Jerusalem, One City Three Faiths*. New York: Ballantine Books, 2005.
'Ata ur-Rahim, Muhammad. *Jesus a Prophet of Islam*. London: Diwan Press, 1977.
Auld, Sylvia and Robert Hillenbrandt. *Ottoman Jerusalme: The Living City, 1517-1917*. London: Altajic World of Islam Trust, 2000.
Aykol, Mustafa. *The Islamic Jesus*. Saint Martin's Griffin US.: St. Martin's Press: 2018.
Ayoub, Mahmoud M. *The Qur'an and Its Interpreters: Volume 2: Surah 3*. Kuala Lumpur: Islamic Book Trust, 2013.

Bond, Helen K. *The Historical Jesus*. London: T&T Clark International, 2012.

Brill, EJ *The First Encyclopaedia of Islam* 1913-1936. Accessed from: https://brill.com/view/db/ei1o

Al-Bukhari, Muhammad. *Sahih Bukhari*. Accessed from: https://www.searchtruth.com/searchHadith.php

Clarke, Howard W. *The Gospel of Matthew and Its Readers: A Historical Introduction to the First Gospel*. Bloomington: Indiana University Press, 2003.

Cotton, Hannah. A Cancelled Marriage Contract from the Judaean Desert. *The Journal of Roman Studies*, 1994, vol. 84. Accessed from: http://www.jstor.com/stable/300870 July 2020.

Drachman, Bernard and Kaufmann Kohler. Ablution. *Jewish Encyclopedia*. Accessed March 2020 from: http://www.jewishencyclopedia.com/articles/338-ablution.

Essig, Mark. *Lesser Beasts: A Snout to Tail History of the Humble Pig*. New York: Basic Books, 2015.

Flaquer, Jaume. The Akbarian Jesus – The Paradigm of the Pilgrim in God. *The Muhyiddin Ibn Arabi Society*. Accessed May 2020 from: https://ibnarabisociety.org/the-akbarian-jesus-jaume-flaquer/

Ginzberg, Louis. *Legends of the Bible*. Philadelphia: The Jewish Publication Society, 1956.

Grabar, Oleg. The Shape of the Holy. Princeton, New Jersey: Princeton University Press, 1996.

Grabbe, Lester L. *Judaic Religion in the Second Temple Period: Belief and Practice from Exile to Yavneh*. London: Routledge, 2000.

Gril, Denis. Jesus, Mary and the Book, According to Ibn al-'Arabi. The Muhyiddin Ibn Arabi Society. Accessed May 2020 from: https://ibnarabisociety.org/jesus-mary-and-the-book-denis-gril/

Gruber, Christiane. "Between Logos (Kalima) and Light (Nur): Representations of the Prophet Muhammad in Islamic Painting." Accessed April 2020: https://core.ac.uk/download/pdf/31069187.pdf

Hakim, Souad. The Spirit and Son of the Spirit. The Muhyiddin Ibn Arabi Society. Accessed May 2020 from: https://ibnarabisociety.org/jesus-according-to-ibn-arabi-souad-hakim/.

Haneef, Suzanne. *A History of the Prophets of Islam vol. II*. Chicago: Library of Islam, 2002.

Horn, Cornelia B. Intersections: The Reception History of the Protoevengelium of James in Sources from the Christian East and in the Qur'an. *Journal of Aprocrypha* 17, 2006.

Hujwiri. *The Kashf Al-Mahjub of Hujwiri.* Reynold A. Nicholson trans. London: Luzac and Company LTD. 1967.

Ibn Abbas, Abdullah. *Tanwir Al-Miqbas.* Accessed from: https://www.altafsir.com

Ibn 'Arabi, Muhiyiddin. *The Bezels of Wisdom.* R. W. J. Austin trans. NY: Paulist Press, 1980.

Ibn 'Arabi, Muhiyiddin. *The Meccan Revelations.* M. Chodkiewicz ed. NY: Pir Press, 2005.

Ibn Ishaq. *The Life of Muhammad.* A. Guillaume trans. Lahore: Oxford University Press, 1974.

Ibrahim, Celene. *Female Figures in the Qur'an:Women and Girls in Revelation's Stories.* Oxford: Oxford University Press, 2020.

Khalidi, Tarif. *The Muslim Jesus.* Cambridge, Mass.: Harvard University Press, 2001.

Ibn Kathir, Ismail. *Stories of The Prophets.* Riyadh: Maktaba Dar-us-Salam, 2003.

Ibn Kathir, Ismail. *Qur'an Tafsir* accessed from: http://www.qtafsir.com

Ibn Kathir, Ismail. *Great Trials and Tribulations.* Riyadh: Darussalam, 2012. Accessed May 2020 from: https://maktabahassunnahblog.files.wordpress.com/2016/02/book-of-the-end.pdf

Al-Jilani, Abd al-Qadir. *The Sublime Revelation.* Muhtar Holland trans. Al-Baz Publishing Inc.

Al-Jilani, Abd al-Qadir. *Utterances.* Muhtar Holland trans. Malaysia: Al-Baz Publishing Inc.

Kabbani, Hisham. Five Commands of Prophet Yahya (a) and Five Commands of Prophet Muhammad (s). *The Fiqh of Islam Vol 8.* Accessed June 2020 from: https://sufilive.com/5-Orders-of-Prophet-Yahya-as-and-5-Orders-of-Prophet-Muhammad-pbuh--5136-EN-print.html

Al-Kashani, Abd ar-Razaq. *Tafsir.* Accessed from: https://www.altafsir.com

Kisai, Muhammad ibn 'Abd Allah. *Tales of the Prophets.* Wheeler M. Thackston Jr. trans. USA: Great Books of the Islamic World, Inc., 1997.

Lane, Edward William. *An Arabic-English Lexicon.* London: Islamic Texts Society, 1984.

Leirvik, Oddbjørn. *Images of Jesus Christ in Islam*. London: Continuum International Publishing Group, 2010.

Lings, Martin. *Muhammad His Life Based on the Earliest Sources*. Rochester VT: Inner Traditions International, 1983.

Macpherson, John. Zacharias: A Study of Matthew 23:35. *The Biblical World*. Vol. 9 No. 1 (Jan., 1897). Accessed from: https://www.jstor.org/stable/3140343 Accessed: 30-10-2019 17:31 UTC.

Madani, Mufti Abdur Rahmaan Kauthar and Mufti Afzal Hoosen Elias. *The Virtues and Laws of Zamzam*. South Africa: EDI Publishers, 2011.

Mahmud, Muhammad Bin Kanvendshah Bin. *The Rauzat-Us-Safa*. E. Rehatske trans. London: Kessinger Publishing, 2010.

Malik, Imam. *Muwatta*. Accessed from https://www.searchtruth.com/searchHadith.php

Matar, Nabil. The Cradle of Jesus and the Oratory of Mary in Jerusalem's al-Haram al-Sharif. https://www.palestine-studies.org/sites/default/files/jq-articles/Pages%20from%20JQ%2070%20-%20Matar.pdf

Maybudi, Rashid al-din. *Kashf al-Asrar tafsir*. Accessed from: https://www.altafsir.com

Muslim, ibn al-Hajjaj. *Sahih Muslim*. Accessed from: https://www.searchtruth.com/searchHadith.php

An-Nawawi, Imam Abu Zakariya Yahya. *Riyad As-Salihin*. Accessed from: https://sunnah.com/riyadussaliheen

Parrinder, Geoffrey. *Jesus in the Qur'an*. London: Oneworld Publications, 2013.

Perry, Paul. *Jesus in Egypt*. New York: Ballantine Books, 2003.

Phillips, Bilal The True Message of Jesus Christ. Accessed Dec. 2019. https://www.islamreligion.com/ebooks/The-True-Message-of-Jesus-Christ.pdf

Al-Qushairi, Abd al-Karim. *Tafsir*. Accessed from: https://www.altafsir.com

Al-Qubrusi, Shaykh Nazim. *To Be a Muslim*. Nikosia, Cyprus: Spohr Publishers Ltd., 2016.

Al-Rabghuzi, *The Stories of the Prophets*. Edited by H. E. Boeschoten and J. O'Kane. Leiden: Brill, 2015.

Reynolds, Gabriel Said. The Qur'an and the Apostles of Jesus. *SOAS* Vol. 76 No. 2 (2013). Accessed from: https://www.jstor.org/stable/24692806 Accessed: 09-04-2020 12:57 UTC.

Saltanat.org. The Official Site of Shaykh Muhammad Nazim Al-Haqqani Online Magazine. http://saltanat.org

Schimmel, Annemarie. Women in Mystical Islam. Women's Studies Int. Forum Vol 5, No. 2. Great Britain: Pergamon Press ltd., 1982.

Schleifer, Aliah. *Mary the Blessed Virgin of Islam*. Louisville KY: FonsVitae, 2008.

Shah-Kazemi, Reza. Jesus in the Qur'an: An Akbarian Perspective. The Muhyiddin ibn Arabi Society. Accessed April 2020 from: https://ibnarabisociety.org/jesus-in-the-quran-part-1-reza-shah-kazemi/

Shelton, Mahmoud. The Red and the White. Temple of Justice Books USA: 2019.

Smith, Johnathan Z. *To Take Place: Toward Theory in Ritual*. Chicago: The University of Chicago Press, 1987.

Sufi Live.com. The Media Gateway of the Naqshbandi-Haqqani Sufi Order in America. https://sufilive.com

As-Suyuti, Shamsu d-din. "Description of the Noble Sanctuary in Jerusalem in 1470." Guy Le Strange translator. Journal of the Royal Asiatic Society of Great Britain and Ireland for 1898. London: Forgotten Books, 2017.

As-Suyuti, Jalaluddin. *Tafsir al-Jalalayn*. Accessed from: https://www.altafsir.com

Al-Tabari, Abu Jafar Muhammad b. Jarir. *The History of al-Tabari vol. IV*. Moshe Perlmann trans. Albany: SUNY, 1987.

Al-Tha'labi, Abu Ishaq Ahmad b. Muhammad Ibrahim. *'Ara'is al-Majalis Qisas al Anbiya or Lives of the Prophets*. W. M. Brinner trans. Leiden: E. J. Brill, 2002.

Al-Tustari, Sahl. *Tafsir al-Tustari*. Accessed from: https://www.altafsir.com

Al-Wahidi. *Asbab al-Nuzul*. Accessed from: https://www.altafsir.com

Williams, Rev. George. *The Holy City or Historical and Topographical Notices of Jerusalem*. London: John W. Parker, 1845.

Wheeler, Brannon M. *Prophets in The Qur'an: An Introduction to the Qur'an and Muslim Exegesis*. London: Continuum, 2002.

Wheeler, Brannon M. Arab Prophets of the Qur'an and Bible. Journal of Qur'anic Studies, vol. 8, no. 2 (2002). Edinburgh University Press. Accessed from http://www.jstor.org

Zahniser, A. H. Mathias. *The Mission and Death of Jesus in Islam and Christianity*. Eugene, Oregon: Wipf and Stock, 2008.

Zucker, Dr. Rabbi David J. Did Pharaoh's Daughter Name Moses? In Hebrew? Accessed April 2020 from: https://www.thetorah.com/article/did-pharaohs-daughter-name-moses-in-hebrew

Picture Credits

p. 21 – Joshua Haviv: The Western Wall, Jerusalem. Shutterstock.
p. 34 – Muntains Hunter: View of the top of Mount Moses at sunrise. Shutterstock.
p. 35 – C. J. Everhardt: Dome of the Rock. Shutterstock.
p. 38 – Painting by contemporary artist Chin Hsung. chinghsun.com/birds/gj82jwk9l49yjuzy1z6aohn83sgo9p
p. 47 –Lenush: Grotto of the birthplace of Mary, Jerusalem. Shutterstock.
p. 56 – Courtesy Abdul Hadi Parsdofer.
p. 66 – Tillottama: Ramses II with wife. Shutterstock.
p. 68 – Arzi: Hagia Sofia mihrab. Shutterstock.
p. 86 – Framalicious: Dome of the Rock at sunrise. Shutterstock.
p. 119 – Studio Basel: closeup of palm tree. Shutterstock.
p. 150 – Jam Travels: sand and oasis, Peru. Shutterstock.
p. 198 Contemporary photograph by Kathrin Swoboda. mymodernmet.com/wp/wp-content/uploads/2019/08/red-winged-blackbird-kathrin-swoboda-2.jpg
p. 228 Contemporary miniature art work by Willard Wigan photo by R.J.R. Baddeley https://www.mbandf.com/medias/parallel-world/2010/wigan/wigan1.jpg
p. 257 Time exposure photograph by Ken Christison. https://earthsky.org/brightest-stars/polaris-the-present-day-north-star

www.ingramcontent.com/pod-product-compliance
Lightning Source LLC
Chambersburg PA
CBHW042127160426
43198CB00021B/2932